THE
NEWS
MANIPULATORS

THE
NEWS
MANIPULATORS

Why You Can't
Trust The News

Reed Irvine
Joseph C. Goulden
Cliff Kincaid

Book Distributors, Inc.

Published by Book Distributors, Inc., Smithtown, New York
Manufactured in the United States of America

ISBN 0-9625053-1-5

Contents

Preface

In February 1993 the news show *Dateline NBC* was forced to eat the most generous helping of crow ever served up on national television. For a full four minutes anchors Jane Pauley and Stone Phillips apologized for the network's fakery of crash tests crafted to prove that certain models of General Motors trucks were "rolling fire bombs" because of the location of their gas tanks. NBC helped "prove" its point by (a) mounting miniature rocket engines next to the gas tanks, which were (b) filled beyond capacity and (c) equipped with caps which popped off when a test car hit the side of the truck.

Unfortunately for NBC, all this chicanery was recorded by a video camera mounted on the dash of a fire truck which had been summoned to the test site in rural Indiana in case the expected conflagration got out of hand. (Contrary to the fireball shown on the NBC show, product of a closeup camera shot, the "holocaust" was a brief puff of flame that caused minor blistering of the truck's paint and a short-lived grass fire.) Curious firemen questioned the fairness of the methodology, and the NBC crew told them all would be explained on the telecast.

NBC did no such thing. Instead, it used the faked film to bolster its claim about the trucks being unsafe. In due course GM learned of the fakery and its lawyers found not only the video evidence but also one of the test trucks with the miniature rocket motor still taped next to the gas tank. Confronted in private, *NBC News* declared fealty to its story, whereupon GM threatened to file a libel suit in Indiana and staged a two-hour press conference in which it laid out the evidence. A GM lawyer threw down the gauntlet to NBC when he declared, "We would be most happy to have an Indiana jury pass judgment on the ethics of *NBC News*." NBC capitulated the next day and ran the retraction, and the president of its news division, Michael Gartner, was among the several persons who lost their jobs as a result of the scandal.

NBC's disgrace itself became the subject of major news stories in both the electronic and print media. Other reporters, especially those for magazines and newspapers, gleefuly flailed NBC for violations of journalistic ethical standards. Editorialists joined in the denunciations. The theme was that NBC's behavior was a journalistic aberration.

Nonsense. For those of us at Accuracy in Media, NBC's disgrace was unique only in that the network was caught cheating and in such red-handed fashion that it had no choice but to confess error. Further, GM had the resources to track down the evidence that proved NBC's lie, and the money to mount a law suit that NBC had to take seriously. The gravity of what NBC did surely was not an everyday occurrence in our media. But the deliberate sensationalism and the willingness to fudge the truth is found in much of the reporting that has undermined public confidence in the media. NBC's motivation was to manipulate the news to make a point—"advocacy journalism," in short.

The News Manipulators gives chapter and verse on some of the media distortions, inaccuracies and outright falsehoods which Accuracy in Media has reported the last several years. These episodes illustrate why a sizable majority of the American public has come to view the media with distrust, even disgust.

How do the media misbehave? Several common threads run through these case histories:

1. Promotion of Leftist Agendas. Unsurprisingly, given the liberal bent of many news people, the issues which the media cram down the public's collective throat fall far left of center. As we write [July 1993] the *cause d'jour* is homosexuality, a lifestyle which the media determinedly depict as mainstream American as motherhood and apple pie. The media fault the Reagan-Bush administrations for the spread of AIDS, rather than the unsafe sex which lured homosexuals into seedy bathhouses and other trysting spots. On our network TV screens, a homosexual march on Washington is given the aura of the boy (and girl) next door out for a pleasant Sunday walk—despite the presence of hundreds of barebreasted women, same-sex couples embracing and fondling, and placards bearing slogans which could not be printed in a family newspaper.

2. Acceptance of Chicken Little Science Scares. In no other single area than environmental news have our media been so consistently wrong over the last decade. The same scientists who in the early 1980s warned of "global chilling" did an abrupt about face later in the decade and began flapping their wings about a new menace, "global warming." Reporters quoted these "experts" without blinking, and without citing long-term climatological records which show no significant change in temperatures.

The list of scare-science stories is seemingly endless. A CBS *60 Minutes* segment on Alar, a chemical used to regulate the growth of apples, relied upon a so-called "scientific report" by an environmental advocacy group which had not been subjected to rigorous peer review. By the time objective scientists debunked the report, the domestic apple industry had suffered an estimated $150-200 million damages. An apology or retraction by CBS? None has been heard.

Or consider farm pesticides. As their use has increased the last two decades, cancer rates have gone down, broadly. Nonetheless, we have ABC's *Nightline* warning that "pesticides on fruits and vegetables may be giving our children cancer"—although the government report on which ABC's Chris Wallace based this alarmist statement was not nearly as emphatic as his language. [June 28, 1993] (Wallace left himself a safety hatch by saying that chemicals *may* cause harm.) At Senate hearings the next day, Senator Richard Lugar asked the principal author of the report, Dr. Philip Landrigan, a pediatrician, if evidence existed as to how often pesticides caused harm to children. "The short answer is no," Dr. Landrigan replied. "We do not have good information on how often these events occur. We can project, of course. That is the essence of risk assessment, but that is projection."

Or radon. The Environmental Protection Agency spends

$50,000 on a booklet instructing journalists on how to write stories on this supposedly deadly gas. Not a whimper of protest is heard from reporters about a blatant attempt at news management. Nor do reporters reveal that as a danger, radon is more myth than menace, and that a citizen faces greater risk of dying in a house fire or from falling off a ladder than being harmed by radon.

3. The Promotion of Odious Leftist Leaders. In reportage of foreign affairs, our journalists are caught in a time-warp, unable to recognize changes in the world since the Reagan years. Any Central American leader who is not far-leftist is a military-backed dictator. A government, even a democratically-elected one, which uses its police powers to suppress violence runs "death squads." Our media reflexively side with any Marxist or terrorist who has the public relations wit to describe himself as leading a "national liberation movement."

The media brush makeup powder over the warts on their leftist favorites. For months the press ignored a story that Winnie Mandela, wife of South African politician Nelson Mandela, savagely beat a teenage boy with a rawhide whip and terrorized her neighborhood with a band of lusty youths euphemistically identified as a "soccer club." The lad was later found dead in a field, his throat cut, and Mrs. Mandela was ultimately tried and convicted for complicity in the murder. (An appeals court months later overturned this conviction but left standing one involving the kidnaping of four youths, one of whom was the murder victim.) Similarly, the media deplored the ouster of Haitian President Jean-Bertrand Aristide, with *USA Today* noting, "A Roman Catholic priest popular among Haiti's poor, he and his populism are loathed by the army and wealthy elite." Civilized Haitians perhaps also loathe Aristide's nasty habit of inciting followers to deal with foes by "necklacing"—that is, draping a gasoline-filled tire around a man's neck and setting it ablaze. The U.S. media didn't tell the American public about that.

4. A Cynicism Towards Organized Religion. Elitist reporters who purport to understand such cultural oddities as deconstructive literature and cubist art are unable to fathom the appeal of religion to the majority of Americans. A good example came right after the 1992 election, when Michael Weisskopf of *The Washington Post* dismissed followers of television evangelist Pat Robertson as "poor, uneducated and easy to command." The statement was utterly false, as the *Post* was forced to admit in a retraction the following day. A poll by the Marketing Research Institute found that in fact evangelicals and other religious persons are better educated and hold higher paying jobs than the general population.

Protestantism is dismissed as the domain of such odd-balls as Jim Bakker or Jimmy Swaggart; Catholicism gets attention through an exposed pedophile priest; for a Jewish rabbi, the swiftest road to media fame is to denounce Israel. And when homosexual activists desecrate St. Patrick's Cathederal during a Mass, hurling condoms at priests and smashing sacraments, a brutish event is transformed into a "demonstration."

5. Political Partisanship. Media researchers Robert and Linda Lichter and Stanley Rothman came up with sobering figures when they surveyed 238 journalists during 1979-80 at the nation's most influential outlets—*The New York Times, The Washington Post, The Wall Street Journal, Time, Newsweek, U.S. News & World Report,* and ABC, CBS, NBC and PBS. In each presidential election from 1964 through 1976, "the proportion of leading journalists who supported the Democratic ticket never drops below 80 percent," they wrote. During the entire 16-year period, less than 20 percent of the journalists ever voted for the Republican candidate.

A continuing pro-Democratic bias was manifested during the 1992 presidential campaign by the media's reluctance to pursue the "character issue." Early that year, the revelation by sometime singer Gennifer Flowers that she had a 12-year sexual affair with Bill Clinton threw the Arkansas governor's presidential campaign into temporary panic. Not to worry. Flowers' candid tapes, which included smutty passages we shan't quote, were virtually ignored by the mainstream media. (Exceptions included the tabloid *Star*, the *New York Post* and the *Washington Inquirer*.) The network morning shows shunned Flowers. So did talk show biggies such as Larry King, Phil Donahue and Oprah Winfrey. So, too, did most of the print media, even after Clinton authenticated the tapes by apologizing for slurring remarks he made on them about Governor Mario Cuomo of New York.

Eleanor Clift, a political writer for *Newsweek*, let the media bias out of the bag in an article on February 10, 1992: "Gary Hart would have given anything for the support Clinton got last week. Truth is, the press is willing to cut Clinton some slack because they like him—and what he has to say. He is a policy wonk in tune with a younger generation of Democrats eager to take the party beyond the liberal stereotype."

Sidney Stark, a columnist for the liberal *Boston Globe*, wrote in a similar vein on March 16, 1992: ". . .many reporters may truly believe a Clinton victory is essential for the good of the country. Still, the question is whether the coverage, as a whole, has become so one-sided that the mainstream press is not giving the public the whole truth. That has clearly happened. Why have so many baby-boom reporters boosted Clinton? In part, it's because they identify strongly with a liberal, semi-hip contemporary who seems to share their values. (The chic professional wife doesn't hurt either.)"

Let us cite one of many Clinton stories that went unpursued by the media. On the Flowers tapes (the ones most of the media wouldn't print) Clinton and Flowers discussed a job with the Arkansas state government, which she got with some extraordinary help from the Governor at the expense of a black woman, Charlette Perry, who lost a deserved promotion. Perry, irked, filed a grievance over her treatment. When Flowers mentioned to Clinton that reporters might ask how she got the job, he advised her to reply that she had never talked to him about it—in short, lie. That is what Clinton himself did the one time a reporter asked him about the Perry case during the campaign.

In arguing against publicizing Gennifer Flowers' accusation, many in the major media took the line that a politician's private life is his own so long as his conduct does not affect his public performance. What hollow reasoning! The Charlette Perry affair was the nexus between the public Governor Clinton and the private philanderer Clinton—yet the story went unreported by much of the national media, although AIM repeatedly called it to their attention.

Clinton ran for president as a supporter of women's and black rights. Yet the press covered up a major hypocrisy in his record: shoving aside a black woman to make room on the payroll for a woman with whom he had a longtime romantic involvement.

6. Pack Journalism. For a group which prides itself on independence, journalists show a remarkable responsiveness to pressure from their peers—to follow the pack, rather than pursue stories that the majority decide no longer exist. A good example is found in the Vietnam War, which had general supportive media coverage through the Tet Offensive of January 1968. Tet was widely—and incorrectly—reported as an American defeat, and soon thereafter Walter Cronkite of CBS and Frank McGee of NBC aired pieces strongly critical of the war. In short order, the press flock followed them into opposition.

Thereafter any U.S. perfidy, suspected or otherwise, was subjected to sensationalized media treatment (i.e., My Lai, the "tiger cages," the incursion into Cambodia, covert operations anywhere). Peculiarly, in the years since the U.S. role in the war ended in 1973, our press has turned a collective blind eye to a lingering scandal—the plight of American prisoners the Hanoi regime retained as "bargaining chips" for future economic aid.

Since the 1973 "Operation Homecoming," and the declaration by the Nixon Administration that all prisoners had been freed, the media have treated the POW/MIA problem as a fringe issue, dismissing grieving family members and refusing to heed occasional spotting reports of live Americans. A few family support groups struggled to keep the issue before the public consciousness, contested both by government obstinance and media skepticism.

Suddenly, in 1993, previously scattered strands of evidence coalesced into a coherent picture—more than 700 Americans in fact had been left behind when the war ended. This evidence included (a) a Vietnamese politiburo report dated 1972, discovered in Soviet archives in early 1993, disclosed that North Vietnam held hundreds more prisoners that it acknowledged; (b) independent interrogation reports of two defectors which confirmed the 1972 document in essential detail; and (c) satellite spottings as recently as June 1992 of distress signals including names and secret authenticator numbers assigned to U.S. pilots listed as missing.

Are Americans still alive in Vietnam? The evidence strongly suggests that they are. The scandal is that our media, with few exceptions, have not presented the evidence to the public. Indeed, the media's ignoring of this scandal has itself become a scandal.

* * *

The varieties (and causes) of press misconduct are endless. In the following pages you will find selected examples of media mischief that Accuracy in Media has addressed in recent years. This material is taken from our Media Monitor radio commentaries, five of which are distributed weekly to stations nationwide, and from our weekly AIM newspaper column.

During radio interviews, a stock question from the host or hostess seems to be, "Just what is Accuracy in Media—and what do you do?" AIM's mission is to do for the media what the media do so vigorously for every other institution in our society except themselves, that is, act as an independent watchdog and critic.

Journalism is an unusual "profession" in that it has no enforceable code of ethics. A lawyer who lies to a judge can be sent to jail and disbarred. A plumber who fouls up too many bathtub installations can lose his license. No such official oversight exists for journalism, the only trade afforded the protection of the United States Constitution. Nor should there be any governmental regulation: we shudder at the thought of a Department of Media Affairs suddenly appearing on the Federal Triangle in Washington, alongside the EPA and the Federal Trade Commission and other bureaucracies.

Yet the media's very independence demands that our press exercise professional responsibility. To be sure, various journalistic lodges (such as the American Society of Newspaper Editors and the Society of Professional Journalists, to name two) have pompous "codes of ethics" which lay out the bounds of acceptable conduct. Yet there is a peculiar omission from these windy statements: nowhere is there found a penalty clause for violators. A journalist who violates his profession's code is not censured by his peers nor told to turn in his press card.

AIM's role is to act as a professional watchdog—to receive and investigate complaints from citizens and others who feel they have been victimized by false or shoddy reporting. In essence we "re-report" the story in question. If it proves valid we say so, and so inform the complainant. If not, we publicize the misdeed in our column, a Media Monitor broadcast, our main publication, the *AIM Report*, which is published 24 times a year, or via a direct communication with the offending media outlet. In sum, we give the media the peer review which they do not do for themselves.

One of the nasty secrets of journalism is the haughtiness with which media people view their consumers—that is, persons who subscribe to a newspaper, or buy the products which provide the advertising which supports the electronic media. *The Washington Post* is one of many papers which has a staff member with the high-sounding title of "ombudsman," a Swedish word which means, in essence, an advocate for the public. The very existence of an ombudsman salves the conscience of *Post* editors and reporters who feel that the ombudsman is a heat shield between them and their readers. But how does the "ombudsman" feel about responsibility to citizens: Here is what Richard Harwood, a longtime Post reporter and senior editor, wrote on October 28, 1990, when he held the ombudsman's job:

> You are not "entitled" to a letter to the editor, to an op-ed piece or even a paid advertisement; if we don't like it, we don't print it. To ask for "equal time" on the evening news or in the morning newspaper is, very often, to bay at the moon. You have no "right" to fair treatment, no "right" to be quoted accurately or in context or even quoted at all in news reports, broadcasts or commentaries.

If you are offended by a Herblock cartoon, your remedy may lie with the United Nations but not here. If your reputation is soiled in a front-page story under a four-column headline, it is most unlikely to be cleansed in the same spot (if it is cleansed at all). The First Amendment to the Constitution, as the Post's executive editor [Benjamin C. Bradlee] once put it with accuracy and candor, protects our responsibilities as it protects innocuous speech.

Since its founding in 1969, Accuracy in Media has laid down an on-going challenge to our nation's press: You can put us out of business overnight if you do your job well, and you respond to reader complaints in timely and meaningful fashion. Alas, the attitude expressed by Richard Harwood suggests that we will be around for years to come. And the media will be reading more criticisms of the sort that you will find in the following pages.

New Book Exposes PBS's Iraq Lies

Let's talk a moment about a big lie about the Gulf War told over the Public Broadcasting Service, and financed by the hard-earned dollars which the Federal government takes out of your pocket for taxes. Like it or not, your money goes to support the left-wing nonsense which PBS puts on the air in the guise of news. And one of the bigger lies of recent years was told in the fall of 1991 by the husband-wife team of Andrew and Leslie Cockburn.

The Cockburns went out to Iraq after the Gulf War ended and came back with a dramatic "news special" which blamed the United States for what they called the "devastating effect of the war on the people of Iraq." The Cockburns said that anywhere from 75,000 to 175,000 children were starving— "due to the public health conditions that we caused."

Accuracy in Media checked out these claims when they first aired and found them to be bogus—that in fact Saddam Hussein was withholding food from his own people for political reasons. As we pointed out, the Cockburns, in their zeal to push their leftist point of view, misquoted relief officials who tried to tell them the truth. We asked PBS brass to run a corrective story, but executives chose to let the tax-financed lie remain on the public record. So much for honesty at the Public Broadcasting System.

Now a new book on the Gulf War further nails the Cockburn team. It is named *Martyr's Day*, and it was written by Michael Kelly, who covered the war as a free-lance journalist, and who is now a Washington reporter for *The New York Times*. As did the Cockburns, Kelly saw starving children in the hospitals of Baghdad. But who is to blame—Uncle Sam, as the Cockburns claimed, or the mad dictator Saddam Hussein? Kelly quotes from an interview with the angry director of Catholic Relief Services in Baghdad. This man

1

said, "The food stocks are at 120 percent . . . but the government will not distribute the food, or allow anyone else to. They are giving out only 25 to 30 percent of what is necessary for the people to be decently fed."

The Catholic relief director continued that for less than $1 million, Saddam Hussein could buy enough powdered milk to stop all infant deaths. But nurturing babies would "take pressure off the United Nations" to lift economic sanctions. So, by starving his own people, including infants, Saddam postures as Iraq's defender against a world of oppressive enemies.

Michael Kelly's new book also sets the record straight about Iraqi deaths on the so-called "Highway of Death" outside of Kuwait City, when Allied planes strafed and bombed Iraqi convoys fleeing the city. Media claims that thousands of persons were slaughtered were a factor in President Bush's decision to halt the advance. Reporter Kelly says the actual toll was only several hundred—that most of the Iraqis fled into the desert. Our question: why does PBS finance liars such as the Cockburns rather than honest reporters such as Michael Kelly? Why leftist lies rather than the truth?

August 4, 1993

Media Ignore Sandinista Terror Story

Throughout the 1980s our media scoffed at hard evidence that the communist Sandinista regime in Nicaragua supplied arms and other assistance to fellow terrorist organizations in such countries as El Salvador and Guatemala. The State Department and CIA convincingly documented how the Sandinistas received arms from Cuba and Libya and dispersed them all over Central America in hopes of spreading their revolution. One of the prime offenders in those years was *CBS News*, which did repeated documentaries, *60 Minutes* segments and other stories arguing that we had nothing to fear from communist-backed revolutionaries in Central America.

Now an extraordinary event in Managua, the Nicaraguan capital, has confirmed what the Reagan Administration was stating in those years. An explosion in a car repair shop on May 23 led police to discover what could be called a "terrorist shopping center," underground bunkers crammed with sophisticated weapons, including 19 surface-to-air missiles, and facilities for manufacturing false passports and other documents.

There was more, much more. In the words of Douglas Farah of *The Washington Post*, who broke the story on July 14, documents found in the building detailed "a Marxist kidnaping ring directed at Latin American millionaires." Six specific kidnapings have since been linked to the headquarters. There is even a suggestion that Nicaraguan passports held by some of the terrorists who bombed the World Trade Center in February came from the Managua facility.

Two points should be stressed. That the bomb warehouse still operated, despite the election of President Violeta Chamorro in 1990, shows that the Sandinistas continue to control much of what happens in Nicaragua. Indeed, former Sandinista Minister of Justice Tomas Borge ran to the scene

3

in his pajamas when he heard of the explosion, even though he no longer holds any government job. And the warehouse shows that the FMLN, the terrorist bunch trying to seize control of El Salvador, remains in fighting form, the existence of a peace treaty notwithstanding. In fact, a leader of one of the five guerrilla factions making up the FMLN admitted her group's connection with the arms dump.

So what attention have our media given this bombshell story? Aside from Douglas Farah's frontpage *Washington Post* article, it has been ignored. The Big 3 TV networks ignored it. So did *The New York Times*, which has prided itself on its exposure of right-wing death squads and massacres by Salvadoran troops.

Let us close with one amusing footnote. A spokesman for a far-left group which calls itself "Fairness and Accuracy in Reporting" discussed the arms dump on the Pacifica Radio station in Washington a day after Doug Farah's story. His explanation? The whole affair, including the explosion, was faked by the CIA, which is still trying to discredit the peaceloving revolutionaries of Central America. We expect such goofiness from the far left—but why haven't our media reported this extraordinary story from Managua?

July 30, 1993

4

Surgeon General Nominee's Record Concealed From Public

It's a fact of life that network news broadcasts don't have enough time to go into detail about important public policy issues. But when the compression of news and information becomes downright misleading, that's another matter altogether. On July 18th, *NBC Nightly News* anchor Garrick Utley narrated a brief report about Joycelyn Elders, who is Bill Clinton's nominee as U.S. Surgeon general. Utley said she was under fire from conservatives because she favors abortion rights and sex education for children.

That's like describing Ronald Reagan as just a former movie actor. Since most people favor abortion under some circumstances, and most people favor some kind of sex education at some stage in a child's life, at least by his parents, Garrick Utley made it sound like Joycelyn Elders was in the mainstream of American thought. In fact, Utley concealed her radical views on abortion and sex education.

Utley could just as easily have said without adding much additional time to his broadcast, that "Joycelyn Elders favors taxpayer funded abortions, and supports sex education for children as early as kindergarten." By adding these few words, Utley could have provided viewers with a more accurate and complete and far different picture of Clinton's nominee. Clearly, he failed to do so because he knew those views are NOT shared by most people.

If Utley had just a few more seconds, he could have provided even more details. He could have said: "Joycelyn Elders favors school-based sex clinics that provide free condoms to high school students, even though condoms have a failure rate of 15 percent. Since Elders took her post as the Director of Health for Arkansas, teen pregnancy rose 15 percent." Utley could have added: "Elders compared sex ed to driver's ed when she said, 'We've taught (kids) what to do in the front seat of the car, but not what to do in the back seat.' She says that prostitutes should be given birth control so they "can continue to sell their bodies to buy drugs."

The national media started paying attention to Elders when her nomination hearing was postponed a week to examine charges of financial irregularities in her background. Those are serious, but as Surgeon General she won't be in charge of the S&L bailout; she'll be the highest ranking public health official. The Family Research Council put the issue this way: "Americans should have concerns about Elders' lack of integrity in her current position, poor record of success in Arkansas, and inability to represent the American people on such sensitive issues as abortion, family life, education, and teen pregnancy."

But that's not the way the national media see it. That explains why Elders' record has been carefully concealed. She is truly a radical, but the media won't use that label to describe her.

July 28, 1993

Readers Kept In Dark About Defense Budget Cuts

Readers are accustomed to getting a point of view on a newspaper's editorial page. And *The New York Times* is no different. But with the *Times*, which considers itself the newspaper of record, a reader should also expect to find that opinion having at least some basis in fact. Yet, when the *Times* ran an editorial in June calling for further cuts in the defense budget, it completely failed to make its case and, worse yet, kept its readers in the dark about the massive defense cuts now underway.

The editorial was titled "Keep Cutting at the Pentagon." What occasioned the editorial was Defense Secretary Les Aspin's order to the military services to find $20 billion in additional cuts in the 1994 Defense budget. The *Times* defended the order, saying the cuts were necessary to bring the Defense budget down to $263 billion. The *Times* neglected to tell its readers that Clinton is already planning to cut the Defense budget more than twice as much as he promised during the campaign. Then, he said he would seek $60 billion in cuts over a five-year period, now he wants more than $120 billion in cuts. Obviously, this is a violation of a campaign promise that the *Times* supports.

Those are cuts from President Bush's proposed Defense budget. In 1994, for example, Clinton wants a defense budget of $263 billion, Bush wanted $275 billion. But even that doesn't tell the whole story. The Bush budget was itself a reduction from the so-called defense budget of the Cold War. In other words, Bush had already set reductions in motion. In fact, they amounted to reductions of $386 billion over five years. If you add Clinton's additional cuts of $120 billion, that means that the Defense budget is being cut by half-a-trillion dollars.

Here are some other facts that the *Times* forgot to men-

7

tion: first, two-thirds of the spending reductions in the Clinton economic plan come from Defense and, second, the percentage of total federal spending taken up by Defense has dropped from 50 percent in 1960 to less than 20 percent today. Even during the Reagan defense build-up of the 1980s, defense didn't take more than about 25 percent of all federal spending.

But that is where *The New York Times* focuses its attention. In calling for the cancellation of new weapons systems, the paper said more reductions can be accomplished because "the United States already has the most advanced weapons in the world" and "no rival could conceivably challenge America's technological edge for at least a decade."

Again, the *Times* omits some critical facts. America has these weapons because we spent money on them and tested them. And they were deployed despite the opposition of some so-called Pentagon watchdogs who used the pages of the *Times* and other papers to argue that they were flawed and wouldn't work.

July 27, 1993

New York Times Goes Overboard For Gays

The New York Times has undergone a sea change regarding its attitude about homosexuals. Whereas it once refused to call them "gay," now it has openly gay reporters doing puff pieces about the gay rights movement. Actually, it goes beyond puff and fluff, to the point of making the movement seem more mainstream than it really is. We have in mind the stories they published about the April gay rights march in Washington. One of those stories was written by an openly gay reporter, Jeffrey Schmalz.

It's getting worse. Picking up a recent Sunday edition of the *Times*, we counted four major articles that served their agenda. If someone didn't know better, they would have sworn the *Times* was an organ of the gay rights movement, like the "gay" *Washington Blade* in the nation's capital.

Possibly the most disturbing and damaging article occupied two full pages in its Style section. Two-thirds of one page was taken up by a photograph of a sweet-looking 17 year old girl who believes she is a lesbian. The story told how she goes into high schools teaching kids that homosexuality is a legitimate alternative lifestyle. Except for a few critical words from an official of the Catholic Church, the tone of the article was positive about the role of what were called "gay youngsters."

But that wasn't all. Turning to another section of the same paper, there was a favorable review of a public television film about two homosexuals who lived together and have now developed AIDS. The film depicts what it is like to die from the disease. The review said the film featured doctor's visits, bodies covered with lesions, and one of the characters so emaciated and weak that he was reduced to wearing diapers. It must have been uncomfortable for the *Times* reviewer, openly gay reporter Jeffrey Schmalz, to see the film, for he,

9

too, has been diagnosed with AIDS. For the *Times* that makes him more qualified to cover the subject.

But that's not all Schmalz was doing for that edition of the *Times*. On the front page of the Metro section, his by-line appeared under a favorable profile of Nicholas Rango, who coordinates AIDS policy for New York State. Rango, too, has AIDS. Finally, the business section featured a major article about employees of major corporations who are coming out of the closet and admitting they are gay. One gay male described the turmoil involved in introducing his boyfriend to company executives. One lesbian, still in the closet, discussed her fear that she would be exposed because she received a fax message at work from a group called "Commando Queers."

The *Times* is really overdoing it: four major articles promoting gays in just one issue of *The New York Times*. Maybe we're asking too much, but perhaps it occurred to the editors of this once-great newspaper that several of the characters mentioned in these stories were either dying or dead. And that is why the homosexual lifestyle must not be promoted, especially to children.

July 26, 1993

A Pesticide Scare That Duped America

Against a backdrop of pictures of sweet-faced kids in grocery shopping carts and in a school cafeteria, ABC's *Nightline* on June 28 pulled out the emotional stops on a new study by the National Academy of Sciences about the use of pesticides in growing fruits and vegetables. Anchor Chris Wallace sounded the theme, "Tonight, a new study sounds an alarm. Pesticides on fruits and vegetables may be giving our children cancer."

The *Nightline* show and stories on network evening shows concerned an NAS study which recommended that the Federal government take a closer look at pesticides. *The New York Times*, which got a one-day jump on the report via a leak, ran it as the lead story on Sunday, June 27, stressing that the Clinton Administration intended to "reduce" pesticide use as a means of "protecting the health of children and the environment." "Pesticide Risk May Be Higher in Children" read the headline in *The Washington Post*.

But how much substance was there behind the scare? The NAS itself admitted that little hard evidence existed to warrant a pesticide panic. In discussing reduced pesticide use, an NAS summary admitted that "a major obstacle to the use of this new approach is a lack of data. Without better information on the food consumption patterns, pesticide residues and toxicity, more accurate risk assessments cannot be widely applied." It found only a "potential for concern."

Nonetheless, the Clinton Administration suited up its biggest environmental gun to advocate greater reliance on expensive organically grown foods. Carol Browner, head of the Environmental Protection Administration, went on *Nightline* to pledge a "real reduction" in pesticide use. "We are prepared to get very tough," Browner said. "We believe there are safer alternatives."

11

Wendy Gordon of "Mothers and Others for a Livable Planet"—successor to the old Meryl Streep Alar scare front group—gushed praise for the "really terrific" attitude of the Clinton people for dictating a "total change of policy" on pesticides. She argued that "big business" supports chemical farming chiefly because "they profit from the sales" of pesticides.

But all this TV and print coverage ignored important parts of the story. Foremost, where is the evidence of any actual harm to children? The week before the NAS report was issued, the Natural Resources Defense Council, creator of the 1989 Alar/apple fraud, reported that "pesticide use has increased dramatically," from roughly 540 million pounds a year in 1964 "to more than one billion pounds in 1991." When wood preservatives, disinfectants and sulfur are counted, "the actual amount of pesticides applied in 1991 was 2.2 billion pounds, approximately eight pounds for every man, woman and child in the country."

If pesticides are as dangerous as NRDC and other environmental groups claim, what effect has this increase had on cancer rates? Cancer statistics compiled by the National Cancer Institute reveal that between 1973 and 1988, "the mortality rates have shown substantial declines in persons under age 55, and especially in children for whom cancer mortality has dropped 38 percent." Although both cancer cases and deaths increased in numerical terms, this was due primarily to "the growing size of the United States population as well as its increasing longevity."

Even the figures showing decline, NCI continued, are skewed by the "relatively high incidence and mortality" of lung cancer, which "often obscures the overall cancer picture." NCI stated, "With lung cancer excluded, the total reduction in the cancer mortality rate since 1950 is 14.1 percent with the largest reductions found in the younger age groups."

The principal author of the NAS study was Dr. Philip J. Landrigan, a pediatrician at the Mount Sinai School of Medicine in New York City. Landrigan worked closely with Dr. Irving J. Selikoff on asbestos scare studies in the 1960s and

1970s which have now been widely discredited. Oddly, the task force ignored such specialists in food safety as Dr. Bruce Ames and Dr. Thomas Jukes, both of the University of California/Berkeley.

Ames points out that 99.9 percent of the pesticides we ingest by weight are put into plants by Mother Nature. Ames says that of the 5,000 to 10,000 natural pesticides we ingest, only 52 have been put through costly rodent tests to determine if they are carcinogens. Of these 52, about half were found to be rodent carcinogens, suggesting that half of those not yet tested are also carcinogens. This does not mean that eating fruits and vegetables is risky. On the contrary, a previous NAS study found that eating large amounts of fruits and vegetables was a good way to reduce the risk of cancer.

The NAS panel ignored the epidemiologic evidence that fruits and vegetables decrease the risk of cancer even if they contain minute traces of man-made chemicals, and it acknowledged that it paid no attention to the natural carcinogens found in food that far outweigh the synthetics. The NAS, the EPA and the media should be ashamed of falling for this junk-science scare story.

June 29, 1993

PBS's *Point of View* Straight From Fidel!

The letters "P - O - V" are a movie maker's shorthand term for "point of view," and in a technical sense it means the eyes or viewpoint from which the camera sees a certain scene. The Public Broadcasting System has adopted the tag *POV* in a different context altogether, as the name of a summer documentary series in which the director is not bound by any canons of journalistic objectivity. In other words, the film is allowed to have a "point of view."

On PBS, unsurprisingly, that "point of view" is firmly on the far-left side of the political and social spectrum. During the several seasons we've watched *POV* shows, we've noted an obsession with homosexuals, lesbians, persons suffering from AIDS, downtrodden prisoners or members of minority groups—you name the cause, and *POV* and PBS have shed the politically correct tears on its behalf. PBS defends the lack of objectivity by stating that since the programs are labeled as having a "point of view," normal documentary standards do not apply.

Given the tiffs that Accuracy in Media has had with the people who run *POV* over the years, we don't get review copies of a season's programs. Like everyone else, we have to wait until they air on the Public Broadcasting System before we can see what the left-wing documentary filmmakers are serving up each season. But sometimes we get advance information on a program from a review in the left-wing press. Thus we give grateful acknowledgment to the socialist weekly paper *In These Times* for letting us know what is coming from PBS in August.

The program is entitled *Miami-Havana*, and according to *In These Times*, it is the work of a "dedicated Fidelista" named Estela Bravo who has "concocted a pseudo-network documentary about Cubans in the U.S. and Miami." Accord-

14

ing to the review, Estela Bravo focuses exclusively on Cubans in the United States who want to return to Cuba, and Cubans in Cuba who doggedly support the revolution. Given the starvation now racking Fidel Castro's tottering dictatorship, we're curious as to how Senora Bravo found enough Castro-supporters to fill up an hour of time, but that's her problem.

But let's get to the summation that the left-wing *In These Times* gives to the PBS documentary. Director Estela Bravo "has narrated the piece with upbeat rhetoric that might as well have come right out of *Granma*, the Cuban government daily." The reviewer continues, "It lacks the integrity of the journalist who genuinely strives for balance and objectivity, and it fails to clearly frame the point of view."

So, taxpayers, there you have it: the Public Broadcasting Service is using your money to air propagandistic trash that even a left-wing paper says is absurdly one-sided. At a time of federal budget crunch, why should your money be wasted on a public relations film for Fidel Castro? In our opinion, PBS's *Point of View* is downright cockeyed.

June 21, 1993

Why Both Sides Are
Not Being Heard On Gays
In The Military

The C-SPAN television network recently aired major portions of an Accuracy in Media conference on the topic of "homosexual disinformation." Many people may have been exposed to this kind of information for the first time in their lives. Much of the information countered the impression that gays are just like ordinary people, that their lifestyle is harmless, and that they are born that way.

Another conference later in the week, sponsored by the Center for Military Readiness, featured a panel that examined why both sides in the debate over gays in the military are not being heard in the major media. One panelist, columnist Richard Grenier, said the media worldview is that the gays, like almost everybody else, are victims of American society. As a result, the media see them as people who deserve compensation from the government in the form of special rights to serve in the military and other sectors of society.

Fred Reed, a columnist who covers military affairs, argued that the media have taken sides in the cultural war, against traditional values. He said many in the media come from the liberal urban centers and Ivy League institutions of the Northeast and have lost touch with the American heartland. He said many of them have had no military service and no exposure to the military. As a consequence, he said that when other reporters hear that he writes about the military, their response is one of disgust.

Fred Reed made the flat-out accusation that there is a "strong homosexual element in the press" that manipulates news coverage of the issues. He said other elements in the press are afraid to tell the truth because they fear being branded as politically incorrect. On the other hand, he said they have nothing to fear from the Pentagon and attack it regularly, because the Pentagon rarely defends itself.

White House pressure on the Pentagon in the debate over gays in the military was revealed when an active duty Navy Lieutenant, David Quint, described how his superiors have tried to prevent him from speaking out in favor of the military gay ban. And when he is allowed to speak out, certain restrictions are imposed on him. For example, he had to appear at the forum in civilian clothes, even though gay Navy sailor Keith Meinhold was photographed on the cover of *Newsweek* in his uniform.

Lieutenant Quint choked up at one point and became emotional over how he has been treated. Clearly, he was taking a risk by even appearing at this forum. He sincerely believes that the admission of open gays would damage the military but is terribly disappointed that he has not been given the freedom he needs to make the case publicly. Asked if he had a future career in the military, he said sadly that he didn't think so.

June 4, 1993

The Real Anita Hill—The News Media Take Sides

TV Guide writer Harry Stein has finally produced a column that qualifies as media criticism. He has questioned why most of the major media seem reluctant to deal with David Brock's new book, titled, *The Real Anita Hill*. The content provides the answer. The book demolishes Hill's claims of sexual harassment which were aired against Judge Clarence Thomas on national television. Though polls indicated most people believed Thomas' denials and he went on to be confirmed to the Supreme Court, the major media have openly taken sides with Hill and have vigorously tried to restore her reputation and credibility.

Stein admits that the Brock book is compelling. But he says the only interview with Brock that he saw was on the NBC *Today* Show, and Brock was allowed to appear only when paired against a lawyer for Anita Hill. Stein says he called a producer for the CNN show *Larry King Live* and asked why they hadn't featured Brock. The terse response was that they just weren't interested.

But the book is important not only because of what it says about Hill, but because of what it says about Senator Paul Simon of Illinois. And here is where reporters have also fallen down on the job. Remember that Hill only came forward after her private allegations against Thomas were leaked to the media. A key question has always been: Who leaked those charges to the press? Suspicions have always centered on liberal members of the Senate Judiciary Committee or their staff aides. A special investigation failed to find the culprit.

But David Brock's book claims to find the leaker. He says that Senator Paul Simon leaked the Anita Hill documents to the press and thus was responsible for what Clarence Thomas called the public lynching of him that followed. At the time of the Thomas-Hill hearings, Senator Simon was among those liberal members of the committee who denied they or their staffs were involved in leaking anything. Since the Brock book came out, we have seen no follow-up, no grilling of the Senator about the charges against him. And Brock's charges are not made in passing; his book devotes 15 pages to how he established that Simon was the leaker.

The treatment of the allegations once again demonstrates the media double standard. They don't want to embarrass Simon because he is perceived as someone on their side of the debate, someone who wanted to stop the conservative Clarence Thomas from gaining a seat on the court.

But, if the Brock book is correct, then Justice Thomas is right when he says that the whole proceeding resulted in an irreparable injustice to him and his family, and Senator Simon played a key role in the affair. It is time for our media— including Larry King—to ask Senator Simon to sit down next to David Brock and get to the bottom of this matter.

May 28, 1993

How Incomplete Reporting Misleads The Public

The Associated Press is a cooperative news service owned by hundreds of separate newspapers and television and radio stations. Given the broad diversity of its owners, the AP since its founding has prided itself on strict objectivity in its coverage. There have been conspicuous glitches, of course, such as Peter Arnett's infamous anti-American reporting from Vietnam. But all in all, America's editors trust the AP to deliver fair and accurate news.

Thus we were surprised to read a woefully inaccurate account in May concerning an Accuracy in Media member, Richard Kania, a retired lawyer and civic activist who lives in Carthage, North Carolina. Earlier this year, Kania and two friends decided to start a postcard campaign to discourage President Clinton from attending any Memorial Day events at such shrines as the Vietnam Memorial. Since Clinton managed to slide around service in Vietnam, they told him in their card, "let's not see you engage in any hypocrisy by attending ceremonies either at the Vietnam War Memorial or at the Tomb of the Unknown Soldier."

The card continued, "While your 'esteemed' conscience led you to organize events that provided aid and comfort to the enemy, American soldiers were maimed and killed obeying the legal processes of representative government."

Soon the three men had more than 300,000 postcards in circulation, and an Associated Press reporter named Lawrence Knutson called Dick Kania to get a story on what was rapidly becoming a national grassroots campaign. Kania talked freely with the reporter, and he was very surprised to read the resultant story a few days later. The AP story went out of its way to stress that Kania was not a Vietnam veteran. The headline, even in Kania's hometown paper in North Carolinia, noted that a "non-Vietnam veteran" was running the campaign.

"Whoa!" Dick Kania said to himself. "I served in the Air Force during the Korean War. Don't these reporters recognize that our country has had wars other than Vietnam?" The Associated Press story had a more grievous error concerning Kania's two friends who were equal sponsors. One of them, John Roberts, a Green Beret, had served five tours in Vietnam. Rolf Kreuscher, another Green Beret, had two tours in 'Nam. During their interview, Kania had offered their phone numbers and addresses to Knutson, who replied that he already had them.

Why no mention of Roberts and Kreuscher and their service in Vietnam? Calling either or both of these men would have taken the Associated Press reporter only a few minutes—and he would have had an accurate story, rather than one that dismissed the campaign as stemming from a non-Vietnam Carolina lawyer. In the next few days Dick Kania received many clippings of critical editorials and columns from around the country in which the writer picked up on the AP's statement that he was not a Vietnam veteran. This is a classic instance of how incomplete reporting can do mischief far beyond the original article.

Knutson offered an excuse through the assistant chief of the AP bureau in Washington, David M. Espo. By Espo's account, Knutson asked Kania whether he was a Vietnam veteran. Kania "did not volunteer the information" that he had served in Korea, Espo wrote. Oh? Given the fuss Knutson made about the no-Vietnam service, why not the logical question a competent reporter would have asked, "Well, are you a veteran of any wars?" There were 142,091 American casualties in Korea—killed, wounded and missing. Many persons who are perhaps a few years older than Knutson considered the Korean War serious business.

Despite this sabotage by the Associated Press, the postcard campaign succeeded. In early May one of Clinton's press agents, Dee Dee Myers, told CNN that "only a few hundred" cards had reached the White House. That was in late afternoon. CNN a few hours later got another count, presumably from another press agent, that was "around 16,000."

Perhaps wisely, the Clinton people by mid-May were no

longer giving out any specific numbers. Columnist Mary McGrory wrote in *The Washington Post* on May 13 that the campaign had "flooded the White House with postcards. . . ."

Accuracy in Media urged the Associated Press to correct the cheap shot it took at Dick Kania and his two Green Beret friends. In response, editor Espo claimed to be "at a loss to understand [AIM's] charge that we took a cheap shot at Mr. Kania and that we violated our own standards of journalism."

Quite simple: When a news service transmits a misleading article to clients, it has an obligation to straighten out the record when the error is brought to its attention. As of the last days of May, AP had done nothing to give its clients an accurate story about the postcard campaign. We fear that this once-respected news service no longer takes seriously its own standards of fairness.

May 24, 1993

How They Censor What They Don't Want You To Know

The National Rifle Association, the NRA, is presented by some in the media as a big powerful political lobby that controls members of Congress through political contributions. But if reporters and editors were honest, they would have to admit that the power of the NRA is actually dwarfed by the power of the media.

In the past, we've noted that the NRA's power has stopped at the headquarters of those in the media business. For example, when the NRA felt it wasn't able to get its side of the story presented in *Time* magazine, the group tried to take out a paid ad. But *Time* refused to take the NRA's money and flatly refused to run the ad. This demonstrates that the power of the press exceeds the power of any special interest group.

More recently, the NRA took exception to a claim by *ABC News* that one-fourth of the guns used in homicides in New York City were purchased in Virginia. The claim was made during a successful propaganda campaign in favor of a proposal to limit gun purchases in Virginia to one a month. But a look at the figures demonstrated that only 824 out of 13,000 guns used in those crimes in New York City were traced anywhere, and less than 200 were traced to Virginia. The NRA called ABC "Anything But Correct."

Now we have another installment in the organization's battle over censorship with the media. The NRA tried to run a commercial on the three broadcast network affiliates in Washington, D.C. presenting its viewpoint that what the nation needs is not more ineffective gun control laws, but reform of America's criminal justice system. The commercial features a criminal laughing as a politician tells a TV audience that he's going to crack down on crime by proposing another gun control law.

In all three cases, the NRA commercial was rejected. Ted Turner's CNN did sell the time, and the NRA commercial was presented to viewers of his network. In addition, the NRA took film clips from the ad and bought space to reproduce them in various newspapers, together with the text of the ad. And the ad did pose a number of thoughtful questions, such as, "Where's the right to free speech, right here in the world's cradle of freedom? Why have these thought police decided you can't think for yourself? Why can they orchestrate the news, but we can't give them the facts? Why is it acceptable for them to dramatize gun violence for profit every night, but it's not acceptable to dramatize the failure of our criminal justice system and offer real solutions?"

The answers from the three broadcast network affiliates that turned down the NRA were not impressive. The ABC affiliate spokesman rejected the ad by saying it is inflammatory; a CBS affiliate spokesman said they rejected the ad and didn't have to say why; and NBC's owned and operated station didn't offer any comment at all. If not for the NRA newspaper ads, most people wouldn't even be aware of the controversy.

May 18, 1993

Where's The Outrage About Our Abandoned Vietnam POWs?

In December 1979, radical Iranians seized the American embassy in Teheran and held 50 of our diplomats hostage for more than a year. The hostage crisis dominated the news for the next 444 days. Jimmy Carter's failure to get the hostages freed outraged America and played a major role in Ronald Reagan's victory in the 1980 election. Later Reagan was to have his own hostage crisis over the handful of Americans held by Moslem extremists in Lebanon. Thanks to heavy media publicity, there was an enormous public outpouring of outrage over the kidnaping of these private citizens.

Now we know for certain that 12 times as many American servicemen have been held hostage by the communists in Vietnam as were held by the Iranian radicals in Teheran. A report by a communist general, Tran Van Quang, that was recently discovered in the Communist Party archives in Moscow, shows that the Communists lied when they claimed in March 1973 that the 591 American prisoners they had just handed over to us were all that they were holding. General Quang's report showed that they were secretly keeping more than 700 additional American POWs to use as bargaining chips.

General Quang said they could do this because the Americans did not know how many of their men had actually been captured. And he proved to be right. Even though we were sure that they were holding more than 591, the Senate in May 1973 defeated an amendment offered by Senator Bob Dole authorizing President Nixon to resume bombing to force the North Vietnamese to give a full accounting of the number of prisoners they were holding.

Thereafter the media and most of the public tried to flush

the 700 hostages down the memory hole. It was mainly the families and friends of the missing servicemen who struggled to keep the issue alive.

Despite media and governmental inattention, over the years much credible evidence accumulated that indicated that Vietnam was holding an unknown number of live American prisoners. In 1979, an intelligence officer named Le Dinh who had defected from the Vietnamese People's Army reported that he had heard from army generals that they were holding 700 American POWs as "a strategic asset." He claimed to have personally seen 33 of these prisoners and talked to three of them in December 1974.

Defense Intelligence Agency agents interviewed Le Dinh in Paris in November 1979. Although he refused to be polygraphed, they were satisfied that he had been a member of an intelligence unit with access to information about American POWs. That assignment ended in 1975, and Le Dinh escaped from Vietnam by boat in 1978. The DIA found some of his information checked out, but they were skeptical of other of his claims, including the story that Vietnam was holding 700 American POWs.

Now General Tran Van Quang's secret 1972 report verifies Le Dinh's story, and Le Dinh's account confirms the validity of the Quang report. Independently, they both put the number of American POWs that were held as hostages at about 700. Le Dinh provided important additional information—that the prisoners were still alive in 1975 and were being held for ransom. These reports not only confirm each other, but they also are confirmed by aerial photography and satellite imagery indicating that POWs have been signaling their presence in Vietnam over the years.

The DIA report on the Le Dinh interview is no longer classified. Copies of it were sent to a number of journalists after General Quang's report came to light. It was ignored by all but one journalist. The Quang report itself was given little attention by the three TV broadcast networks that most Americans depend on for their news. They mentioned it a total of only six times in the three weeks after it was released. The print media have given it more attention, but they have focused more on those who are trying, in vain, to discredit it than on the evidence that it tells the awful truth that we abandoned 700 of our men. Almost none of the reporting brought up the evidence that many of those men are still alive today, praying to be rescued.

Former Congressman Billy Hendon revealed on *Larry King Live* that in June 1992, satellite imagery spotted the authenticator codes belonging to two American aviators, Major Henry Serex and Lt. Peter Mathis, tramped in the grass in fields near a prison our investigators have never been allowed to visit. Incredibly, that sensational revelation has not been reported as news. *Dateline NBC* has aired two strong segments on the photos of authenticator codes, most recently on April 27. They showed one of the photos. The numbers were distinct and unmistakable even on the TV screen. Again, no other reporters picked up on this story.

If the media would give this story the coverage that they gave to the hostages in Teheran and Lebanon, the resulting public outrage would send a message powerful enough to get the action necessary to free the American hostages held by Hanoi. It is hard to understand why we must ask, "Where is the outrage?"

May 4, 1993

What TV Did Not Show About Homosexual Parade

The television networks and the rest of the media faced a unique challenge in trying to cover the April 25 march on Washington by hundreds of thousands of homosexuals. Much of what happened on the public streets of the nation's capital was too obscene and disgusting to display on national television, or to describe fully in family newspapers.

NBC News gave a bare hint—and we don't intend any pun in using those words—of the sexuality which it dared not show when a correspondent noted that several lesbians chose to march topless, their breasts exposed to onlookers. The NBC camera showed a discreet, from-the-back view of several of these marchers. But the topless demonstrators were tame compared to other marchers whose conduct can only be described as raunchy.

For instance, a number of homosexual men chose to march stark naked. We're sure this blatant exhibitionism was appreciated by tourists who happened to be in Washington on a pleasant spring Sunday with their small children, and who came upon the parade. Just how flaunting of public nudity on Pennsylvania Avenue is a civil rights issue is something we've yet to understand. Other marchers carried the exhibitionism a gross step further, outfitting themselves with grotesque artificial sexual equipment which made a mockery of the human body.

C-SPAN did a live telecast of about six hours, wisely concentrating not on the march itself, but the so-called "formal program" at the end of the Mall. This consisted, in the main, of musical numbers and windy speeches by homosexual activists and their supporters in the media and in politics.

For instance, talk show host Phil Donahue showed up to affirm his allegiance to the homosexual movement. Massachusetts Rep. Gerry Studds railed at the Navy for the

Tailhook scandal involving aviators, gliding around his own problems arising from his seduction of a 16-year-old House page whom he plied with grape juice and vodka. Larry Kramer, a founder of ACT UP, "outed" Secretary of Health and Human Services Donna Shalala again, denouncing her for denying that she is a lesbian and for doing nothing for homosexuals.

But these were the tamer moments, for even the so-called "official" program had moments which are difficult to describe in a family newspaper. Four-letter words and their many variations were heard in abundance on the C-SPAN telecast. WPFW, Washington's far-left Pacifica radio station, broke off its live coverage in mid-afternoon, saying it feared trouble with the Federal Communications Commission if it aired some of the song lyrics.

One of the many masters of ceremonies—a lesbian comic wearing a man's pinstripe suit—chatted about how the United States finally had a First Lady with whom she'd like to make love. She used the vulgar four-letter word to express her desires. Another lesbian performer sang about her jaded life and fantasized about "getting it on" with Anita Hill. C-SPAN's cameras, during roving crowd shots, picked up the occasional bare breast, but C-SPAN shied away from frontal male nudity.

Television decided to exercise the responsibility and judgment which some of the homosexual demonstrators were unwilling to exercise for themselves, but the conduct at this parade was tame compared to the outrageous public displays of sexuality that have characterized gay pride parades elsewhere.

The media-savvy homosexual leadership, of course, is trying to present the public as pristine a view of their community as possible. The strategy was revealed last Nov. 15 by Jeffrey Schmalz, a gay *New York Times* reporter, who wrote about the public relations campaign intended to force the Pentagon to accept homosexuals.

As Schmalz wrote, "Now that they have settled on it [the military] as a main issue, gay groups have become adept at picking the test cases, choosing only those who are telegenic

29

and have near-perfect records." This is why the Washington march organizers tried to downplay the more flagrant homosexuals, the leather-and-chains crowd, for instance. Traditionally, a lesbian motorcycle group named "Dykes on Bikes" had been the lead contingent in gay pride marches. For the Washington affair, they were relegated to the last place in line. The North America Man-Boy Love Association, which usually has a contingent in gay parades, was missing altogether.

The media coverage did not give a true picture of what happened that spring Sunday in Washington, and what happened, offensive and tasteless as much of it was, did not show how the homosexuals celebrate their sexual obsession when the whole nation is not watching.

April 27, 1993

Television's Anti-Religious Bias Revealed

Michael Medved's new book, *Hollywood vs. America*, describes how filmmakers have assaulted traditional American values, including religion. But Ralph Reed points out that television is waging a war on religion as well. Ralph has a vested interest in the subject, being the executive director of the Christian Coalition. But he made several valid points in a recent column published in the *Wall Street Journal* about how television is distorting the role of religious people in society.

It's not that reporters are ignoring what religious people do. On the contrary, one national news magazine carried a cover story titled, "In The Name of God," which focused on the cult leader in Waco, Texas, and the New Jersey sheik suspected of having some link to the World Trade Center bombing. But the focus was on their religious views and how they were related to violence and death. The coverage was reminiscent of when a so-called terrorism expert on the Larry King radio show claimed that the events in Waco represented "Christian fundamentalism."

Ralph Reed noted the same media tendency in the coverage of the shooting death of an abortionist in Florida. Many reporters portrayed the killer as some kind of pro-life religious nut. But less widely publicized was the fact that his church had removed him from membership after he had rejected counseling. Ralph Reed noted that he was beleaguered by marital problems having nothing to do with abortion and that he erupted into fits of violence without warning. He was certainly a troubled man who committed a horrible crime, but it is far less certain that his religious or pro-life views played any role in what happened.

An anti-religious bias drives some of this coverage. Ralph Reed noted, "More than 100 million Americans attend church every month and approximately 30 million attend church four times a month or more. Yet few of our nation' s journalists, professors and intellectuals can be found in the pews on any given day."

No one is going to force those journalists into the pews. But Watergate figure Charles Colson, who now runs a religious group for prisoners called Prison Fellowship, has come up with a compromise. During a recent speech to the National Press Club, he put the conflict this way: "We have often seen the media as being in league with the People for the American Way and the ACLU hatching plots in the basement of CBS to grind our altars into dust . . . You, in turn, [see] every church [as] a carnival of corruption."

Colson said each side needs to re-evaluate, and that the media should start covering the good things that religious people do. He cited his own group, which sends 50,000 volunteers into the prisons and delivers hundreds of thousands of Christmas gifts to inmates and hundreds of thousands more gifts to forgotten children. One thing is certain: faith will come in handy as Colson waits for the coverage to take a turn for the better.

April 13, 1993

32

Arts & Entertainment Network Perpetuates A Lie

Some argue for the abolition of public television by saying that private cable channels like the Arts & Entertainment Network offer the same kind of programming. Unfortunately, that's the case, as A & E recently demonstrated when it offered viewers an extreme left-wing treatment of anti-communism in America during the 1950s. Titled, *The Un-Americans,* and presented on the program, *Time Machine with Jack Perkins,* A & E purported to offer a "comprehensive look at an era of suspicion, repression and fear" and claimed to expose the" disastrous effects of anti-communist witch-hunts on (the) lives of ordinary Americans." A & E is available to 60 million households in the U.S. and Canada via more than 8,400 cable systems.

One of the prominent villains, of course, was Wisconsin Senator Joseph McCarthy. In many cases, the network contended that the anti-communists went after people who were totally innocent. Frank Wilkinson of the "First Amendment Foundation" is presented as someone harassed, persecuted and eventually fired from his job for "political reasons." It was never mentioned that Wilkinson was identified under oath as a member of the Communist Party.

A & E admitted that some other "victims" were, in fact, communists. But the network portrayed them, too, as simple political activists operating within the legal and constitutional framework of society. The worst thing that was said about the Communist Party USA was that it failed to criticize the Soviet Union.

The network acted as if the Cold War had not been decided in our favor and that the archives of the former Soviet Union had not been opened. The evidence demonstrates beyond a shadow of a doubt that the Communist Party USA was a subversive force sponsored by Moscow. Even *The*

33

Washington Post has admitted in a front page story that the archives reveal that the party was secretly financed and directed by the Kremlin.

But even without those archives, the evidence is overwhelming. Members of the party like Judith Coplon and Julius Rosenberg did spy for the Soviet Union. And Alger Hiss, convicted of perjury for denying he was a Soviet spy, was a top aide to President Franklin Roosevelt and was identified as a member of a Communist cell by defector Whittaker Chambers. The 1990 book, *KGB: The Inside Story*, by Oleg Gordievsky, the Soviet KGB's former station chief in London, identified another Roosevelt aide, Harry L. Hopkins, as the "most important of all wartime (Soviet) agents in the United States."

In other words, the passage of time has proven that Senator McCarthy and other opponents of communism were essentially right about the danger we faced. In fact, they could be criticized for understating the magnitude of the threat. A & E should do a program about that.

April 8, 1993

How *The New York Times* Uses Its News Columns To Help Candidates And Causes

The New York Times recently tried its hand at media criticism. It attacked Rupert Murdoch, the Australian-born entrepreneur who has built an international media empire, which includes the Fox TV network and television stations, newspapers and magazines in the United States. Last month, Murdoch stepped forward with an offer to buy the *New York Post*, the feisty tabloid that was on the verge of collapse. Murdoch was widely hailed as an angel for offering to take on the considerable financial burden of keeping the 192-year-old paper afloat.

Murdoch had owned the *Post* from 1976 to 1988, changing its orientation from liberal to conservative. He had to sell it in 1988, when the Federal Communications Commission, bowing to political pressure, refused to renew the waiver that had permitted him to own both a TV station and a newspaper in the same city.

Unhappy about the prospect of Murdoch's return as one of its few remaining competitors, the *Times* said in an editorial, "He may save the *Post* as a daily journal, but there should be no illusions that he is a healthy influence on American journalism." It denounced his newspaper journalism as "politically and professionally dishonest," charging, "He used his papers to grind the axes of his political buddies, to promote a reflexive conservatism . . ." It claimed that when he previously owned the *Post*, he "made unabashed political use of its news pages." That, said the *Times*, violated "the ethical standards crafted by American journalists since World War II."

The editorial explained that "the standard today is to keep the news pages fair and maintain a strong dividing line between the editorial and news departments." This was described as "a triumph for the newsroom staffs (at the best papers) and the handful of publishers who put probity ahead of profit." Gone were the days when the owners of the papers dared used them for "political manipulations."

But the use of newspapers to achieve political goals or promote causes is not a thing of the distant past. Editors and reporters also have axes to grind, political favorites to elect and ideologies to promote. They indulge in these practices frequently, unashamedly and sometimes with disastrous results, as the record of *The New York Times* itself proves. Here are some examples.

Herbert Matthews was a *Times* reporter who avidly promoted Fidel Castro in his news stories when Castro was holed up in the Sierra Maestra mountains struggling to survive. Castro's success in toppling Batista has been widely attributed to the role Matthews' stories played in gaining international support for the revolutionaries.

In 1963, the *Times* correspondent in Vietnam, David Halberstam, was one of three reporters who, according to President Kennedy's press secretary, Pierre Salinger, openly boasted that they were going to topple Vietnam's President Diem. They wrote story after story accusing him of persecuting the Buddhists. Investigations showed the charge was false, but not before the media-generated uproar helped persuade President Kennedy to sanction the coup in which Diem was murdered.

In 1974-75, *Times* reporter Sydney Schanberg ignored evidence and warnings from the American embassy in Cambodia that a communist victory would result in a terrible bloodbath. He wrote that their victory would mean "a better life for most." His stories contributed to their victory, and the killing that took at least a million Cambodian lives promptly ensued.

In 1991, the *Times* pumped life into a conspiracy theory that the 1980 Reagan campaign team had delayed the release of the American hostages in Iran to help Reagan win the election. It then ignored breaking news that discredited this conspiracy theory. It finally conceded that the theory was baseless after Congress wasted millions of dollars investigating it and came up empty-handed—after the 1992 elections.

Last year, the *Times* supported Bill Clinton for president when it suppressed or downplayed information that would have seriously hurt his campaign. For example, there was good evidence that Clinton had invoked powerful political influence to help him dodge the draft. We called it to the attention of the executive editor in writing and discussed it with the publisher a month before the election. They ignored it; publication would have hurt their candidate.

Rupert Murdoch may at times openly use his papers' news columns to help candidates or causes he favors. The editors and reporters of *The New York Times* do it covertly with the tacit consent of the publisher. The *Times* calls this "the signal professional triumph of American journalism in this century." Some might call it hypocrisy.

April 6, 1993

"Reporters Are Not All That Hard To Manipulate For A Cheap Headline"

Many reporters in Washington like to think of themselves as the adversary press, ready to pounce on government wrongdoing. Usually, that has meant scrutiny of a Republican White House and serving as a mouthpiece for a liberal Congress. Details of the sophisticated propaganda operations that have been jointly conducted by the press and Congress are detailed in a new book by Eric Felten called *The Ruling Class: Inside the Imperial Congress*.

Felten recalls the great Alar scare of 1989, when mothers got so alarmed about a growth regulating chemical used on apples that they poured apple juice down drains. Felten notes that, all along, Alar was perfectly safe. But he says the scare occurred because of a publicity stunt staged by Congress and a special interest group to get media attention. The initial attention came when *60 Minutes* gave unwarranted publicity to a flawed report of the Natural Resources Defense Council alleging that Alar was a health danger, especially to children.

The appeal of Felten's book is that he also details the role played by Congress in keeping the scare going. He writes, ". . . one scare story on TV is a good start, but anti-Alar hysteria would never have taken off without teamwork: the combined efforts of federal regulatory agencies, interest groups, and Congress are needed to yield such bountiful press coverage." Within a month of the *60 Minutes* story, he points out, a Senate subcommittee was holding hearings featuring "child victims, a press in full gallop, and, best of all, an honest-to-goodness movie star, Meryl Streep." Of course, Felten says that "they never actually produced any real victims; they only produced witnesses who talked about theoretical children being at risk."

A similar *modus operandi* was at work when the media and Congress promoted a national scare over lead in the environment and its alleged threat to children. Felten describes how another environmental group, the Environmental Defense Fund, worked with a Senate subcommittee headed by Senator Harry Reid to create a panic that was echoed by the media. In both of those cases—Alar and lead—the key was finding alleged victims. Felten says, "Victims make compelling news . . . Members of Congress know this better than anyone, and they do their best to oblige by cramming their hearings full of victims."

After describing these and other cases, Felten concludes, "The media are crucial to the success of these efforts. And, although the press has a reputation for cynicism and street smarts, reporters are not all that hard to manipulate for a cheap headline." He calls it a Barnumocracy. And the solution lies in cultivating a habit of disbelief when it comes to Congressional hearings.

April 5, 1993

Were Media Too Involved In Waco Story?

A lawsuit filed by a federal agent in mid-March insures that much attention is going to be devoted to the media's role in the prolonged hostage standoff by members of a religious cult outside Waco, Texas. The officer claims that someone on a Waco newspaper tipped members of the Branch Davidian group that agents of the Federal Bureau of Alcohol, Tobacco and Firearms, or ATF, intended to make an early Sunday raid to search for illegal weapons. The cult members were ready, and four ATF agents died in the ensuing shootout; the suing agent was among the several officers wounded.

The agent's charge about the media tip is just that—a charge—and it is roundly denied by an editor of the newspaper. Nonetheless, the fact remains that media people showed up for the early-morning raid, including a camera crew for a Waco TV station which got gritty footage of the shootout. We don't think the media wandered onto this rural scene by accident, and the circumstances suggest that the Federal agency was happy to have cameras present to record the raid. We've seen enough news footage of guys with the letters "ATF" or "FBI" on the backs of their windbreakers smashing down doors to know how cops and the media play this particular backscratching game.

Live films of officers carrying out a raid—for drugs, for guns, for whatever—make for good ratings for TV stations. They also provide splendid publicity for the officers, who get the chance to show what a great job they are doing. But there must come a point where the line is drawn between law enforcement and show business. The more people who know a secret, the less likely it remains a secret. We don't know what happened in Waco—but law enforcement agencies take the media into their confidence at their own risk.

There is also strong evidence that media coverage

encouraged cult leader David Koresh to prolong the siege. At one point Dallas radio station KRLD let Koresh broadcast a 58-minute taped message. Koresh began and ended the harangue by promising that he and his followers would come out "immediately"—that's his word—after the broadcast.

Well, Koresh got his air time, then refused to surrender, leaving KRLD looking rather silly. The station defended its decision, saying it had hoped to break the standoff. At this point the FBI asked the media to stop airing interviews with Koresh and also had the media move back more than a mile from the compound. Whereupon the cultists put a banner out a window reading, "God help us. We want the press."

This banner summarized the agenda David Koresh adopted once he got himself in a hostage situation. The murder of the four federal agents made it obvious that he and key followers are going to be spending decades in a federal slammer. All that was left for this misguided messiah was to try to coax the media into giving him a forum for a last hurrah of publicity. Our suggestion for the media in such situations? Cut off the microphones, turn out the lights, and see how long a nut such as Koresh can last without publicity.

April 1, 1993

Media Glorify Black Panther Thugs

Our media seem to be starting a campaign to rehabilitate the reputation of one of the more notorious, bloodthirsty groups of the 1960s and 1970s—the infamous Black Panthers. Think back to the pictures of such Black Panther leaders as Huey Newton and Bobby Seale brandishing automatic weapons and vowing to kill every cop in sight—to "off the pigs," to use their language. Although essentially a band of street gangsters, the Black Panthers managed to convince our ever-gullible leftists that they were in the vanguard of a revolution that would transform America.

In time, the Black Panthers fell apart, victim of their own thuggery. Perhaps appropriately, Huey Newton was shot dead during a drug deal only a few blocks from where he had murdered a 17-year-old girl. The remnants of the Panthers scattered—to prisons, to academia, to exile abroad. Now, the media have rediscovered the Cult of the Thug. *The New York Times* recently devoted more than a full page of a Sunday edition to an article glorifying the Panthers and other radical retreads of a generation ago. The article said, "Yippies, black militants and other radicals, once criminals who were wanted by the authorities and feared by the American mainstream, are now folk heroes, complete with their own autobiographies, lecture tours and film deals."

Prominent among these re-emerging Panthers is their former leader, Elaine Brown, who has just published a book called *A Taste of Power*. Press reports say that Pantheon Books paid Brown a whopping $450,000 advance, and she has been busily promoting it on the talk show and lecture circuit. A reviewer for the *Los Angeles Times* called her book "beautiful ... touching ... astonishing." The *MacNeil/Lehrer NewsHour* put her on a panel as an authority on black

America. Perhaps she qualified by telling the *Los Angeles Times*, "I hate this country."

We recommend that the starry-eyed reporters writing about Elaine Brown read an article in the magazine *Heterodoxy* by David Horowitz. Entitled "Black Murder, Inc.," the article is a former insider's hard-eyed look at the realities of the Black Panthers. During the Panthers' heyday Horowitz edited the radical magazine *Ramparts*, and he was closely associated with the group.

One project was a learning center in Oakland, the Panther headquarters. To summarize a very complex story, Horowitz persuaded a female auditor from his magazine to help the Panthers keep their books. She asked unwelcome questions about money for the center that was going for limousines and other luxuries for Panther leaders. She disappeared and her body was found in the bay weeks later, her head bashed in. Horowitz makes a convincing case that Elaine Brown—the writer now lionized by our media—could answer key questions about the murder.

Why aren't our media more skeptical about such people as Elaine Brown? As David Horowitz writes, "The existence of a Murder Incorporated in the heart of the American Left is something the Left really doesn't want to know or think about. Such knowledge would refute its most cherished self-understandings and beliefs." The media prefer to ignore reality.

March 29, 1993

Who Was More Racist— L.A. Police Officer Or Bryant Gumbel?

As the co-host of the NBC *Today* show, Bryant Gumbel is one of the more visible blacks on network television. But we've noticed an unfortunate shortcoming in Gumbel's professionalism over the years. Time and again Gumbel has let his own racial prejudices affect his commentary on stories with a racial angle.

We saw a good example of this late last month when Gumbel interviewed Sgt. Stacey Koon, one of the four Los Angeles police officers being tried on the charge of violating the civil rights of Rodney King. Gumbel seemed upset that the trial judge had refused to permit testimony about supposedly racist remarks contained in the draft manuscript of a book Sgt. Koon wrote about the case.

Koon's lawyer, Ira Salzman, interjected that the judge had decided to restrict testimony to events of the night of the incident—and for that reason he would not permit testimony about many details of King's criminal record. Besides, Salzman continued, Koon did not make the remarks on his own—he was simply quoting what other officers had said in discussing the King case. But Bryant Gumbel disagreed. He showed his displeasure, shaking his head and saying, "I think the prosecution would say that they were trying to speak to his own racial attitudes."

It would appear that Bryant Gumbel had not read Sgt. Koon's excellent book, *Presumed Guilty*, which is available from Accuracy in Media. It tells a lot about his racial attitudes, and they are not at all what Gumbel was implying. Koon tells an interesting a story about a black transvestite prostitute who had been arrested and who suddenly stopped breathing. Other officers did nothing. Koon said that he knew the chances were great the prostitute carried the AIDS virus. Nonetheless, he gave him CPR. As Sgt. Koon wrote in *Presumed Guilty*, "Would someone with racial bias deep enough to beat a prisoner simply for being black also go to the aid of another black who was a potential AIDS carrier, giving him mouth-to-mouth resuscitation?" Koon continued, "I think not. Draw your own conclusion."

Sgt. Koon also wrote about the effort he spent fighting the police bureaucracy to get proper benefits for a fellow officer who was injured on duty, and who was being ignored by department brass. Koon became so persistent that he put his own career in jeopardy, but he won, and his fellow officer got what was due to him. The fellow officer was black.

Koon's book was certainly available to the staff of the *Today Show*—even to Bryant Gumbel himself. Gumbel mentioned it during the interview. But instead of giving Sgt. Koon a chance to tell the story about how he risked getting AIDS in his attempt to save the life of a stricken black man, Gumbel tried to give his viewers the impression that the treatment of Rodney King was racially motivated. Bryant Gumbel is quick to apply the racist label to whites with whom he disagrees. In this instance, we ask, "Who was more racist—Sgt. Stacey Koon or Bryant Gumbel?"

March 29, 1993

45

How What ABC Left Out Misled Viewers

There is no question that the drug lobby is galvanized by the election of a President and vice president who are admitted former marijuana users. And here on Media Monitor we've commented previously on the media tendency since the election of Clinton to promote the notion that we've lost the war on drugs. But now we're starting to see some in the media return to a tactic they tried in the '60s and '70s—glorification of the drug culture.

The New York Times tried this in a recent story that carried the headline "Repotted." The story was about how marijuana users are regrouping in the '90s and promoting pot by claiming it has many beneficial uses as paper, fiber, fuel, medicine and even food. The story was helpful in the sense that it may have alerted concerned parents to how dopers are trying to market their product. But it was also damaging in that the dangerous health effects of marijuana were glossed over.

Here's how the author of the article, Ian Fisher, dealt with it. Almost as an afterthought, he said, "And, of course, marijuana is a drug." He then quoted Herbert Kleber, formerly of the National Drug Policy Office, as saying that marijuana impairs memory, energy and motivation, and that it has long-term harmful effects on the lungs and immune system.

When it comes to cocaine, the media are not yet trying to tell people that the drug has many beneficial uses. But they are attacking the government's efforts to eradicate the source of supply. Perhaps the most glaring example of this came last December when Peter Jennings narrated an *ABC News* special program titled, "The Cocaine War . . . Lost in Bolivia." The title reflected the content, as Jennings stated up front that the United States and its Latin American allies could not win the war against cocaine. Clearly, Jennings was hoping to find a sympathetic ear for this attitude of defeatism in the Clinton Administration. He said his broadcast was as much for Clinton as it was for the rest of us.

Let's hope not, because the head of the U.S. Drug Enforcement Administration fired off a letter to Jennings taking issue with much of what he broadcast. Robert Bonner said the information was outdated and misleading. Bonner also charged that Jennings completely ignored the successful anti-drug operations.

Here's how Jennings did it. Bonner noted that ABC emphasized that a key cocaine trafficker in Bolivia, known as Danilo, had escaped during a raid. But Bonner added that ABC failed to tell viewers that he was arrested a short time later, and that information he provided led to the dismantling of his organization. Bonner went on to say that ABC knew about his arrest because they used his arrest photo on the air. Bonner said these facts indicate that ABC's omission "appears to be deliberate." We agree. This is ABC's equivalent of the phony NBC exploding truck story. ABC should correct the record and apologize.

March 29, 1993

60 Minutes Short On Truth On El Salvador

On successive Sundays in March the CBS news show *60 Minutes* did hatchet jobs both on the government of El Salvador and on the Reagan-Bush administration for giving it economic and military support. The thrust of the two segments was that the United States funneled money to a band of bloody thugs who killed peasants, priests and nuns for no apparent reason other than that they were political leftists. The stories were grossly incomplete, even by *60 Minutes* sloppy standards. Here are some of the things CBS didn't tell you about El Salvador.

First, and foremost, the governments which Washington supported during the 1980s were freely-elected, voted into office by citizens who resoundingly rejected the communist umbrella group, the FMLN, as it is known by its Spanish acronym. That the elections were free was attested to by observers from the U.S. Congress, which was controlled by Democrats. But the FMLN wouldn't accept democracy. Instead, it turned to insurrection, trying to win through bloodshed what it could not achieve at the ballot box.

Second, the FMLN pushed its cause through selective terror. Here we saw a repetition of a pattern familiar in communist guerrilla warfare throughout the world. The FMLN used selective killings to goad the military into retaliatory violence of its own. The military violence—and not that of the FMLN—got world media attention, especially in the United States, where our press historically has closed its eyes to communist bloodshed.

The third omission is that the root cause of the violence— the communist insurrection against a democratic government—is shoved into the background and not mentioned by the media. The second of the *60 Minutes* segments dealt with the murder of six Jesuit priests in November 1989. *60 Min-*

utes didn't mention the context—that these killings came during an FMLN offensive in San Salvador, the capital city, that began with an attempt by a death squad to murder President Alfredo Cristiani. This murder attempt should have been no secret to the research staff of *60 Minutes.* It was reported on the front page of *The New York Times* on November 13, 1989 by staff writer Lindsay Gruson.

We don't condone murder by any side in a civil war. But throughout the 1980s, our media constantly harped on government violence while ignoring the bloodshed by the left. In a sick sort of way, the media's reporting was about like that old skit on *Saturday Night Live* when the announcer would give "partial baseball scores." New York, 7. That's all. No mention of what the other side did.

What we've seen in the America media the past days—notably on *CBS News*—is an attempt to denigrate the triumph of democracy in El Salvador. For an entire decade the American press savaged the attempts of war-torn El Salvador to survive under a constant insurgency that wrecked much of the country's economic infrastructure and brought misery to millions of persons. The FMLN finally gave up and let democracy prevail. Why can't our media call off its mindless campaign against democracy?

March 22, 1993

The Story Of A
Misleading Headline

"Clinton Plan Enjoys Strong Public Support" was the headline over a page one *Washington Post* story. The headline was based on a *Washington Post-ABC News* poll. It's true that 60 percent expressed support for the plan. But as Congressman Newt Gingrich pointed out at a news conference one day later, the headline was extremely misleading.

The *Post* pulled out one finding from the poll that made the President look good. Congressman Gingrich noted that the paper could just as easily have run a headline indicating that the public thought the Clinton plan didn't go far enough in cutting spending. That's because buried in the actual poll results carried back on page 8 was the revelation that 75 percent of the people thought the spending cuts were not large enough.

Gingrich noted that the *Post* could just as easily have run the headline, "Clinton Fails to Re-establish Trust in Government." The poll found that only 21 percent trust government always or most of the time, the lowest level reached in the history of the poll and lower than after the Watergate scandal or after the four disastrous years of Jimmy Carter. Gingrich attributed this low figure to President Clinton's abandonment of several campaign promises, including a middle-income tax cut.

The *Post* did note in the early paragraphs of its story that the findings indicate an anti-Washington mood is still strong in the country. But the paper waited until the 24th paragraph to reveal the details. The *Post* put it this way: "Americans are more willing now to reduce the size of the federal government than they were during the height of the Reagan revolution in the mid-1980s. . ." The *Post* said this finding "could clash with Clinton's activist approach to government." The survey found 67 percent wanting smaller government, while 30 percent wanted bigger government. Again, that's much better news for conservatives than during the height of the Reagan revolution in 1984. Then, 49 percent favored smaller government. Now, the figure is 67 percent.Then, 43 percent favored bigger government. Today, that has shrunk to 30 percent.

The *Post* understated or played down the significance of other findings in the poll. Congressman Gingrich, for example, said the headline over the story could have been "Clinton Disapproval Twice Reagan's and Two and a Third Times Bush's." That was a reference to the fact that, at this point in their Administrations, Clinton has 33 percent disapproval, Reagan had 16 and Bush had 14.

The news out of this poll was mostly bad for the Clinton Administration. But the *Post* pulled out one finding that gave the President a glimpse of light at the end of the tunnel. Republicans like Gingrich don't have to be told that it's the result of partisan liberal bias.

March 19, 1993

Another *60 Minutes* Deceptive Report

The president of *NBC News* recently lost his job because of his defense of the tactics of advocacy journalism, but advocacy journalism still rides high at CBS. On March 14, *60 Minutes* aired a classic example of this type of reporting in a segment glorifying, of all things, a notorious practitioner of advocacy journalism. Correspondent Ed Bradley set out to refurbish the reputation of Raymond Bonner, who, as correspondent for *The New York Times* in El Salvador in 1981-82, was so helpful to the communist rebels that the U.S. ambassador described him as one of their "tools."

In January 1982, Bonner had two stories in the *Times* that aided the communist cause. One, published on January 11, charged that American military advisers in El Salvador had attended a torture-training session for Salvadoran troops. It claimed that American Green Berets watched while Salvadoran military instructors tortured two teenagers suspected of being guerrilla sympathizers. It was based on uncorroborated charges by a Salvadoran army deserter named Carlos Gomez.

Leftists in Mexico had been peddling Gomez's story but had found no takers among American reporters until Bonner picked it up, eight months after Gomez's desertion. *The New York Times* gave it big play, even though it was uncorroborated and full of holes. The *Times* eventually acknowledged that it should not have been published, and Bonner agreed, writing in 1984, "I now believe that I should not have written Gomez's account without seeking a second source to verify what he related. . . . I suspect now that he embellished what had happened, and I do not believe that the American advisers had been present as he described."

The other Bonner story was about the massacre of civilians in El Mozote, a hamlet in rebel territory. Salvadoran troops had made a sweep through the area in December 1981.

52

Escorted by guerrillas, Bonner toured the region a few weeks later. Alma Guilliermoprieto, a reporter for *The Washington Post*, also signed up for the guided tour, entering as Bonner was leaving. In stories published in the *Post* on January 27 and the *Times* the next day, both reported that a large number of non-combatants had been killed by the army. The *Post* story said that a housewife had counted about 170 men and women, not including children, being rounded up and carried away to be killed. She said the village population was about 500.

Bonner said that the peasants had compiled the names of 733 persons murdered by the soldiers in the El Mozote area, but that the Human Rights Commission of El Salvador had put the total at 926. He claimed that the peasants had tallied 482 killed in El Mozote alone, including 280 children. That would have left 20 survivors if Guilliermoprieto's source was right about the population.

These stories ran just before President Reagan had to certify to Congress that El Salvador was making progress in human rights if it was to continue to get American aid. Assistant Secretary of State Thomas O. Enders testified before a Congressional committee that there was no evidence that civilians had been massacred systematically at El Mozote or that the number killed even remotely approached the figures cited in Bonner's story. He added, "In fact, the total population of El Mozote canton last December is estimated locally at only 300, and there are manifestly a great many people still there."

60 Minutes pointed out that investigators have now exhumed 146 skeletons, of which 132 were children under the age of 12 at just one burial site. Others are expected to be located. CBS saw this as vindication of Bonner and Guilliermoprieto, who *60 Minutes* said had been attacked by the Reagan administration as "tools of a left-wing propaganda campaign."

Displaying Accuracy in Media's newsletter, the *AIM Report*, Ed Bradley said that "after the El Mozote story appeared, an ultra right-wing media newsletter said that he (Bonner) had been worth a division to the communists in Central America.'' Bradley neglected to mention (1) that AIM never disputed that non-combatants may have been killed at El Mozote, but did question the elastic numbers, and (2) that the *AIM Report* describing Bonner's value to the communists was published six months after the El Mozote stories and was based on an analysis of 51 Bonner stories in the *Times*. It showed that Bonner had been a conduit for a broad range of rebel propaganda, the most glaring example being his tall torture tale.

Ed Bradley ignored all of AIM's evidence supporting the charge that Bonner was acting as an advocate for the rebels. He didn't point out that Bonner made no bones about his desire to see the rebels win in El Salvador. His articles in the *Times* were reminiscent of arguments made about China, Vietnam and Nicaragua—that the rebels were not communists, that they had no outside support, and that the people were overwhelmingly on their side. El Salvador was spared the fate of those countries because we had leaders who recognized communist disinformation even if it was in *The New York Times*.

March 16, 1993

ABC Sacrifices A Big Scoop In Order To Help Clinton Campaign

Last October, shortly before the presidential election, ABC's *PrimeTime Live* invited viewers to provide examples of biased coverage of the election campaign. They promised to air a program based on the viewers' response, but they didn't get around to doing so until March 11.

They received about 8,000 letters and 90 percent of them complained that the media coverage was biased against President Bush. Here is what they reported as examples of this bias: (1) The choice of photos of the candidates by newspapers in Chicago and Richmond; (2) Evidence of pro-Clinton bias in headlines and news stories in *The New York Times*; (3) *60 Minutes* putting Ross Perot on the air to make an outlandish charge against Bush on the eve of the election; (4) NBC's Tim Russert commenting negatively about Bush's address to the Republican Convention before the speech was delivered; (5) ABC's Sam Donaldson introducing an interview of Bush with a negative comment and ending an interview with Clinton with an upbeat remark; (6) CNN's Larry King interviewing Bush and letting Clinton's communications director call in to grill the president; (7) ABC's Carole Simpson interjecting snide comments about Bush and Perot while moderating the second debate.

These examples showed the pervasive bias, but most of them are small potatoes. There was no mention of the fact that most of the media, including *ABC News*, had failed to report that Bill Clinton had invoked powerful political pressure to obtain his draft deferment. Senator J. William Fulbright pressured the University of Arkansas ROTC colonel into certifying that Clinton was enrolled in the ROTC when he was not even enrolled in the university. That was a clear violation of federal law, but the media ignored it.

Nor were voters told the story of Charlette Perry, the black secretary who was denied an expected promotion in her Arkansas state government job. A fix was on. The job was given to Clinton's girl friend, Gennifer Flowers.

Charlette Perry filed a grievance. The committee that heard her complaint agreed that she had been discriminated against and recommended that she be promoted and given back pay. The Clinton administration in Arkansas ignored that. So did the pro-Clinton media.

One of the worst examples of pro-Clinton bias involved the sacrifice of a big scoop by *ABC News*. They got the letter that Clinton wrote thanking the ROTC colonel for saving him from the draft, but they sat on it for three days, allowing Clinton to release it himself. ABC's Ted Koppel told Clinton's people that the letter had been leaked by the Pentagon. That was false, but it was the basis of a diversionary Clinton maneuver—attacking the Pentagon. That night, Ted Koppel had Clinton as the only guest on *Nightline*, helping him to put the damaging letter in best possible light. The executive producer of *PrimeTime Live*, a close friend of a top Clinton adviser, denies allegations that he had a hand in this. His program on media bias showed his own bias by not exposing the biased media cover-up of Clinton's misdeeds.

March 15, 1993

Red Faces At The *Orange County Register*

Orange County, California, is considered one of the most conservative areas of the country, and its area newspaper, the *Orange County Register*, generally takes conservative stands on the issues. But one of the paper's positions that has troubled many readers is its opposition to the war on drugs. Rather than seek a crack-down on the use of illegal drugs, the *Register* has basically said that the war on drugs is lost, and that we should try something else. That something else is presumed to be decriminalization or legalization of drugs like marijuana and cocaine.

That position has been embraced by a small fringe group, including a few columnists, mayors and a group called the Drug Policy Foundation. This group was a key source of information to the *Orange County Register*. But now we know that this paper's raising of the white flag in the drug war may have been due to something other than an intellectual retreat. The *Register* was hit by a drug scandal.

The *Register* stated its opinion in an editorial that ran last September, titled, "Losing the Drug War." The paper said that the federal government was wasting its money and resources fighting drugs. The paper admitted that the war was being won in the sense that drug use has been declining, but it claimed this had nothing to do with the involvement of the federal government, and that the decline actually slowed down or leveled off after the feds got involved.

It also claimed that the effort to keep drugs illegal and prosecute drug traffickers and users was responsible for the increase in violent crimes and homicides linked to the drug trade. The paper claimed that "between 5,000 and 6,000 people per year are murdered because the government insists on waging a War on Drugs."

That's a strange way to put it, since the federal government is trying to eliminate a key part of the problem—illegal drugs. It is apparent to most people that the murders are being committed by thugs and drug dealers, not by law enforcement authorities. But this peculiar reasoning was put in a different perspective a month after that editorial was published when it was announced 76 employees at the *Register* had been forced to resign or were disciplined as the result of an internal investigation of drug use in the work place. That was 76 out of a total work force of 2,800. The paper admitted that the investigation was launched after employees described the sale and purchase of drugs at company offices.

We don't imply that the editorial advocating surrender in the war on drugs was linked to the use of illegal drugs. The paper never admitted what departments the 76 employees fired or suspended for drug use were based in. But this timing of events does suggest that it's worth a second look by readers when a paper or magazine tries to tell you that the war on drugs is over or can't be won. That rhetoric could be a tip-off that the publication has a drug problem that it doesn't want exposed.

March 15, 1993

It Sounded Convincing—
But It Was Not True

Its almost endless agitating on behalf of gay rights earned *The New York Times* the reputation of being a virtual house organ of the homosexual lobby. It wasn't surprising to see several editorials a week promoting the gay agenda. In November, after then-President-elect Clinton reaffirmed his stand for gays in the military, the *Times* weighed in with an editorial insisting that the president was right, and that experience abroad shows that gays "cut the mustard" in other armies.

The *Times* went so far as to claim that the Israeli Army, one of the most effective fighting forces in the world, requires homosexuals to serve their country, and that there is no discrimination against gay soldiers. The paper added, "Homosexuals are not denied promotion because of their sexual orientation; they serve in even the most elite fighting units, on critical frontiers."

That sounds pretty convincing—except for the fact that it's not true. And we know it's not true because the *Times* itself two months later finally admitted the truth. In a story datelined Jerusalem that ran on February 21st, correspondent Clyde Haberman spelled out the details, and they weren't helpful to the gay rights cause. The first relevant fact that needs to be emphasized is that in Israel, in contrast to the United States, there is military conscription. That means everyone—including gays—is subject to the draft. The *Times* said the conscripts are not asked if they are homosexual, and those who are openly homosexual are not drummed out of the service because of it.

That may sound like non-discrimination, and favorable to the gay rights cause. But seen in another way, it only means that the Israelis do not want people claiming homosexuality as an excuse to avoid military service. If the Israeli Army auto-

59

matically excluded declared homosexuals, it would serve as a convenient excuse for some to dodge the draft.

If they do claim homosexuality, *The New York Times* article made clear that they are discriminated against. They are required to undergo psychological and security tests. The paper said the Army regards them with distrust and concern that their sexual orientation might reflect emotional disorders. And contrary to what that *Times* editorial said last November, the *Times* article in February said identifiable homosexuals are restricted from serving in highly sensitive units like intelligence, and from some combat units where soldiers are together for long periods of time and under stress.

Contrary to what the *Times* said last November, when it was so eager to back Clinton's plan, the case of Israel argues against homosexuals in the military. And that leaves only a few countries that allow homosexuals to serve in the Armed Forces without restriction. Those military powerhouses include Luxembourg, Denmark, Norway and Sweden. If the American people want to follow the advice of *The New York Times*, then our military will join that distinguished list.

March 12, 1993

Is ABC At Clinton's Service?

What's cooking with Fidel Castro? On March 4, ABC's *PrimeTime Live* aired a very friendly interview with Castro by Diane Sawyer. She stayed with the kid-glove treatment that Castro is used to getting from American television journalists. It was never justified in the past, but now that the Cuban economy is so obviously down the drain, no self-respecting reporter should treat Fidel as anything but a failed tyrant whose departure is long overdue.

At the time Sawyer was conducting her interview, Castro was going through the motions of holding an old-fashioned communist sham election, with only one slate of candidates. Instead of exposing this as a farce, Sawyer asked Castro if the American system of quadrennial presidential elections seemed crazy to him. She probably didn't know that when he seized power 34 years ago, Castro's No. 1 promise was to restore constitutional democracy to Cuba.

Sawyer sat silent as Castro explained that four years was too short a period to accomplish anything, and eight was only a little better. He said that one could do a lot in twenty years, not blushing at the thought of his 34-year record of wrecking the economy and establishing the most totalitarian dictatorship in Cuba's history. Diane Sawyer didn't even blink when Castro derided *our* economic and foreign policies as insane.

Sawyer appeared to be on a mission to promote a dialogue between Castro and the Clinton administration, first interviewing President Clinton, asking what he would say to Castro, and then asking Castro what he would say to Clinton. What did Castro think of the new president and his wife? Would he welcome an invitation to meet with him? She summed up after the interview saying that Castro seems ready to start talking with a new administration and a new generation of Americans.

Could this be President Clinton's first attempt at electronic diplomacy to complement his electronic town meetings? The executive producer of *PrimeTime Live*, Rick Kaplan, is a close friend of Clinton adviser Susan Thomases. Thomases, though not a government employee, has a White House pass that gives her easy access to both Bill and Hillary Clinton. Kaplan himself has played golf with Bill Clinton. At a minimum, the White House gave Diane Sawyer's mission to Havana its blessing.

The involvement of *ABC News* in the move to ease pressure on Castro goes beyond *PrimeTime Live*. The same day Sawyer's interview aired, Peter Jennings, the anchorman on ABC's *World News Tonight*, told students at Howard University that he favored improving relations with Cuba. He said, "I have never thought it was particularly productive to keep any country at arms length." Reminding the audience that he was a Canadian, Jennings said, "I think Canadians have always felt that dialogue was better than rejection and that democratic nations, particularly the United States, have always done better by inviting their enemies in and their adversaries in, rather than rejecting them continually."

Jennings hasn't always felt that way. In June 1986, he devoted three quarters of his evening newscast—17 minutes out of 22—to a long-distance telephone interview with Bishop Desmond Tutu in South Africa. Bishop Tutu used this unprecedented amount of time to urge the United States to impose harsh sanctions on South Africa. The sanctions were imposed even though polls showed that the majority of South Africa's blacks opposed them. They are now credited with playing an important role in bringing about the dramatic political changes that are now taking place in South Africa.

In his talk at Howard University, Jennings was critical of the Cuban refugees who oppose lifting the embargo. He referred to them as "the Cuban lobby" whose "more conservative Cuban-American agenda has had a lock on the political discussion for a very long time." He said they had "prosecuted [sic] Castro and everyone else who lived on the island." Since the refugees have been in no position to put Castro in the dock, Jennings must have meant "persecuted."

The idea of Castro's victims persecuting their oppressor is, to say the least, a unique concept.

Unfortunately, there are no Cuban Tutus—residents of Cuba who are free to go on an ABC newscast to urge keeping the heat on Castro. Only those who have escaped can speak freely, but Peter Jennings thinks that our Cuban policy should be guided by Canadians, instead of Cubans who want "Cuba Libre" to become a reality, not just a drink enjoyed by Canadian visitors to Cuba Comunista.

March 9, 1993

How They Spread
Disinformation About Guns

The value of the C-SPAN television network has been demonstrated time and time again. Recent coverage of the Conservative Political Action Conference in Washington had an additional feature; it showed representatives of gun ownership groups directly blasting the major news media for blatant bias.

John Snyder, director of the Citizens Committee for the Right to Keep and Bear Arms, summarized the major gun control proposals as a ban on certain kinds of guns, a waiting period for gun purchases, and limits on the number of guns a person can buy in a certain time period. Snyder turned these proposals around to the detriment of the news media, asking what the press lords would say to laws forbidding journalists from using certain kinds of computers, from buying a certain number of pens or pencils, or using certain kinds of technology for information purposes.

Wayne LaPierre, president of the National Rifle Association, presented a strong case that the major media are actively promoting the erosion of second amendment rights by publicizing disinformation on the gun issue. He called the national media "our biggest problem" in preserving the right to keep and bear arms.

NBC, he charged, had created the impression that an armor piercing bullet was generally available to the public which could go through police body armor. He said the coverage led to 20 different bills being introduced in Congress to ban so-called "cop-killer" bullets. In fact, he said the ammo was never in wide circulation, and that the network obtained the bullet from a narcotics officer who presented proper identification.

LaPierre said columnist Jack Anderson caused a similar panic when he claimed there was a plastic gun available and that 3,000 were being purchased by Libyan terrorist leader Muammar Qaddafi. The implication was that Qaddafi's terrorists could smuggle these through airport metal detectors. The truth, he said, was that the gun was never undetectable because it had 20 ounces of steel in it, and Qaddafi never bought any of them. Nevertheless, 20 bills were introduced in Congress to ban it.

Finally, LaPierre cited the "one-gun-a-month" proposal of Virginia Governor Douglas Wilder, who claims guns from Virginia are fueling criminal violence in New York and other cities. LaPierre said the facts are that authorities confiscated 13,000 guns in New York City, and of the 800 that were traced, 190 came from Virginia. About half of those were possessed by generally law-abiding citizens who simply got caught with a firearm. Of the remainder, only 3 were used in murders. Nevertheless, LaPierre said ABC had led off a national news report claiming that 1 out of 4 guns found at murder scenes in New York City had come from Virginia. He said that when the NRA called ABC asking for documentation, they admitted they had none.

March 9, 1993

Peter Jennings Distorts The Facts

Peter Jennings, the suave Canadian who anchors ABC's *World News Tonight*, has been more discreet than his counterparts on NBC and CBS in confessing his liberal political bias publicly. Recently Jennings addressed journalism students at Howard University, a predominantly black school in Washington, D.C., and even though the talk was being aired by C-SPAN, Jennings gave some astonishing replies to questions from the students that clashed sharply with the image he likes to project on the air.

Responding to a question that was critical of media coverage of the landing of American troops in Somalia, Jennings said: "We had just come out of Desert Storm, which to this country's disgrace and to the media's disgrace and to the government's disgrace, and I would also argue to the public's disgrace which did not up and yell and cry about it, the media was totally locked out of a military operation. The access of the U.S. press to the operation Desert Storm was so negligible as to be virtually nonexistent."

The Gulf War was covered by well over a thousand correspondents and camera crews. They couldn't all be permitted to roam freely in the front lines, but pools were created to give reporters access to the troops. Daily military briefings both in Riyadh, Saudi Arabia and in Washington were beamed directly into millions of homes throughout the country. True, the military, having learned a bitter lesson in Vietnam, imposed censorship. But it was very mild, and the public overwhelmingly supported it. The breadth and immediacy of the coverage was unprecedented.

But here is why the media were allowed to cover the landings in Somalia, according to Peter Jennings: "The military had also come to understand that its failure to give anything other than the most controlled coverage of the Persian Gulf had left them with a victory in which the American people did not share."

"A victory in which the American people did not share?" It is a disgrace that the students at Howard University didn't rise up and yell and cry about that outrageous statement. The truth is that the American people were deliriously happy about the victory in the Gulf War, which had been achieved so quickly and with so few casualties.

Far from feeling that they didn't share in that victory, eight out of 10 Americans felt that the coverage of the war had been excellent or good according to a *Times Mirror* poll. Eighty-three percent approved the restrictions the military had placed on the coverage. Thanks to his successful prosecution of the war, President Bush's popularity soared to record heights. Thanks to their coverage of the war, there was even a sharp improvement in the popularity of the television news anchors. Ironically, Peter Jennings showed the biggest gain. The percentage that viewed him favorably rose to 43 percent in the March 1991 survey, a gain of 16 percentage points over his rating two years earlier.

March 8, 1993

Carl Rowan's Failed Attempt At Damage Control

Syndicated columnist and commentator Carl Rowan has a big problem. Twenty-five years ago he wrote an article blasting Martin Luther King Jr., the father of the civil rights movement, and linking him to communists. This is a problem for Rowan because he is black, and because he is a liberal who nowadays complains about red-baiting. Lately, Rowan has been traveling around the country promoting his book about the late Justice Thurgood Marshall, the first black on the Supreme Court. But Rowan still can't get away from that 1967 article he wrote about King. Rowan is so embarrassed by the article that he is suppressing the distribution of tapes featuring his comments about it.

The fiasco occurred on the Diane Rehm radio show in Washington, D.C., when Rowan appeared as a guest promoting his book on Marshall. A caller raised the subject of the September 1967 *Reader's Digest* article written by Rowan about King. The caller noted that the article strongly criticized King for attacking the Administration's policy of fighting Communist aggression in Vietnam. The caller added that the article quoted people as connecting King with communism.

At that point in the show, Diane Rehm must have noticed Rowan shifting uncomfortably in his chair, for she said, "Where are you going with this?" And Rowan jumped in, saying, "Yes, I'm familiar with it. What's your question?" The caller said his question was simply whether Rowan held the same opinion of King now that he had then. Rowan countered, "You're making it appear that I was some kind of enemy of Martin Luther King." When the caller said he was only quoting the *Reader's Digest* article, Rowan accused him of quoting it "way out of context."

Then, Rowan provided his "historical perspective" on

the incident. He said he wrote the article at a time when black leaders were telling King that he shouldn't link the civil rights movement to calling President Johnson "a killer" for his prosecution of the Vietnam War. Rowan added, "There was no suggestion on my part that Martin Luther King was a communist." On the contrary, he said he had written a book about FBI campaigns against King.

The essential facts, which contradict Rowan, are less important than his unwillingness to have his explanation preserved for posterity. We say this because after the Diane Rehm program advertised the tape of the program for re-sale purposes, her staff suddenly announced that the hour of the program featuring his defense of his *Reader's Digest* article was NOT available. Her assistant told someone interested in the tape that "Mr. Rowan would not release that hour" for reproduction purposes. That's too bad for Carl Rowan because the contents of the conversation were already out in the public domain, and his effort at damage control fell short. This may be more embarrassing than the original article.

March 5, 1993

Dirty Election Tricks By CBS

Congressman Bob Livingston, a Louisiana Republican, says that *60 Minutes* set out to smear him during last year's campaign, using deception similar to that practiced by *NBC News* in its attacks on GM pickup trucks and the Forest Service. NBC used footage to make its points, but the film was not what it was represented to be. Livingston says that *60 Minutes* tried to portray him as a tool of the radical animal rights advocates, which, he says, couldn't be further from the truth. The program was scheduled for airing last October, but it was dropped from the schedule when Livingston won re-election in the primary a month before the general election.

As aired on January 24, the *60 Minutes* segment portrayed Livingston as a villain for having initiated an investigation into a research project being carried out by Dr. Michael E. Carey of Louisiana State University. Dr. Carey, a professor of neurosurgery, had spent some $2 million of taxpayer funds shooting anesthetized cats in the head to gather information on brain injuries. This was funded by the Army, which thought that the research might be useful in the treatment of wounded soldiers.

Bob Livingston says, "No one wants more to help the soldier than Bob Livingston, and I have always supported animal research *if it is legitimate*. But when questions arose about the quality and value of Carey's research, I turned it over to the General Accounting Office (GAO) for the experts to evaluate. The GAO learned that . . . Carey had published no papers and had no discernible results to talk about despite more than six years of effort. Only after the investigation began, did he start to publish papers on his research, and to this day, no private drug or medical companies are known to have shown any interest in Carey's findings."

It was on the basis of the report issued by the GAO, not

70

because of any pressure from Livingston, that the Defense Department decided to terminate its contract with Dr. Carey. Livingston says he agrees with the decision, because we had nothing to show for the research but a lot of dead cats.

60 Minutes muddied the waters by showing clips of animal rights extremists marching in the streets, giving the impression that the termination of Dr. Carey's research was being driven by the protests of crazies like People for the Ethical Treatment of Animals. The footage of the animal rights demonstrations used by CBS had absolutely nothing to do with the case of Dr. Carey and his cats.

60 Minutes didn't say that Bob Livingston was serving as point man for the animal rights crazies, but any viewer could be forgiven for drawing that conclusion. Since the Carey contract was canceled in 1991, we wondered why *60 Minutes* was doing a story about it at this late date. Livingston's office said *60 Minutes* shelved its smear job when Livingston won re-election in the primary and was no longer vulnerable. They resurrected it on January 24th when a segment they planned to run that night was canceled at the last minute and they needed a replacement.

March 2, 1993

Another *NBC Nightly News* Faking Scandal

A few days after his network was caught rigging crash tests of GM trucks, *NBC News* president Michael Gartner made an impassioned speech to demoralized staff members. Move on, Gartner exhorted, follow our standards. "We can't let ourselves be defined by 57 seconds," he said, referring to the length of the controversial video of the tests.

Unfortunately for the embattled Gartner, *NBC News* has been caught in another faking scandal that shows that their problem is a lot more serious than Gartner would have us think. On January 4, an "America Closeup" segment on the *NBC Nightly News* set out to prove that logging is killing fish in national forests. NBC made its "case" by misrepresenting the facts and using misidentified film footage. The main thrust of the story was that the national forests are being denuded by logging and that something must be done to keep the Forest Service from permitting trees to be cut at the rate planned. That is false.

The report focused on the Clearwater National Forest in northern Idaho. To make the point that there had been excessive clearcutting there, NBC showed footage of an area that had been cut to salvage the timber after a forest fire. It also showed footage of an area overcut by design, but it was in the Olympic National Forest in Washington state. Annual new growth in the Clearwater is estimated at 250 million board feet per year. The Clearwater National Forest plan provides for annual sales of up to 173 million board feet per year for ten years. Last year, a mere 26 million board feet were actually sold because of program gridlock caused by numerous environmentalist lawsuits and appeals. Over 60 percent of the Clearwater has never been logged at all.

In addition to trying to create the impression that the trees were vanishing, NBC claimed that logging in the Clearwater was polluting the streams and killing the fish. To prove this point it showed viewers a man in waders in a stream netting fish that correspondent Robin Lloyd said had been killed by the water pollution. Another shot showed several large fish floating belly-up in a stagnant pool, presumably victims of pollution caused by logging in the Clearwater National Forest.

This was even more phony than the rigged tests of the GM pickup trucks. The fish that were being netted had been stunned by electro-shock to facilitate a fish count to measure the stream's health. The man doing the netting was a biologist. NBC had obtained this footage from the Idaho Public Broadcasting Service, which was properly incensed by the use made of it. The footage of the large fish that were floating belly up came from an unknown source. The timber people assert it wasn't shot in the Clearwater National Forest.

NBC claimed that 70 percent of the streams in the Clearwater were in violation of water quality standards. The industry claims that water quality standards adopted in the mid-1980s were based on flawed assumptions that set standards that could not be met by 47 percent of the streams in wilderness areas that had never been logged. They note that while 70 percent of all the streams failed to meet some of the new standards, this doesn't mean the streams are being poisoned. They point out that two of the most productive cutthroat trout fisheries in the country are on Clearwater streams in areas that have been logged. The pollution rap against logging is simply that building logging roads increases silt in the streams.

The Intermountain Forest Industry Association demanded that NBC retract its incorrect story. NBC did nothing until February 24, when Tom Brokaw delivered the following statement at the end of his *NBC Nightly News* program: "Last month we reported on Forest Service employees in Idaho's Clearwater National Forest who felt the forest was overcut, causing fouled streams and endangering fish. At one brief point we inadvertently used footage of dead fish from another forest further south, not from Clearwater. We also showed workers conducting tests on water in the Clearwater where fish appeared to be dead. In fact, they were not; they had been stunned for testing purposes. And finally, we showed a large area of land that the timber industry claims was burned and not cut. Our information remains that the video accurately portrayed clearcuts, although some portions may have been cut after a fire. We regret the inappropriate video to illustrate what was otherwise an accurate report."

Tom Brokaw should have said, "The misrepresentation of the video footage in this story occurred because the producers were determined to convince you of the truth of allegations that are simply not true. Lacking bonafide footage that would support their story line, they falsely described what you were shown. We learned of this immediately after the program was aired on January 4, but, as with our story on GM pickup trucks, we tried unsuccessfully to brazen it out. Those responsible for perpetrating the deception and the coverup have all been fired. If you know of any openings for a slightly tarnished anchorman, please let me know."

February 23, 1993

Helping Hide The Real Hillary Clinton

Reporters have been debating recently about how to cover Hillary Rodham Clinton, whose name used to be Hillary Clinton, and before that, Hillary Rodham. Marian Burros, who covers food for *The New York Times*, recently obtained an exclusive interview with Mrs. Clinton. It dealt with her taste in food, what's going to be served at White House dinners, and her banning of smoking in the White House. This front-page story featured the dramatic news that broccoli, a vegetable hated by President Bush, was back in favor.

But even more newsworthy than that was something not reported by the *Times*: as a condition of the interview, the paper was reportedly told it could not ask anything at all about Mrs. Clinton's role as a policy maker. So the question remains: how and when are reporters going to hold Mrs. Clinton accountable for the role she plays beyond that of First Lady.

The *Times* interview appeared to be the first shot fired by Mrs. Clinton in a campaign to divert attention away from her policy-making role. She is taking such an active role in policy, especially in the health care field, that she is being talked about as the co-president. But Mrs. Clinton doesn't want to talk too much about that. Soon after the *Times* article about her food habits appeared, Mrs. Clinton's social secretary appeared on not one, not two, but all three morning programs to discuss Mrs. Clinton's style as First Lady. These are the operations in the White House East Wing.

But Mrs. Clinton also has an office in the West Wing, where President Clinton and his top advisers are based. This is where Mrs. Clinton is laying out reform of our health care system. She was appointed the chairman of a task force on health care by her husband, the President. In this role, she coordinates the activities of 6 members of the president's cabinet. This is the area of concern that *The New York Times* was told it could not ask about.

The question is, why? It appears that Mrs. Clinton is hiding behind the traditional status of First Lady in order to escape scrutiny as presidential adviser. Some might say that First Ladies have always performed such a role, and that Nancy Reagan, for example, played a role in policy matters. But Nancy Reagan's motive seemed to be solely protection of her husband. She did not have a distinctive ideological agenda apart from his. Mrs. Clinton is known to have an ideological agenda and may, in fact, be even more liberal than the President.

It's time for the major media to subject both Clintons to some tough questions. Among them: isn't her role, though unpaid, in violation of the federal law against nepotism? And what was the significance of her changing her name after the election? And why has her task force on health care, in possible violation of federal law, been holding meetings in secret? It's time for answers, not more stories on broccoli.

February 23, 1993

Why They're Called
The Media "Elite"

The term "media elite" has been used over the years to refer to those editors, reporters and commentators in top positions of power in the media business. But they're also called elitists because many think of themselves as above and apart from the masses of ordinary Americans. Don't think we're exaggerating when we say this. *NBC News* veteran journalist John Chancellor recently gave an amazing speech denouncing the power of average people to affect political change. He admitted that he sounded elitist, but that didn't bother him one bit.

Chancellor's remarks were triggered by the incredible outburst from the American people over President Clinton's plan to admit open homosexuals into the military. Part of the outrage was funneled through radio talk shows around the country. Chancellor said he didn't like the growing popularity of these shows on radio or TV and their influence in the political process.

Turning his attention to the political campaign, Chancellor let it be known that he didn't like the fact that candidates went on the talk shows and avoided the so-called mainstream media. He didn't like the kinds of questions that were asked by the hosts of these programs or their audiences. Chancellor said, "Ordinary folks are not trained to conduct a serious interview with candidates. It is perilous to turn everything over to the people of the United States. You shouldn't reduce the dialogue to the lowest common denominator."

According to a story about his speech in *Broadcasting* magazine, Chancellor acknowledged that his remarks sounded "undemocratic" and "elitist." But he said, "you need a better way of running the country . . . than turning it over to the people." Chancellor claimed that politicians who talk directly to the people through talk shows may turn into "demagogues," and that, he said, will be a real worry.

The real worry is that unelected media elites such as Chancellor have turned into demagogues. The criticism of President Bush used to be that he was isolated from the people. Well, John Chancellor makes Bush look like a man of the people. It would do John Chancellor good if he sat down on some radio and TV talk shows and listened to what the people had to say for a change. For far too long, he's been giving commentaries on *NBC Nightly News* without feedback.

The basic flaw in his argument is that he mistakenly believes that the people are incapable of understanding the important issues and knowing how to question the candidates accordingly. He presumes that only a few top editors, reporters and commentators have the knowledge necessary to probe the issues and keep government going in the direction they want. The good news it that John Chancellor's arrogance won't be a problem for us much longer. This dinosaur, the last of the evening news liberal commentators, will be retiring in June. Good riddance.

February 19, 1993

Do Cellular Phones Really Cause Cancer?

People calling into CNN's *Larry King Live* program recently may have had second thoughts if they were calling in on a cellular telephone. The reason—the show was about claims that cellular phones cause brain cancer. The completely unsubstantiated charge is that the cancer is somehow linked to the radio waves, frequencies or energy generated by the phone.

Despite the fact that no medical evidence for the claim was presented on the air, CNN permitted a Florida man to argue that he believed a hand-held cellular phone had given his wife a brain tumor. The sensational claims may have generated good ratings for Ted Turner's CNN, but the end result of the frenzied chain reaction that Larry King set in motion was that the stock of two major cellular companies eventually fell 9 percent.

Steve Young, a business reporter for CNN, followed up with a report on the controversy that noted that a "blizzard of negative stories" had appeared about cellular phones. That was true. Unfortunately, his story was part of the blizzard that began on his own network. In fact, his report was worse because he peddled what he admitted was "runaway speculation" that several personalities in the news, including former GOP chairman Lee Atwater, had gotten brain tumors from the use of hand-held cellular phones. He provided no evidence that the speculation was true.

But the worst performance was turned in by someone who should know better—ABC's medical expert, Dr. Tim Johnson. In a story that aired on ABC's *20/20* program, Dr. Johnson interviewed a couple of people who thought their brain tumors had been caused by the phones. But he then provided important evidence that the claims couldn't be true. First, an expert from the Medical College of Virginia who is studying the matter said the claim of a cancer link to the phones was "probably not" true, but that he couldn't say anything for sure. Second, Dr. Johnson provided an analysis of the data on brain cancer cases. The data showed that the number of cases had risen from 5 per 100,00 in 1973 to only 6 per 100,000 in 1989. Since cellular phones came on the market in 1984 and there are ten million in use today, one would expect a larger increase if phones were the cause.

Furthermore, Dr. Johnson interviewed another expert who noted that the new cases do not show the tumors developing behind the ear, which is where they would develop if they were linked to the phones. The expert said the pattern of placement of tumors continues to be random in nature.

But after essentially debunking the cancer scare, Dr. Johnson fanned the flames of the controversy by telling *20/20* moderators Hugh Downs and Barbara Walters that if he had such a phone, he would use it only "occasionally" or "intermittently" and not "for hours on end." The doctor was unwilling to criticize his colleagues in the media for unnecessarily scaring the public.

February 16, 1993

"That's Not What We Said At All!"

The days before the Super Bowl game, the media blossomed with stories about how wives and other women could expect to be slapped around in great numbers by men inflamed by watching the violence of professional football. The story was hawked by a far-left outfit named Fairness and Accuracy in Reporting, or FAIR, which describes itself as a media watchdog group. FAIR press agents put out a news release warning women, "Don't remain alone with him during the game." Now, it turns out, FAIR was hoodwinking the very media it claims to be monitoring for fairness and accuracy.

The story which FAIR peddled to reporters through its so-called "women's bureau" was supposedly based on a study by Old Dominion University in Virginia that found that beatings and hospital admissions of women rose 40 percent each time the Washington Redskins won a football game. FAIR's story got air time on the Big Three TV networks—ABC, CBS and NBC—as well as in such newspapers as the *Boston Globe* and *San Francisco Examiner*. CBS and the Associated Press warned women about what they called "a day of dread." NBC, which telecast the Super Bowl, was browbeaten into airing a public service announcement during the game which urged men not to mistreat women.

But one reporter decided to look beyond the press release put out by the left-wing FAIR. Ken Ringle of *The Washington Post* talked to the Old Dominion University researchers who did the report cited by FAIR. One of the researchers listened to Ringle read the FAIR press release and retorted, "That's not what we said at all!" The university in fact had done a study of emergency room admissions, but researchers found no association between football and increased injuries.

The *Post's* Ken Ringle found other FAIR prevarications.

A Chicago psychologist, who is an expert on battered women, stated that FAIR created from whole cloth a quotation attributed to him in a press release. And a Denver psychologist who was cited by FAIR as an expert on Super Bowl spouse abuse said the claim was "news to me"—that is, false.

A woman who helped spread the misinformation was Linda Mitchell, described as head of FAIR's "women's bureau." Mitchell admitted to Ken Ringle that she knew that the Old Dominion University study was misrepresented by a women's right advocate who spoke at a FAIR press conference in Pasadena, the Super Bowl site. Why, then, reporter Ringle asked, did not Mitchell step in and make a correction? This is what Linda Mitchell of Fairness and Accuracy in Reporting replied, "I wouldn't do that in front of the media. She has a right to report it as she wants." End of quote.

And, in our opinion, the end of FAIR's credibility as well. Instead of battered women, what got battered by FAIR was the truth. And as *The Wall Street Journal* noted in an editorial about the FAIR fiasco, the circulation of the false story could end up hurting efforts to curb the real problem of spouse beating.

February 8, 1993

NBC Fakery Exposed: The Truth About The Phony GM Truck Crash

NBC News has learned an embarrassing lesson from General Motors: if you fake auto-crash tests, make sure that bystanders don't have video cameras. On November 17 NBC's *Dateline* aired a segment alleging that GM full-size pickup trucks made from 1973-1987 were rolling firebombs because their two gas tanks were located on the sides outside the main frame of the vehicles. The segment included a test segment supposedly showing a GM pickup set afire when hit at 30 miles an hour.

Dateline correspondent Michelle Gillen said: "In one crash at about 40 miles per hour there was no leakage and no fire. But in the other, at around 30 miles per hour, look what happened." The film showed a wall of flame seemingly coming from the side of the truck after the collision, but it quickly cut away. Gillen explained, "At impact a small hole was punctured in the tank. According to our experts, the pressure of the collision and the crushing of the gas tank forced gasoline to spew from the gas cap. The fuel erupted into flames when ignited by the impacting car's headlight. The pickup's tank did not split wide open. If it had, the fire would have been much larger."

NBC refused to provide GM with scientific data on the tests and told them the vehicles couldn't be inspected because they had been junked. But in mid-January GM discovered that the group that had conducted the tests for NBC, The Institute for Safety Analysis (TISA), had rigged the trucks with incendiary devices that were ignited just before each vehicle was hit in an effort to ignite a fire. TISA does work for personal injury lawyers who specialize in auto safety cases.

GM investigators went to Hendricks County, Indiana, and took statements from firemen and a deputy sheriff who witnessed the tests. They obtained a video that a fireman made showing the NBC crash from a different angle and some still photos. According to the firemen, 'pyrotechnic people" had fitted four to six model rocket engines on the underside of each pickup around the gas tanks to ignite any leaking gas. These were ignited just before impact by a radio control device. GM investigators scoured area junkyards and found the truck that had ignited the fire. One of the rockets was still in place, held by duct tape.

Physical and X-ray examinations of the truck's gas tank failed to detect the small hole Gillen claimed had been "punctured in the tank." A fireman told GM investigators that the testers had "topped off" the tank from gas cans just before the test. For safety reasons, tanks are designed so they fill only to within five gallons of capacity from a conventional pump. Manually, they can be filled to the intake, which is apparently what the NBC testers did. Then they "sealed" the tank with a non-GM cap that popped off when the truck was hit. By overfilling the tank, using a cheap, non-GM cap, and firing the rockets around the tank, the NBC testers managed to start a fire.

How much of a fire? It looked impressive as shown on *Dateline*, but they cut away quickly. Thanks to video and audio tapes made by the firemen and others who witnessed the test, we know why. After the brief burst of flame upon impact, a patch of grass alongside the truck burned for about 15 seconds. The truck body showed minor paint blistering from the grass fire. Voices can be heard on an audio tape made near the fireman's video as the grass burns. "There ain't that much fire," one man comments. "It didn't do what we wanted it to do,' comes the reply. "You can survive that." "So much for that theory!' someone quips, and there is laughter.

According to the witnesses, the minor fire came after the first crash, which occurred at a speed of at least 39 miles per hour, according to GM's experts who analyzed the NBC video. Disappointed, NBC tried again, this time upping the speed of the crash car to 47 miles per hour, according to GM, not the 40 claimed by NBC. This time, despite the higher speed, the incendiary rockets, and the same overfilling of the gas tank, no fire resulted.

In the broadcast, NBC showed the second test first, leaving the impression that they had proven that the pickups were a fire hazard. If they had honestly admitted that despite all the rigging, they didn't get much of a fire on the first test and failed utterly on the second try at the higher speed, their case would have been blown sky high.

GM announced on February 8 that for the first time in its history it is suing a media company for defamation. It had a strong case. The fakery involved in the tests was outrageous, but so too was the one-sided, emotion-laden but statistics-poor presentation that preceded it. GM's evidence that the safety of its pickups compares favorably with its competitors is compelling, and NBC's *Dateline* was forced to admit that the test had been rigged and to make an apology on the air.

February 8, 1993

What Mainstream News Reporters Really Think Of Mainstream Americans

Are you angry about President Clinton's attempt to force-feed homosexuals into an unwilling military? Are you tired of Washington politicians ignoring the laws that apply to the rest of us? If the answers are yes, you'll perhaps be surprised to learn that you are "poor, uneducated and easy to command," obeying voices that you hear over "Thug Radio."

Something remarkable is happening in America these first weeks of 1993. The general public is standing up and telling the mainstream press that it no longer accepts the media's agenda on such issues as ordering the military to admit homosexuals, or believing that an attorney general-nominee who violates immigration and tax laws is fit to hold office.

Through talk radio and fax and phone messages, citizens are bypassing the media and taking their angry protests directly to the Congress and President Clinton. So how are our media responding to citizens who don't accept the press's self-assigned role as the arbiter of acceptable behavior? Our media are frightened silly that the American people are speaking out and in effect telling hot-shot commentators, columnists, network anchors and even reporters to get lost.

Democracy particularly offends columnist Anthony Lewis of *The New York Times*. Lewis is an unusual fellow. Many years ago, when he started writing a column tagged "Abroad At Home," he chose Boston as his home base, explaining to readers that he did not want to risk being steeped in the Washington/New York mindset. The political peculiarities of Boston perhaps explain why Lewis is so out of touch with average Americans, as reflected in a February 1 piece in which he ranted about the dangers of "mass participatory democracy."

Listen to Lewis: "The danger of mass participatory

democracy is that it can be manipulated: shaped by ideologues and demagogues.'' He conceded that the outrage over Zoe Baird ''seemed genuine,'' coming from a public ''sensitized by the scandals of recent years. . . . But the protests against President Clinton's plan to end the ban on gay men and women in the service were different. To a considerable degree they were orchestrated by the religious right and conservative extremists. . . . The extreme-right talk shows hosts on Thug Radio also denounced the Clinton plan.''

Lewis misses the point. He does not comprehend the depth of public revulsion at a presidential scheme that threatens to put the entire military establishment in jeopardy. His shrill protest is a sign that he and other pundits feel their accustomed control of public opinion is slipping.

Michael Weisskopf displayed the same arrogant elitism in a front-page article in *The Washington Post*, claiming that the flood of calls on the military gay ban ''demonstrated the power of the religious right to mobilize its masses for the kind of political action that shook official Washington.'' Weisskopf spoke of ''the gospel lobby,'' and listed a number of Christian evangelical radio and TV programs, among them those of Jerry Falwell and Pat Robertson. ''Their followers', he said, ''are largely poor, uneducated and easy to command.''

Flooded with angry calls protesting this put-down of evangelical Christians, the next day the *Post* ran this correction in its early editions: ''An article yesterday characterized followers of television evangelists as 'largely poor, uneducated and easy to command.' There is no factual basis for that statement. According to a nationwide Gallup Poll conducted in November, 38 percent of Americans identifying themselves as 'Evangelical-Born Again' Christians had some college education, compared with 45 percent of all Americans. Thirty-five percent of evangelicals had incomes of more than $30,000 a year, compared to 43 percent of the population as a whole.''

It was a good correction, but someone at the *Post* didn't like it. In the paper's final edition it was reduced to, ''An article yesterday characterized followers of television evangelists Jerry Falwell and Pat Robertson as 'largely poor, uneducated and easy to command.' There is no factual basis for that statement." The *Post's* ombudsman said the change was made because Weisskopf had not smeared all evangelicals, only those who listen to Falwell and Robertson, and the Gallup Poll was not limited to them.

Liberals who dominate the media worked hard to put their favorite, Bill Clinton, in the White House, expecting to bring about a cultural revolution. Not sharing or understanding the values of the majority, they expected to see the homosexual lifestyle win the seal of military approval by the stroke of Clinton's pen. They are in a state of shock to find that there are still millions of Americans who don't agree with their agenda and are willing to stand up for the values they hold dear. These Americans are not "easy to command" "yahoos" and "thugs." They are the kind of people who made this nation great and who have risen in their wrath to show that they want to keep it that way.

February 2, 1993

Why *Time* Magazine Took Rush Limbaugh's Picture Off Its Cover

The October 26th issue of *Time* magazine was very popular—the second best-selling issue of the year. If you just saw the cover story, you would have wondered why. It was about the discovery of a frozen stone age man and whether it would yield new clues as to what life was like in 3300 B.C. But the secret to the success of this issue could be found inside—an article about and an interview with the nation's most popular radio talk show host, Rush Limbaugh.

Limbaugh, who toots his own horn, had heavily promoted this issue in advance to his millions of radio listeners. And he thought he would be on the cover. *Time* magazine photographers had been taking pictures of him that he was led to believe would produce a cover shot. It wasn't to be: for reasons still not clear, Limbaugh was replaced on the cover by a stone age ice man. It is apparent that a decision was made not to give him the additional exposure that a cover photograph would bring him. But Limbaugh's promotion of the issue meant that it would be a big seller nonetheless.

Limbaugh was quick to make the point on his TV show that it wasn't the ice man who made that issue such a big seller. An actual ice man was placed in front of Limbaugh on TV as he interviewed him about the current issues of the day, such as condoms in the schools. The ice man was silent and responded with drips as he thawed out in front of Limbaugh's TV audience.

It's Limbaugh with the opinions, and he was quick to give them in the *Time* interview. He discussed why he supported Pat Buchanan against President Bush in the Republican presidential primary, and why he opposed Bill Clinton. He attacked feminism and rigorously defended the rights of the unborn. The article next to the interview was not complimentary to Limbaugh—it was headlined, "Conservative Provocateur or Big Blowhard?" That is hardly the choice as seen by fans of Limbaugh. They see him as a man with common sense about America's problems.

Time magazine's treatment of Limbaugh demonstrated the double standards of the liberals who hate him. First, he was accused of implying that women become feminists because they're ugly—something he never said—and the magazine then made fun of how Limbaugh looks, noting his 300 pound frame. Second, *Time* reported the charge that one bookstore in Portland, Oregon, had refused to stock his best-selling book because it was outspokenly conservative. *Time* didn't call that censorship.

Time magazine was aware of his selling power; that's why they decided to do a big story about him, together with an interview. But in the final analysis, its own liberalism overcame its best news judgment. A decision was therefore made to drop him from the cover, replacing him with a relic from the stone age. Limbaugh had the best answer to this kind of news management—he laughed at it.

February 1, 1993

Censorship At
Time Warner

Here's a good example of media hypocrisy in the raw. Time Warner Inc., the entertainment conglomerate, doesn't mind earning millions of dollars by huckstering rap music that advocates murdering police and sexually abusing teen girls. Wrapping the First Amendment around his shoulders, Gerald Levin, the company's CEO, insists that doing so is vital to protecting free speech.

Why, then, are Levin and other Time Warner executives in a tizzy about Accuracy in Media's attempt to enable the company's shareholders to read for themselves the sort of obscene filth they are peddling? Here is how Time Warner worked itself into a ridiculous censorship situation that is attempting to protect management from shareholder wrath.

One of the highlights of last summer's annual shareholders meeting came when actor Charlton Heston read lyrics from some of the songs the media conglomerate was distributing for rap singer Ice-T.

Many of the thousand shareholders present best know Heston's magisterial voice from such movie roles as Moses in "The Ten Commandments." Therefore, many of them reacted with visible disgust as Heston read unexpurgated passages from the album "Cop Killer." These included the title song, which advocates murdering police officers, and "KKK Bitch" about a fantasy Ice-T and his thuggish friends had about sexually-abusing Tipper Gore's two 12-year-old nieces. Another song in the album, "Momma's Gotta Die Tonight,' suggests that youngsters who don't like what their mothers are doing should murder them.

Heston charged that Time Warner was defending these records out of greed, not out of principle. He said that because he was speaking out, "It will be a cold day in hell before I'm offered another picture from Warners or get another good review in *Time* magazine."

Heston's appearance put Levin on the defensive. Ignoring the lyrics, he argued that "Cop Killer" did not advocate violence against police. He said that his defense of Ice-T reflected the unanimous view of the company, but he rejected demands that individual directors speak for themselves.

Levin seemed nervous about letting the general public hear the trash his company is peddling to the youth of America. He barred TV cameras and tape recorders from the meeting. This meant that the Big Three TV networks, CNN, and radio stations could not let the public hear one of the more dramatic performances of Heston's career.

But pressure mounted on Time Warner to disassociate itself from "Cop Killer." NBC's *Today* show aired a videotape of an interview Ice-T gave during the Los Angeles riots in which he advocated killing police officers and declared that he personally would like to blow up "some [expletive] police stations." That pulled the rug from under Levin's claim that Ice-T didn't mean what his records said. Time Warner quickly announced that Ice-T was voluntarily removing the "Cop Killer" song from the album. But the other "vile and irresponsible" songs—that's the way *Time* magazine described them—remained in record shops.

Keeping the heat on Levin, AIM proposed a resolution for inclusion in the proxy material for the 1993 Time Warner annual meeting. It asks that the board repudiate Levin's defense of Ice-T and his songs and assure the public that their repetition or continuation will not be tolerated. AIM's supporting statement quoted excerpts from the unexpurgated lyrics of "Cop Killer," 'KKK Bitch" and "Momma's Gotta Die Tonight."

Time Warner asked the Securities & Exchange Commission to agree to let it omit AIM's resolution from the proxy material, arguing, among other things, that it dealt with matters that were none of the shareholders' business. But it let the cat out of the bag by appending this footnote: "If, for any reason, the [SEC] does not concur with our request to omit the proposal, we would appreciate the opportunity to discuss with the staff omitting certain portions of the supporting statement which we feel may contain language which, while artistically supportable, may be inappropriate for inclusion in a proxy statement distributed to the general public.''

Time Warner proxy statements are not distributed to the general public. They are distributed to the company's owners—the shareholders. It is the Ice-T albums that are distributed to the general public, mainly young people. Time Warner's management obviously doesn't want the owners to see what vile material they are selling to our impressionable youth. The question is, will the SEC agree with Time Warner's argument that this is none of the owners' business? [*Note: Sad to say, it did.*]

January 26, 1993

How The Networks Made Bush Look Bad

President Bush complained emotionally at a recent news conference about a network production technique that had made it appear as though he didn't care about the loss of American lives in Panama. The technique, called a split-screen, was used by *CBS News, ABC News* and CNN on December 21 when they aired a live White House news conference, during which President Bush was upbeat about the invasion of Panama, and, at the same time, showed the flag-draped caskets of dead soldiers coming home.

The President, who was seen smiling and even bantering with reporters at the news conference, was unaware that viewers of the three networks were also seeing the dead Americans on a different part of the television screen. Roger Ailes, media adviser to Bush's presidential campaign, blasted the networks, saying, "To run them both together and not tell the President, that is dirty pool." Ailes said the networks could have taped one event and then played it later, or used their standard technique of announcing an interruption of the broadcast for more important news.

Spokesmen for the networks denied that they tried to embarrass the President. But only *ABC News* announced that it was abandoning the split-screen approach. *ABC News* president Roone Arledge was said to have agreed "in essence" with the President. Spokesmen for *ABC News* and CNN also said that, after the use of the split-screen approach, they informed their viewers that the President didn't know about the juxtaposition of the images.

Nevertheless, the White House was apparently bombarded with angry mail and telephone calls. The President said, "I could understand why the viewers were concerned about this. They thought their President at a solemn moment like that didn't give a damn." His voice breaking with emotion, the

President told the news conference, "And I do. I do. I feel it so strongly. So please help me with that if you would."

The President said he would respectfully request the media to inform him if there were another urgent news development, so that he could stop his news conference. But, except for *ABC News*, the networks announced that they didn't think it would be appropriate to inform the President in advance. The controversy was covered in some detail on the evening news programs on ABC, NBC and CNN. However, *CBS Evening News* anchorman Dan Rather reported only that President Bush criticized some television networks because "he did not like the showing of flag-draped coffins coming home at the same time his last news conference was going on."

On the *NBC Nightly News*, anchor Tom Brokaw added what some observers thought was a strange sidelight. Referring to Bush's conduct at the December 21 news conference, during which he also joked about his stiff neck, Brokaw said some unnamed White House official said that the President "may have been a little light-headed" because "he had taken a muscle relaxant for his stiff neck."

It's difficult to see the relevance of this comment. It only reinforced the media's effort, perhaps unconsciously, to make the President look bad.

January 18, 1993

When *ABC News* Didn't Tell The Whole Story

A longtime staple for investigative reporters has been the "See, we did it!" story. Several years ago *CBS News* exposed lax security at airports by smuggling weapons past the guards. A senior editor at *Business Week* got Vice President Quayle's personal credit report and published it in his magazine to show that it was easy to obtain another person's financial history, if you were willing to lie and risk being prosecuted. We have seen reporters test the honesty of auto repair shops by taking in a car with a wire disconnected to see if they will be charged for an unnecessary expensive repair job.

This makes for interesting and often useful stories that can bring about reforms. But what happens when journalists set up an elaborate test to show that something doesn't work as it's supposed to and they get caught? Do they publicize their failure and give proper credit to those who caught and exposed them? That might make a very amusing story, but it would be at the expense of egg on the face of the journalists, and they don't go for that. When this happened recently to the *ABC News* program *20/20*, it could not bring itself to admit being outwitted by the U.S. Customs Service while reporting a segment on drug interdiction along the U.S-Mexico border.

ABC's crew set out to prove that it is easy for drug smugglers to circumvent a sophisticated air system along the border which combines balloon-borne radar sensors, chase aircraft and helicopters. ABC correspondent Tom Jarriel had a cute idea. He and a crew went into Mexico in a single-engine Cessna 182 aircraft and bought a taco and wrapped it in an *ABC News* pouch. The plane then flew into Arizona, dipped down to 250 feet, dropped the taco pouch and returned to Mexico. The taco, of course, was a substitute for narcotics.

But the Customs Service wasn't fooled. One plane flew along behind the craft carrying Tom Jarriel, while another tracked an ABC van that picked up the package. In other words, the Customs Service interdiction worked. Had Jarriel and his crew smuggled cocaine, rather than a taco, the whole crowd could have gone to jail. Arizona newspapers had much fun with the story about ABC's failure. *The Arizona Republic* headline read *20/20* Crew Smuggles Taco, May Eat Charges." A headline elsewhere over a widely-printed Associated Press story read "Customs Passes '*20/20*' Test."

The Customs Service, too, felt it had "passed" the ABC test. But when *20/20* aired its segment on December 8, Jarriel never mentioned his network's failed exercise. Instead, he talked at length about drug smugglers running rings around the Customs Service on the border, and how the radar detection system was an outright failure. He claimed that there are "dead spots" with no radar coverage where drug smugglers can sneak over from Mexico.

Tom Jarriel wasn't honest enough to admit that Customs caught the ABC network redhanded in trying to breach the system—that ABC wasn't able to get even a taco across the border, much less any dope, without getting caught. Further, an *ABC News* crew had spent two days with Customs officials receiving detailed briefings on how the interdiction system worked. Even with this insider's information ABC could not foil Customs.

At the end of the segment Jarriel made a peculiar statement about the ABC crew having unspecified problems with the Customs Service. Viewers were left to figure out for themselves exactly what the fellow was saying; even with foreknowledge of the taco incident (which Jarriel never mentioned) we had trouble following him. What dishonest journalism!

Bill Anthony, a press spokesman for the Customs Service, tells us that the *20/20* segment was replete with errors—for instance, Jarriel's claim that "$2 billion is spent each year on the air interdiction system." In fact, Customs says it spends $227 million annually, which is 11 percent of the amount claimed by ABC.

Most importantly, Customs asserts that its program is working, that airborne smuggling is about 25 percent of the 1982 level, as measured by a complex formula involving smuggling-related air crashes, stolen aircraft reports, and actual seizures. *ABC News* did not give viewers this information.

Jarriel also claimed that no one from Customs would give *ABC News* an interview. Anthony replied that this was rank nonsense—that a Customs official talked with Jarriel's crew, on-camera, for an hour. Customs did break off talks with ABC after the taco smuggling ruse. David Hooper, the Service's spokesman, told why in a letter to *20/20*. He wrote, "*20/20's* actions were the equivalent of pulling a fire alarm without a fire and sitting back to see what happened. It endangered the lives of Customs agents and air crews, jeopardized other operations, and cost taxpayers money—all in the name of TV ratings."

Bill Anthony had a biting comment about the ethics of *ABC News*. *Current Affair*, the tabloid TV show, also tried to sneak a test plane by Customs. It, too, was caught. *Current Affair* decided the Customs program worked, so it killed the segment. In Anthony's opinion, *Current Affair* demonstrated that it has a higher ethical code of journalistic conduct than *ABC News*. We agree. In the name of basic honesty, *ABC News* should have shown viewers its failed taco-smuggling caper.

January 15, 1993

Another *New York Times* Story Is Proven Wrong

For our arrogant press, few events are more humiliating than to have a story proved wrong. This has just happened to *The New York Times*, which was responsible for one of the more egregious journalistic outrages of the still-young '90s decade. In April 1991 two-thirds of the *Times'* Op-Ed page was filled with an article charging that the Reagan-Bush campaign conspired with Iran to fix the 1980 election by delaying the release of the embassy hostages. The author, Gary Sick, had been on President Carter's National Security Council staff, responsible for Iranian affairs. Sick thus bore much blame for a foreign policy debacle that humiliated the United States. Therefore he had a motive for finding someone else to blame.

Sick's article was long on surmise and short on facts. His "October Surprise" conspiracy thesis had been pushed by leftist fringe journalists since 1981—and rejected by competent investigative reporters as nonsense. But the extraordinary play the *Times* gave Sick's article resonated throughout the media. The long-ignored kooky theory took on a new life, and the Democrat-controlled Congress was finally persuaded to appoint two special committees to investigate it. No doubt the main instigators hoped to find material that would damage President Bush's campaign.

Unsurprisingly, nothing emerged. The special Senate counsel, Reid Weingarten, so stated in a report given his Democratic bosses on September 15, 1992 but not released until November 24—three comfortable weeks after the election. Weingarten said he found "no credible evidence" supporting the "October Surprise" and so stated, in 156 pages.

The New York Times, apparently disappointed at the repudiation of Gary Sick's sick story, was reluctant to provide this information to its readers. Its headline over a story by David

Johnston read, "80 Hostage Dealings by G.O.P. Verged on Impropriety, Panel Says." Not until the third paragraph did the reader learn that "no credible evidence to substantiate the accusation at the center of the investigation" was found. The fourth paragraph revealed that "the great weight of the evidence is that there was no such deal."

An editorial the next day reflected further disappointment by the *Times*. Under the title "October Surprise: Not Proven," it bemoaned the fact that the Senate wasted only $75,000 on this fruitless investigation. It stated that the $1.3 million House inquiry might provide "a fuller, fairer understanding" of what actually happened. (The already completed House report came to the same conclusion as did Mr. Weingarten, but its release was delayed even longer.)

The Washington Post and the *Washington Times* carried front-page stories reporting the findings. The *Post's* headline read, " 'October Surprise' Story Unfounded, Report Says." *The Washington Times* headline said, "Reagan-Bush Officials Cleared in 'Surprise.' " *The Washington Times* account stated, "The report says delays in releasing the Americans were directly tied to the Iranian government's dislike of President Carter. In his report, Mr. Weingarten said U.S. intelligence officers and national security records suggested that Iran's rulers not only refused to release the hostages until after the election, but delayed the release of the Americans until after noon on Inauguration Day 'simply to humiliate President Carter.' "

When the Sick article first appeared, we urged Arthur O. Sulzberger, then *The New York Times* publisher, to have his news staff investigate the allegations, rather than let the paper rely upon an unsourced article by a questionable authority. The *Times* did not do so. Worse, it consistently ignored or downplayed the evidence developed by other reporters that undermined Sick's theory.

The *Times* also permitted columnist Leslie Gelb (like Sick, a veteran of the Carter Administration) to publish a piece which violates the standards by which decent people live. Gelb's column in the *Times* on April 17, 1991, contained these sentences: "Hardball politics is one thing. But Presidential candidates or their aides interfering in life-and-

100

death, war-and-peace decisions of a sitting President is quite another. *It is treachery.*" [Emphasis added.] *The Boston Globe* on May 2, 1991, also spoke of "the allegation of treachery."

Now the *Times* has capped its anemic coverage by devoting only two brief paragraphs to the principal finding of Weingarten's report. Why? And why hasn't columnist Gelb retracted his slander? Apparently because cold, hard facts have refuted the "October Surprise" theory that the Times had done so much to promote.

December 4, 1992

How They Concealed The Good Economic News To Help Clinton Win

NBC's Katie Couric, the chipper half of NBC's *Today* interview team, began a segment on November 24, 1992 by cheerily asking economist Fabian Linden of the Conference Board, "Good morning! Nice to have some good economic news for a change, isn't it?" Linden was appearing to analyze a report that consumer confidence was up some 10 percentage points in the last month, a sharp turnaround from the decline since midyear.

Writing in the *New Republic* less than two weeks after the election, columnist Michael Kinsley admitted, "Scant days ago, before the election, Clinton was pooh-poohing George Bush's claims that the economy is on the mend. Now he can afford to admit that Bush well may be right." The stridently-Democratic Kinsley, who is also co-host of CNN's *Crossfire* show, conceded that "huge layoffs in corporate America are part of a historic restructuring," a tacit admission that Reagan-Bush economic policies were not totally responsible for the high jobless rate.

During the campaign President Bush argued valiantly—but futilely—that the economy was stirring, citing six straight quarters of growth in the domestic national product. But the media, especially the Big 3 TV networks, ignored him. The Center for Media and Public Affairs reported in October that "the economy has been evaluated negatively by 91% of the sources interviewed on the network nightly newscasts over the last two years." That rose to 96 percent in the third quarter of this year.

Something remarkable happened to the media's reporting immediately after Bill Clinton won. Reporters suddenly found silver linings on clouds that until Nov. 3 had been uniformly

102

dark. Here are the major economic stories from *The New York Times* immediately after the November 3 election:

—On November 6, a business-page headline read, "Growth in October Lifts Retailers' Hopes for Holiday Sales." Kenneth Gilpin wrote, "The nation's big chain stores reported further sales gains in October, *continuing a trend that began in August* and raising hopes among analysts that for the first time in four years retailers will not have a cold Christmas." (emphasis added)

—The same date, the *Times* reported from Washington: "New unemployment claims in late October fell to 360,000, the lowest in more than two years, the government said today. ... In another report, [the Labor Department] said the productivity of American workers increased at a seasonally adjusted annual rate of 2.6 percent during the July-September quarter, the best showing in six months."

—On November 11, the lead story on the business page read, "Producer Prices Up Only 0.1 %," reflecting a continuing slowdown in the rate of inflation.

—On November 13, a front-page article reported, "Banks Increase Loans to Business in a Reversal of 2-Year Downturn." On the business page, the *Times* noted, "The number of Americans filing for jobless benefits fell to a two-year low in late October and *remained under 400,000 for the sixth consecutive week*."

—On November 14, the lead story on the front page reported, "Economic Reports Are Showing Signs of a Quicker Pace." Robert D. Hershey, Jr. reported that retail sales rose nine-tenths of one percent during October and that "pollsters at the University of Michigan found consumer confidence soaring in the first half of November." Hershey wrote that "the exceptionally sluggish business recovery may finally be gaining some momentum."

—On November 18, the *Times* had an important story on the front page. "Lower Mortgage Rates Give Consumers Money to Spend." Refinancing home mortgages at lower rates was "roughly equivalent to a $50 billion tax cut," the *Times* noted. The infusion of cash helped drive up consumer spending during the July-September quarter "at a 3.4 percent annual pace after being virtually unchanged during the spring." Americans had "an additional $2 billion each month in their pockets as a result of savings in 1991 and 1992 from refinancing their mortgages or from the lower rates on their adjustable-rate mortgages." Paradoxically, this story stressed a theme of Bush stump speeches—that lower interest rates were helping Americans. The *Times* could have written this story at any time during the past year. It did not appear until two weeks after the election.

Nonetheless, Clinton continues to talk about a stagnant economy, despite the statistical evidence of an upswing. CBS economic correspondent Robert Krulwich suggested two reasons for Clinton's "gloom" on *CBS This Morning* on November 24. Krulwich said that Clinton intends to ask Congress for "sacrifice and cuts" in January, and he can't do so if the economy seems to be turning upward. "The second thing," Krulwich said, "if the economy bounces back right away, doesn't it seem like George Bush did it, and just got a little unlucky by a few weeks?"

Host Harry Smith asked an unnecessary question: "And the last thing they [the Clinton people] want to do is give him credit for it?"

We would rephrase Smith's question: "And the last thing the media want to do is to give Bush credit for it?"

November 27, 1992

Hiss "Exoneration" Story Proves To Be Bogus

The Russian general who claims to have exonerated Soviet espionage figure Alger Hiss has admitted to us that his work was based on a slipshod and incomplete review of USSR intelligence archives.

The admissions by Dmitri A. Volkogonov dash attempts by die-hard supporters to clear the name of Hiss, America's most notorious traitor since Benedict Arnold. Hiss, a former State Department official, was convicted of perjury in January 1951 for lying about his Soviet espionage activities. Despite overwhelming evidence of his guilt, Hiss remains an icon to an aging generation of American leftists and fuzzy-thinkers who consider him a victim of "Cold War McCarthyism." The latest attempt to rewrite history was made in October by Volkogonov, overseer of Russia's military intelligence archives.

In a story first given exclusively to *The New York Times*, Volkogonov claimed that on the "basis of a very careful analysis of all the information" available in Soviet files on foreign espionage, Hiss "was never an agent of the intelligence services of the Soviet Union." Volkogonov said his review was based on material provided to him by Yevgeny Primakov, head of the Russian Intelligence Service (RIS), successor to the KGB. He acknowledged to us that he did not review the files personally.

Volkogonov commissioned the review at the request of John Lowenthal, a left-wing filmmaker and sometime lawyer for Hiss. Lowenthal has argued for more than a decade that the diplomat was framed. He contacted Volkogonov in Moscow at the end of August through auspices of The Nation Institute, the research and fund-raising adjunct of *The Nation* magazine.

Volkogonov informed Lowenthal on September 25 that

105

his search had been completed and that there was nothing that incriminated Hiss. Lowenthal surfaced the "exoneration" claim on October 29 through *The New York Times*. Other media picked up the story, generally accepting the line that Hiss had been "cleared." (The *Times* identified Lowenthal only as a "historian and filmmaker who has long studied the Hiss case," not mentioning his legal work for Hiss or his pro-Hiss bias.)

But Volkogonov has now grudgingly admitted to Accuracy in Media that his research was sorely flawed. During an appearance in Washington on November 11, Volkogonov stated he did not review files of the Communist International, or Comintern, for which Hiss spied. The Comintern provided the apparatus through which Moscow used domestic communists, in the U.S. and elsewhere, for espionage.

The omission is important. Whittaker Chambers, the acknowledged American communist who worked with Hiss as a Soviet spy during the 1930s, testified repeatedly that he passed the material gathered by Hiss to Moscow via the Comintern. Given the importance of the Comintern in the Hiss case, had Volkogonov sought out its archives as part of its search?

"I have not seen these documents," Volkogonov told us. "I have not had the opportunity to see these documents . . . only foreign intelligence archives in Russia which contained information on agents. . . . I definitely will take a look at that," he said of the Comintern archives.

In testimony the same day before the Senate Select Committee on POW/MIA Affairs, Volkogonov described the chaotic condition of files of the GRU, the military intelligence branch of the Red Army, a rival of the KGB. The GRU is the other Soviet intelligence agency to which Hiss provided material, again through Chambers. This conduit was mentioned frequently by Chambers both in his autobiography, *Witness*, and in testimony before Congress and at Hiss's perjury trials.

Volkogonov's comments about the GRU files came when Sen. John Kerry (D., Mass.), asked if he was getting the access he needed to GRU materials. At the start of his POW/MIA work in early 1992, Volkogonov replied, "We had serious problems with the GRU, serious obstacles." But after he complained to President Boris Yeltsin, "the situation has improved drastically. There is a new leadership at GRU with whom I had spoken and who has agreed to give me all the documents requested."

The main problem with the GRU, he said, is disorganization of the files. "You will never find a single file folder labeled 'Information About POWs,'" Volkogonov said. Instead, the material is scattered through such sections as "foreign affairs," he said, requiring almost a folder-by-folder search. "You must go through a number of documents page by page. . . . literally hundreds of thousands of documents." This requires "many weeks work," Volkogonov said.

Volkogonov's admission is significant because of his statements that he spent less than a month looking for Hiss materials. But he told the *Moscow Times* on September 25 that "he had been devoting the majority of his time to research in the presidential archives" on the POW/MIA issue. How, then, could he have directed a serious search of massive Soviet intelligence files?

A reporter who did such slipshod research would be demoted to the obituary desk. Yet our media gave prominence to Volkogonov's flawed findings. Leftist celebrators of Hiss's "innocence" should recork their champagne.

November 20, 1992

[Note: On November 24, 1992, a Moscow newspaper published a letter from General Volkogonov in which he admitted that his search for files on Alger Hiss had been inadequate to determine whether or not Hiss had spied for the Soviets. The New York Times published an interview with Volkogonov on December 17 in which he expanded on that statement. He said, "All I said was that I saw no evidence. What I saw gives no basis to claim a full clarification. There's no guarantee that it was not destroyed, that it was not in other channels." This retraction did not get the media attention given to the first story. The Washinton Post, for example, ignored it completely.]

Why Exposé Of Ted Kennedy Was Not Seen On NBC-TV

When trash biographer Kitty Kelley sank her claws into Nancy Reagan a year ago, our mainstream media fell over themselves in publicizing a book that contained some stories that . . . let us be charitable and say only that they sounded like whoppers. *The New York Times* ran a story on the front page of its Sunday edition, and La Kelley simpered at length on the TV morning shows.

Another sizzling unauthorized biography isn't getting nearly so much media attention. *The Senator* takes the reader into the hot tub with Teddy Kennedy as he snorts cocaine and cavorts with an uncountable succession of girl friends. One more or less steady paramour has to "deal with" two pregnancies by Teddy—after (she says) he breached promises to divorce wife Joan and marry her.

The Senator was written by Richard Burke, who worked for Kennedy from 1971-1981, first as a student volunteer and driver, and finally as administrative assistant. Burke became a de facto family member as he shepherded Kennedy, Joan and their children through a succession of crises during the decade. He adds graphic detail—sex, drugs and alcohol—to the Kennedy's October 1991 "mea culpa" speech at Harvard in which he recognized "my own shortcomings . . . the faults in the conduct of my personal life . . ."

Burke, however, carries clouds of his own. He resigned from Teddy's staff after falsely claiming terrorists had shot up his car. He admits he had a problem with cocaine addiction—and he writes that Kennedy introduced him to the drug. He has had subsequent money problems as well.

But given Burke's insider position, why haven't our media let you hear his story? NBC's *Today* show recently canceled a scheduled interview with Burke. Jeff Zucker, executive producer of *Today*, was asked about this on the CNN program *Reliable Sources* on October 3. Here's what Zucker said:

"Well, you know, the fact is that we didn't know what was inside the book until last Friday night. With the secrecy surrounding the book, we didn't get a copy until two nights, two nights before he was supposed to be on the air, and so it wasn't until last weekend that I got a chance to look it over. And after looking it over, that's when I became very uncomfortable with promoting this. And so that's what happened. It was only, only a last minute decision to, not to do the book, because I wasn't comfortable with it."

Panelist Gloria Borger of *U.S. News & World Report* came to Zucker's aid, saying: "A lot of people say these are political decisions, that you're doing it because it's Ted Kennedy, Ted Kennedy is so powerful. I think it's a journalistic decision more than a political one."

Zucker welcomed Ms. Borger's exoneration. He said, "Absolutely. You know a lot of people say we got a lot of pressure from the Kennedys." "Did you?" he was asked. "Well, absolutely," he responded. "The Kennedy office called us and tried, tried to convince us not to do it. Now if anything's going to make us want to do it, it's more pressure like that. So we made this decision knowing that people out there were going to say . . ."

He was interrupted by host Bernard Kalb, who commented, "But you got pressure." "Yes, but when somebody pressures us, you know that gets our back up," Zucker said. "We're going to do it." Only in this case they decided to cancel the Burke interview in spite of the pressure from Kennedy, not because of it, he claimed.

Panelist Hodding Carter, who was State Department spokesman in the Carter administration, added a skeptical note to the discussion, saying, "The problem with that book is not the accusations. The problem with that book is the identity of the accuser. You knew the identity of the accuser. You knew a great deal about that guy before you jerked him. It can't be what was in the book. Most of what's in the book has been out in the public domain for a long time. You're not trying to tell me that book is too irresponsible for a guy who was involved in a number of things Senator Kennedy has allegedly been involved in, or has been involved in on the record."

Kalb supported Carter's suggestion that NBC had good reason to know that the book would involve scandal and suggested that they may have had ratings in mind in booking Burke. Zucker acknowledged that "we originally booked the book because we were told it was going to be a blockbuster book with a lot of allegations." Nevertheless, he would like you to believe that the allegations, not the pressure from Kennedy, were too much for Today.

We can understand Teddy's concern. Much of *The Senator* is gamey stuff. For instance, we find the blind-drunk Senator stripping naked and invading a woman's shower after a tennis match. A "screaming fight" ensued as she evicted him. "He's a pig, Rick," she told Burke. According to the index, "sexual relations" are discussed on 74 of the book's 321 pages (we found none mentioning Kennedy with his wife); "alcohol and drug use" are on 36 pages.

Did conscience or cowardice make *Today* cancel the interview? Does the tarnished Kennedy mystique still dazzle reporters who should know better? Was NBC protecting the feelings of its superstar Maria Shriver, a Kennedy niece? Read *The Senator* and judge for yourself.

October 9, 1992

110

How A U.S. TV Network Helped An Enemy

The media tried to make CNN correspondent Peter Arnett into a hero for remaining in Baghdad during the Gulf War to broadcast to the world. He has been honored with journalistic awards and a hefty advance for a book. However, many people thought that if Peter Arnett deserved any awards they should have come from Saddam Hussein, because Arnett was permitted to remain in Baghdad with the understanding that he would report only what Saddam wanted him to broadcast. That meant he was Iraq's propaganda conduit to the outside world.

Those who feel this way have been joined by General Norman Schwarzkopf, the man who led our troops to victory in that war. The general was recently a guest on *Larry King Live*, and King, one of those who had tried to make a hero of Arnett, asked Schwarzkopf if Arnett had been a hindrance to him during the war. Gen. Schwarzkopf said: "I gotta tell you there were times when I saw the Iraqis leading Peter around . . . saying, 'The Americans say they are trying not to damage civilian places. That's a lie. The Americans are damaging civilian places and look here. Here's all this bombing that took place, and this civilian place was destroyed. Therefore, obviously the Americans are lying.' "

Gen. Schwarzkopf said this was what CNN was broadcasting at the very time we were "trying to knock ourselves out and risking our pilots' lives to avoid civilian damage." He added, "You know when you are looking at a building you don't know whether it's an American bomb that destroyed that building or all this stuff that they're shooting up in the air at you that turns around and comes down when it doesn't hit anything and it lands on their own places. When they were suppressing the Shiites, they fired at random into civilian areas and destroyed all sorts of stuff and then later tried to blame it on us." Nothing of that sort was ever mentioned by Peter Arnett in his broadcasts.

Pressed by King to say what Arnett had done that was good, Gen. Schwarzkopf tried to oblige, saying, "Well, what he was doing, he was keeping the American public informed, and that's something that needs to be done. It's important in molding public opinion." The general seemed to forget that he had just said what Arnett was doing was helping Saddam Hussein mold public opinion by telling lies about our air war.

King didn't ask him to give an example of what Arnett had done to keep the American public informed about the truth of what was happening in Iraq. Instead, he said, "So if you were running CNN, you would have had Peter Arnett in Baghdad reporting, wouldn't you?"

"No, I don't think I would have," Gen. Schwarzkopf replied. He said that when the Iraqis told CNN, " 'We will only let you in if you abide by our rules,' I would have told them to go suck an egg . . ."

King tried again to get the general to endorse the policy of having our own reporters broadcasting enemy propaganda from the enemy capital in time of war, saying, "But isn't it better to be there than not there? As opposed to no picture?" Gen. Schwarzkopf did not buy that. He told King, "I [am] a man who's spent 35 years in the military, and I gotta tell you it sticks in my craw when I see an American broadcasting what is obviously blatant Iraqi propaganda, enemy propaganda, and that's what was being broadcast." He concluded by saying, "You asked me if it bothered me. Yeah, it bothered me. Sure it did. . . . You know, you've got to have favorable public opinion to fight a war. If you don't have it, you have a Vietnam on your hands, and that's the worst of all possible situations, where you're over there fighting a war that the American people don't support."

Saddam Hussein's one hope was that anti-war propaganda would erode public support for the Gulf War as it had during the tragically and unnecessarily prolonged Vietnam conflict. Because President Bush didn't make Lyndon Johnson's mistake of thinking that as commander-in-chief he should be the chief strategist and tactician, the military were able to fight the Gulf War to win a quick victory. That spared us the ordeal of seeing public support for the war eroded by CNN and the other media organizations that didn't tell Saddam to go suck an egg when he offered to let them broadcast from Baghdad if they would air his propaganda line.

October 9, 1992

Clinton And The Draft— What They Didn't Tell You

Back in 1988, the media were working feverishly to find evidence proving that Dan Quayle had used political influence to get into the Indiana National Guard. A lot was said about this, no evidence to support the charges was found and the story died.

But just suppose that reporters had found that back in 1968, Dan Quayle had invoked the aid of the senior Senator from Indiana, the Governor of Indiana and the head of the state Selective Service System to help him escape the draft. Suppose that these men had all applied pressure the Indiana National Guard to certify that Quayle was eligible for a defer-ment on the strength of a promise that he would enlist in the Guard nine months hence. Suppose that the Commander of the Indiana National Guard had given in and delivered the desired certification even though it was clearly in violation of the law. Finally, suppose that Quayle had already received his induction notice when this action was taken, adding to the illegality of the action.

Is there the slightest doubt that all of this would have been treated as the lead story on the TV news programs and in every newspaper and news magazine in the country? This scandalous affair would have been featured in the news every day as long as Dan Quayle remained on the ticket. It would not have taken many days of pounding to force his withdraw-al, if Mr. Bush didn't dump him summarily. Quayle would have been destroyed politically.

But everything that we have asked you to suppose about Quayle is exactly equivalent to what was actually done to enable young Bill Clinton to escape the draft. Only in Clin-ton's case it was the ROTC, not the National Guard, that pro-vided the illegal escape hatch. And there was another major difference. Clinton reneged on his promise to enroll in the

ROTC two days after he drew a number in the draft lottery high enough to insure that he would not be drafted. He never donned the uniform.

The biggest difference of all is the media response to Clinton's unethical and illegal maneuvering. He had a July 28 induction date staring him in the face when he appealed to Arkansas' senior Senator, J. William Fulbright, to put pressure on the ROTC director at the University of Arkansas to inform his draft board that he had qualified for an ROTC deferment. This was illegal because the law required that he be enrolled as a full time student in a school with an ROTC program in order to qualify for that deferment. Clinton was not enrolled at the University of Arkansas Law School at that time or ever. Moreover, he had already received his draft notice, making it illegal for him to shop around for alternatives.

The appeal for Senator Fulbright's help was disclosed by the *Arkansas Democrat* and *The New York Post* last March. They reproduced a copy of the memo written by Sen. Fulbright's top aide, saying that Clinton needed the ROTC deferment and that the head of the ROTC unit at the University of Arkansas would be calling about this on July 16, just twelve days before Clinton was to report for induction. That sensational discovery went unmentioned by the great national media. *The New York Times* didn't get around to telling its readers about it until September 19. The others never mentioned it.

Cliff Jackson, a Little Rock attorney, revealed last April that he had helped his friend and Oxford classmate, Bill Clinton, by getting Arkansas Governor Winthrop Rockefeller and Colonel "Lefty" Hawkins, head of the state Selective Service System to join Fulbright in pressing for the ROTC deferment. Colonel Clinton Jones, the former executive officer for the ROTC, has confirmed that he had received calls from the offices of Fulbright, Rockefeller and Hawkins about Clinton.

On September 2, the *Los Angeles Times* reported that Senator Fulbright had played a key role in getting Clinton's draft board to delay his induction to enable him to go to Oxford in 1968 on his Rhodes scholarship. It reported that this was confirmed by the lone surviving member of Clinton's draft board, who said he and other draft board members had received calls from a Fulbright aide.

Even that was ignored by other Big Media. Finally Colonel Eugene Holmes, the ROTC director at the University of Arkansas on whom this enormous pressure was applied, made public a memo in which he described the pressure applied by Senator Fulbright. That story broke on September 16, with most of the attention being devoted to the colonel's denunciation of Clinton for having deceived him. Fulbright's string pulling was barely mentioned, but it did finally get into *The Washington Post* and *The New York Times*. But it was not treated as a scandal. Indeed, *The New York Times* followed with a long article about how Quayle got into the National Guard, followed with an editorial suggesting that what the two men did was a wash and that the draft issue should be put to rest.

September 25, 1992

Why Didn't They Report This Bomb In Clinton's Baggage?

Thanks to ABC's resuscitated *Viewpoint* program, night owls who normally tune in to *Nightline* had an opportunity to learn about one of the bombs hidden in Bill Clinton's baggage that the media have helped keep from exploding. Reed Irvine, one of the guests invited to participate in a *Viewpoint* discussion of media bias in campaign coverage at Rice University on Sept. 16, asked panelists Roone Arledge, president of *ABC News*, and John Stacks, deputy managing editor of *Time* magazine, to explain why none of the national media had ever reported the case of Charlette Perry.

Charlette Perry is a black employee of the state of Arkansas who had been recommended last year for promotion to supervisor of the secretarial pool in which she worked. She was shocked and disappointed when the job went to an outsider, an attractive white woman. The job description had been changed to require public relations skills and knowledge of computers, freezing out Ms. Perry, who lacked those skills. The woman who got the job tailored her resume to fit the revised job description, having been tipped off about what the revised job description would require.

Angry at the agency's flouting its policy of promoting from within, Charlette Perry filed a complaint. A grievance committee held hearings and found that the hiring procedure was "improper" and that Ms. Perry had been treated unjustly. It said that the job did not require public relations and computer skills, and that the vacancy should have been filled by promoting from within. Its findings and recommendations were rejected by a Clinton political appointee. The white woman who got the job that should have gone to Charlette Perry was Gov. Bill Clinton's good friend, Gennifer Flowers.

117

On the Flowers-Clinton tapes, there are discussions of Clinton's helping Flowers get the job and of Charlette Perry's grievance hearing. There is a discussion of Flowers' concern that reporters might ask her how she got the job. Clinton is heard saying, "If they ever ask if you've talked to me about it, you can just say no." In other words, lie.

Pointing out that this was an important example of the nexus between an official's private life and how he does his job and carries out his responsibilities, Irvine asked, "Why has this story not been told by the national media? It was the subject of a 3,600 word story in *Newsday*, and as far as I know, that is the only place in the media that it has been reported."

Roone Arledge, the president of *ABC News*, responded, "I don't have an answer to that. I'm not familiar with that story. I think one of the criticisms that has been leveled at the press—I'm sure you loved the Gennifer Flowers episode—but most of the critics of our coverage complained just the opposite, that we focused on Gennifer Flowers and scandals like that rather than on issues. I am not aware of this story."

When it was pointed out to him that this was not the story of Gennifer Flowers, it was the story of Charlette Perry, a black woman who was "cheated out of a job," Arledge said, "I think if the name Gennifer Flowers were not connected to this you would not be on national television talking about it."

Nor would the discussion have been taking place if it had been George Bush, not Bill Clinton, whose name was involved. If it had been Bush, the story would have led the TV evening news programs and Charlette Perry would probably have been invited to appear on *Nightline, Donahue* and *Larry King Live*. She probably would have accepted, but the victim of Bill Clinton's favoritism, who is still working for the state of Arkansas, is so intimidated that she has refused all requests for interviews by TV and the print media.

Addressing the point that this case showed that there was a connection between Clinton's private life and public performance, Arledge said, "One of the issues we wrestle with on a regular basis . . . is to what degree (candidates') private lives are fair game for the press. . . . We have normally come down on the side that if it affects their work, if it has something to do with their performance in their job, or if the candidate himself responds to these charges, then it becomes news. If this had been an issue that was widely distributed—I don't know where *Newsday* got that story from, or where you got if from, or even if it's true—I'm not saying it isn't true. Perhaps it is. It probably would have been covered in some degree . . ." John Stacks, *Time's* deputy managing editor, said he agreed with Arledge completely.

The Charlette Perry story was reported by newspapers and on TV in Little Rock, where the records of the grievance committee hearings are available for all to see. Clinton's involvement was proven when the tapes and transcripts of the Flowers-Clinton phone conversations became readily available. It would take a determined effort for those covering Clinton to avoid stumbling over this story, but the pro-Clinton media were equal to the challenge.

September 18, 1992

Media Savagery At The Republican National Convention

The overriding message that came out of the Republican National Convention is that Messrs. Clinton and Gore now enjoy a strong ally for the November election: the bulk of America's mass media.

Coverage of the Houston convention was an exercise in media savagery, as if reporters, editors and TV producers deliberately set out to confirm conservative protests that a "cultural elite" dominates communications in this country.

Put most directly, the media did not like, nor understand, the strong conservative message out of Houston. They don't consider conservatism a subject fit for public consumption. Instead of giving serious attention to why Americans voted for a conservative presidential candidate in each of the last three elections, the media spent a full week proclaiming that the GOP had fallen into the hands of "extremists" and the "radical Christian right."

Never have we seen a convention where the reality of what happened on-site was at such sharp variance with that portrayed by the press. To the mainstream press, the convention was in turmoil over abortion and homosexual rights. Floor reporters gave viewers a steady flow of "dissidents" who disagreed with party planks touching these subjects. The Rev. Pat Robertson was finally moved to comment on CNN's *Larry King Live* show that the media were deliberately "trying to drive a wedge in the party."

A tipoff that fairness was due a rough week came the day before the convention opened, when we marveled at CNN's ability to find, for "man in the street" interviews, a succession of persons who were either Bush-bashers or avowed

Democrats. We felt a Republican or two might have been in town for the convention. If so, CNN couldn't locate them.

CNN suited up an all-hostile panel to discuss the Reagan and Buchanan speeches (David Broder of *The Washington Post*, Jack Germond of *The Baltimore Evening Sun*, Gloria Borger of *US News & World Report*, and host Catherine Crier). Broder shuddered about having to listen to two conservatives back-to-back: "There is no limit to how far this party will go to tip its hat to the far right." Buchanan's denunciation of Los Angeles rioters became "racist" when put into this media mixmaster.

NBC's Andrea Mitchell was particularly adept at finding scattered pro-abortion voices in the sea of delegates. We began to fantasize about her first question should she be assigned to do the locker room story at next year's Super Bowl: "Coach, congratulations on a great victory. Now, are you a decent pro-choice American, or are you a captive of the religious right?"

Mitchell also denounced as "wrong"—she emphasized the word—repeated charges by speakers that Hillary Clinton had equated marriage with slavery ("Speak for yourself, Hillary," Pat Buchanan jibed). Actually, Hillary Clinton came close to saying just that in a 1973 article, "Children Under the Law," in which she discussed the plight of individuals who "are incapable or undeserving of the right to take care of themselves."

She continued, "Along with the family, past and present examples of such arrangements include marriage, slavery and the Indian reservation. The relative powerlessness of children makes them uniquely vulnerable to this rationale."

Semanticists can—and will—argue what Hillary Clinton meant in this passage. But Mitchell's pronouncement that GOP speakers were "wrong" went beyond the reporter's function, and showed her willingness to use her network position to advance a partisan position.

Indeed, on the "Hillary issue" the media helped the Democratic Party achieve a major campaign goal at Houston—to brand any criticism of Governor Clinton's wife as "sleaze" and "Hillary bashing." Given her primary-season suggestion that she would serve as an assistant president if her husband is elected, Hillary Clinton's politics should be fair game. But the media have now decreed that such discussion is dirty politics.

Fortunately, many American viewers saw through the media's bias in Houston. During the convention, Accuracy in Media did more than a hundred radio interviews around the country. Time and again callers (and hosts) told us how dismayed they were at the disparity between what they were seeing on C-SPAN and what they were being told by the other media. One man quipped that CNN was beginning to sound like the "Clinton News Network." He had a good point, and it applies to the Big 3 networks as well.

August 28, 1992

Hiding Candidate Clinton's "Bimbos"

Are our media letting a $2,000 a day private eye hired by the Clinton campaign decide what is fit to print about the "bimbos" the Arkansas governor enjoyed during his days as an admitted adulterer? *The Washington Post* ran an extraordinary story on July 26 about investigator Jack Palladino. Clinton campaign aide and longtime intimate advisor Betsey Wright told the Post she was using Palladino to investigate women causing "bimbo eruptions."

The eruptions are many—no less than 17 since Clinton's nomination, according to Wright, to go along with five during the primaries, including Gennifer Flowers, who had tapes to back her story of a lengthy affair with Clinton.

By Betsey Wright's account, Palladino is digging up dirt (she used the euphemism "deflect allegations") on women bold enough to confess intimacies with Clinton. The dirt is then fed to journalists to discourage them from reporting on the women.

We thought this a startling story—after all, Ross Perot was pilloried over accusations of his use of investigators to probe competitors and to insure that his children did not get involved with unsavory characters. *The New York Times* denounced Perot as a "sinister gumshoe with an uncommon taste for intrigue, investigations and conspiracy." But neither the *Times* nor any of the Big Three TV networks picked up the *Post's* story about Clinton's pricey private eye.

Then Bush deputy campaign manager Mary Matalin tossed Betsey Wright's words right back in a press release, written in Q&A fashion and titled "Sniveling, Hypocritical Democrats." One of Matalin's questions—the last of 22 challenging Clinton stands—asked which campaign had to spend "thousands of taxpayer dollars on private investigators to fend off bimbo eruptions?"

123

Astonishingly, all three TV networks used the Matalin memo to accuse Bush of introducing sleaze into the campaign, as if the "bimbo watch" was his idea. CBS White House correspondent Susan Spencer said the press release "broke the President's personal promise to avoid sleaze." On ABC's *World News Tonight*, Forrest Sawyer said that although the campaign was barely underway "mudslinging has already become a campaign issue." ABC's Brit Hume was the only reporter to state that the term "bimbo eruptions" came from the Clinton people.

John Corcoran of *NBC Nightly News* called the memo a "three-page tirade." He continued, "Pressed to defend [Matalin's] charge, Bush campaign aide Torie Clark said, 'It's the truth, pal.' " Corcoran did not go on to report that the charge indeed was true—that Clinton had hired such an investigator, and that he was being paid with taxpayer dollars given Clinton under federal election finance laws.

Palladino's dirt-digging seems to be sparing Clinton some bimbo grief. During the Democratic National Convention, former Miss Arkansas Sally Perdue appeared on the *Sally Jesse Raphael* television show to detail a three-month affair with Governor Clinton in 1983. She said he would drop by in his state limousine to tryst with his "Long Tall Sally." Love and affection were not involved, Perdue said, "only fun and games." When Clinton's passions were exhausted, he would flick the porch light to summon his driver.

Except for this interview (for which Perdue received no money) the media ignored Long Tall Sally; she was even blacked out in New York, where WABC-TV carries the *Sally Jessy Raphael* program.

Why the lack of attention? *The Post* cited Long Tall Sally in its article about Palladino. It said Palladino and a partner called "former associates and estranged relatives of the woman seeking damaging comments about her credibility." One of these persons with damaging information told *The Post* that Palladino asked her to talk to reporters about Perdue.

Why didn't the media bring out these Palladino-supplied "sources" for public scrutiny? Perhaps some of these persons were simply settling grudges with Perdue. We don't know.

But to discredit Perdue through anonymous sources smacks of McCarthyism.

And where is the line between investigation and intimidation? A woman who admits to a sexual affair with a married man—even a charming Southern governor—is apt to have other matters in her past which she does not wish discussed publicly. What are Palladino and his gumshoes telling the many prospective "bimbos" to frighten them into silence?

The Clinton people are obviously praying that voters are spared further evidence of his adultery—an issue many Americans feel bears directly on his fitness to be president. And our media are playing along with the Clinton line that any attempt to publicize Clinton's paramours is sleaze or dirty tricks.

We heard stories from Arkansas recently that Clinton's reputation as a voracious, indiscriminate womanizer date at least to his Oxford student days. Will our media let Clinton keep these "smoking sheets" hidden in the closet, as they did for Jack Kennedy in 1960?

August 7, 1992

Time-Warner Hides
Ice-T Shame

What a cynical display of corporate arrogance! Time Warner Inc. is the biggest media conglomerate in the world, with major interests in both the electronic and print media. But when the media giant faced its day of shame in Beverly Hills on July 16, 1992, it barred not only TV cameras, but also still photographers and tape recorders.

Time Warner was trying to minimize coverage of a massive protest against its distribution of the infamous rap song, "Cop Killer," by an ex-convict who performs under the name of Ice-T. "Cop Killer" is a primer on how to murder a policeman. Ice-T is a practitioner of what is known as "gangster rap."

The meeting, and the concurrent protest by law enforcement officers from around the country, drew enormous media attention. A score of TV camera crews milled outside the Beverly Wilshire Hotel, where the meeting was held. We didn't even try to count the pen-and-pencil press or radio reporters.

Inside the hotel's grand ballroom, the press section was crammed with reporters—but not a single news photographer was permitted to enter. (Generously, Time Warner let print reporters bring in their pencils and notebooks.) But the visual scene was left to a single artist, who busied himself making sketches of the speakers.

Time Warner didn't want its embarrassment recorded even for its own archival purposes. Corporations routinely tape-record their annual meetings. Not so for Time Warner; it didn't bring in its own audio or video crews—and this from a company which boasts of the power of television and its great technological prowess.

Under heavy pressure from police organizations and pension funds around the country, Time Warner did agree to let

126

their representatives address the meeting. In all, 17 persons spoke, including victims of attacks who survived, even though gravely injured, and the widow of a murdered officer.

Time Warner's strategy was cynical. Let the aggrieved people blow off steam, but safely out of sight of the TV cameras that would put their disgust on network TV, or on the cable channels controlled by Time Warner. The censorship meant that the raw anger would not be seen by people who might stop buying *Time, People* or *Sports Illustrated* magazines, or quit Book of the Month Club, or bypass the theme amusement parks owned by the conglomerate.

The unrelenting attack on Time Warner began immediately after routine opening business. The majestic Charlton Heston arose to say that he had "come as a shareholder" to condemn the company's response to demands that the album be withdrawn. These cries have come from beat cops all the way up to the President of the United States, plus more than 60 members of Congressmen.

Heston pointed out that Time Warner had even sent copies of the album to disc jockeys in miniature plastic body bags. Heston wondered if the person who thought up this sick "promotional gimmick" was the same clever chap who proposed as cover art on another album a gunman lurking near the White House with an Uzi, waiting for President Bush.

Heston put the blame on Time Warner president Gerald M. Levin, who claims "Cop Killer" doesn't advocate killing police. Heston suggested that Levin could have said, "Look, I don't have time to listen to rap lyrics. If some clown in the record division screwed up, we'll deal with it."

Instead, Heston said, "He tried to claim the moral high ground, with protestations of Time Warner's respect for the artist's creative freedom. Mr. Levin, come on. I've been doing this for a living all my life. I know, at least as well as you do, that an artist's creative freedom depends on the success of his last work and the demand for his next.

"Let me ask you," Heston continued. "If that song were titled 'Fag Killer' or if the lyrics went 'Die, Die, Die, Kike, Die,' would you still sell it?" Levin did not answer.

Heston shocked many in the audience by quoting—expletives included—the unprintable lyrics of "Cop Killer" and another record in the album, "KKK Bitch." The latter describes Ice-T's fantasy of having sex with two 12-year-old girls—the nieces of Tipper Gore, the wife of the Democrats' vice presidential nominee.

"This is the matter Time Warner is defending," Heston said. "Not out of principle. Out of greed." He and other speakers demanded that Time Warner withdraw "this vile and irresponsible record"—the description used in *Time*, one of the conglomerate's own magazines.

Mr. Levin's reply, prepared in advance, was: "Time Warner stands by, and will continue to stand by, its commitment to freedom of expression—whether or not we agree with what is said."

In other business in Beverly Hills, Time Warner reported a rise in revenues in 1991 of nearly 9 percent, to $3.1 billion; a second-quarter profit of $9 million versus a year-ago loss of $32 million; a four-for-one stock split; and a 12 percent increase in its quarterly dividend.

The moral, we suppose, is that songs about killing policemen pay—so long as the blood on the money doesn't make you squeamish.

July 17, 1992

ABC News Caught In Outrageous Lie

ABC News needs a purge of liars. Convincing evidence shows that its management can't trust underlings to tell the truth when challenges are raised about the veracity of news stories. If the people at *ABC News* can't tell the truth to one another, why should the public trust what this network reports?

We have caught *ABC News* in an outright lie involving a 1988 broadcast on *World News Tonight* in which a fantasy-weaver named Richard Brenneke made sweeping accusations about Donald Gregg, a career CIA officer who served Vice President Bush as national security adviser. Brenneke, a real estate operator from Portland, Oregon, claimed to have been a covert arms merchant and CIA employee. Frank Snepp, an ABC reporter (himself a CIA veteran), interviewed Brenneke for many hours and believed his stories. ABC aired reports based on Brenneke in April and May 1988.

Brenneke's major charge was that Gregg let narcotics be transported in the Nicaraguan contra supply operation. Brenneke claimed that when he brought this to Gregg's attention, Gregg replied, "Never mind. That's not your business. It's none of your business. Just do what you were hired to do."

Brenneke offered no proof other than his own dubious word that he had ever talked to Gregg. He showed a log purporting to prove he had telephoned Gregg, but the number was that of Vice President Bush's military aide. However, he had the phone number wrong. The CIA, in a rare public disavowal, noted that the man who signed Brenneke's purported employment letter had left the agency years before the date of the document. We pointed out these and many other discrepancies to ABC management beginning in 1988. ABC stood behind Brenneke, even when two Senate committees (controlled by Democrats) and other news organizations wrote him off as a nut.

Brenneke, meanwhile, expanded his fantasy to claim he was in Paris in October 1980 when candidate Bush allegedly plotted with Iranians to delay the release of the embassy hostages until after the election, thereby assuring Ronald Reagan's election. He thus became a key figure in the "October Surprise" yarn.

Then Brenneke overreached. He contracted with a Connecticut writer, Peggy Adler Robohm, to do a memoir, and gave her his financial records. When Robohm got into the papers, she discovered that on dates he claimed to have been in Europe on "October Surprise' missions, his own credit cards and diaries put him in the Pacific Northwest. Outraged, Robohm gave the material to Frank Snepp, now a writer for *The Village Voice*. Snepp wrote a lengthy article about Brenneke's lies and concluded that the information "inevitably undercuts the credibility of everything he touched."

Given this refutation by ABC's own reporter, we thought that the network would have the decency to retract the slurs against Gregg. Network brass had defended Brenneke at shareholder meetings in 1989, 1990 and 1991, and in private meetings and letters to Accuracy in Media. Incredibly, Walter Porges, *ABC News* vice president of news practices, wrote that Snepp's revelation "does nothing to change our minds on our reports of several years ago." He claimed that "sources other than Brenneke provided critical information used in our reports."

At the Capital Cities/ABC shareholders meeting in May we demanded again that ABC retract the story. But Stephen Weiswasser, another *ABC News* vice president, claimed that Snepp himself had said "that he had other sources for the story, and on that basis we stand by the story . . ."

Chairman Thomas Murphy promised to check out the source. Reed Irvine said, "Good. That's all I'm asking. You get the name, and if it doesn't exist . . . you might consider getting rid of the people who are lying if it turns out they are lying." Murphy later wrote us that "after a thorough review I am convinced that we acted responsibly in this matter." He conceded that he did not "myself determine the identity of the secret *ABC News* source" because "our policy is to limit very strictly the number of people to whom such sensitive information is given."

So we did what Murphy should have done himself. We finally succeeded in locating Snepp and told him of the ABC claim that sources other than Brenneke had verified his conversation with Gregg. Snepp unhesitatingly replied:

"If that's what they have communicated to you, there has been a misstatement . . . I can say categorically there was no such source [other than Brenneke himself] for the Gregg-Brenneke contact." Snepp said there were additional sources for other parts of the story, chiefly allegations of Israeli involvement in the Iran-contra affair. He also told us he recently told *ABC News* that Brenneke was the sole source on the Gregg material.

What does this mean? Tom Murphy's subordinates are caught in an outrageous lie. Rather than confess error, they apparently lied to the chief executive officer of their company, causing him in turn to give false information to the public and shareholders. People who lie don't belong in the news business. Murphy should fire the *ABC News* executives who caused this public embarrassment.

July 10, 1992

Big Name News People Level False Anti-Semite Charge

We're waiting to hear some big name media figures apologize for smearing Patrick Buchanan as an anti-Semite because he had the audacity to defend a retired Cleveland auto worker accused of Nazi war crimes. We refer to the case of John Demjanjuk, who was convicted in an Israeli court of being a Nazi death camp guard called "Ivan the Terrible." When Demjanjuk was deported to Israel in 1988 and sentenced to death, his family pleaded that a horrible mistake had been made.

Columnist Patrick Buchanan was one of the few journalists who took the trouble to examine the quality of the evidence the Justice Department used to deport Demjanjuk. Much of the documentation had been supplied by the KGB, the Soviet secret police. Buchanan agreed with the family that major discrepancies marred the case—that "Ivan the Terrible" was in all likelihood another man named Ivan Marchenko. Buchanan urged that the case be reexamined lest an innocent man be hanged. He accused Justice Department lawyers of suppressing evidence favoring Demjanjuk.

When Buchanan challenged President Bush in the Republican primaries, critics used the Demjanjuk case as a pretext for calling him an anti-Semite. The attacks were vicious. A.M. Rosenthal, a *New York Times* columnist, denounced Buchanan for his "smarmy defense of war criminals and the attacks on American prosecutors who dared track them down." Editor Eric Breindel of the *New York Post* accused Buchanan of having a "one-track mind" for defending Demjanjuk. Breindel felt that Demjanjuk's "guilt is clear," although he agreed that "honorable folks may differ." In a background sheet distributed by the Anti-Defamation League,

132

Abraham Foxman cited the Demjanjuk case as evidence of Buchanan's supposed anti-Semitism.

All in all, pretty tough stuff. But these Buchanan bashers ignored evidence developed by other journalists that the Demjanjuk case was flimsy. In 1990, for instance, the CBS news show *60 Minutes* aired convincing evidence that Ivan Marchenko—and not Demjanjuk—was actually "Ivan the Terrible." Demjanjuk's lawyers and family continued scouring files in the former USSR for more evidence.

Now Demjanjuk's defenders appear to be succeeding. After reviewing the suppressed evidence, an Israeli court agreed to reconsider the case. In Washington, the Justice Department announced an investigation of whether lawyers in its Nazi-hunting unit, the Office of Special Investigations, or OSI, hid evidence supporting Demjanjuk's mistaken-identity claim. The federal appeals court in Cleveland that upheld Demjanjuk's extradition is now demanding that Justice Department lawyers return to try to prove they didn't use tainted evidence. And in an astounding front page story on June 13, *The New York Times* reported that a former lawyer in the unit, George L. Parker, revealed that he warned superiors—years ago—that Demjanjuk might not be "Ivan the Terrible."

We congratulate *The New York Times* for publishing this story. But why were our mainstream media so tardy in getting onto a story that Pat Buchanan has written about for years? Buchanan wrote about misconduct by the Office of Special Investigations in 1989—three years ago. He charged that Demjanjuk "may be the victim of a greater miscarriage of justice than Alfred Dreyfus," and said that it was time that "Congress summoned the moxie to take a hard public look at OSI." Events are now proving that Pat Buchanan was right on target.

A Washington group named the Coalition for Constitutional Justice and Security (CCJS) documented abuses by OSI as early as 1986 but had trouble interesting the mainstream media in doing stories. (One exception was Robert Gillette of the *Los Angeles Times'* Washington bureau, who wrote several stories casting doubt on the quality of evidence used by the

Nazi hunters.) Indeed, *The Washington Times* in October 1986 rejected a paid advertisement criticizing OSI reliance on the KGB for evidence in Nazi hunt cases.

A major scandal is before us—evidence that our Justice Department deliberately used tainted evidence to send an innocent man to his death. Is Demjanjuk "Ivan the Terrible," or a lesser war criminal? We don't know. But we do know from what is now emerging that the case is not cut-and-dried.

A secondary scandal is the refusal of media figures to retract some nasty statements that have been printed about Pat Buchanan. A.M. Rosenthal's *New York Times* column denouncing Buchanan ran under the headline "Forgive Them Not." Is Abe Rosenthal a decent man? Perhaps he is. So let him show it by apologizing to Buchanan, in print.

June 26, 1992
[Note: On June 30, 1993, U. S. District Judge Thomas A. Wiseman, Jr., who had been asked by the Sixth Circuit Court of Appeals to review the Justice Department's handling of the Demjanjuk case issued a detailed report. He said new evidence found in Soviet archives cast "a substantial doubt on Demjanjuk's guilt" and that the Justice Department's office of special investigations had not been sufficiently skeptical of some of the information it used. It has also denied the defense access to materials that would have been helpful to it.

On July 29, 1993, the Supreme Court of Israel agreed that the wrong man had been brought to trial and ordered that Demjanjuk be set free. We've seen no apologies from Rosenthal and other journalists who attacked Pat Buchanan for defending John Demjanjuk.]

How Bryant Gumbel Manipulates Guests

Bryant Gumbel, the co-anchor of NBC's *Today* show, began an interview with Sen. John Breaux (D., La.) on June 15 by noting that "for whatever reason," Jesse Jackson had not appeared as scheduled for the segment. No matter. Gumbel performed admirably as a Jackson substitute.

The subject was Bill Clinton's challenging the wisdom of inviting rap singer "Sister Souljah" to speak at a weekend conference of Jackson's Rainbow Coalition. Clinton quoted what Sister Souljah told *The Washington Post* in a taped interview printed on May 13: "I mean, if black people kill black people every day, why not have a week and kill white people?"

Clinton told the Rainbow meeting that these words were "filled with a kind of hatred" and said such an influential entertainer, who is heard by thousands of black youths, was an inappropriate speaker for Jackson's group. According to a *Washington Post* reporter who was present, Clinton's repudiation "stunned" the audience and angered Jackson.

Breaux, the chairman of the Democratic Leadership Conference, appeared on *Today* to argue that Clinton acted correctly in rejecting an advocate of racial violence. The unspoken significance of the Clinton statement was his shove-off message to Jackson—that he can run for president without having to cater to him. But Gumbel seethed that Jackson had been crossed. "In retrospect," Gumbel asked, "do you think that Governor Clinton's remarks were ill-advised, inconsiderate?"

To the contrary, Breaux said: "Clinton's remarks were right on target and showed he would not cater to special interest groups, but speak his own mind."

Gumbel was not persuaded. "What's bothering a lot of people," he said, was that Clinton "was really trying to show

135

intentionally . . . that he is trying to appeal to white voters at the expense of African-American voters."

Not at all, Breaux said: "Clinton deserved praise for saying what must have been difficult to say to this particular audience."

Gumbel pressed on: "At the very least, Senator, do you not think that he was somewhat guilty of insulting the very people who had invited him to be their guest?" (The corollary argument could be made, of course, that Jackson insulted the putative presidential candidate of his own party by deliberately associating him with Sister Souljah.)

Breaux rejoined that he didn't think the audience agreed with Sister Souljah's remarks.

Still not satisfied, Gumbel insisted on reading Sister Souljah's full *Post* quote "to clarify what she said and put her remarks in context." He read it: "I mean, if black people kill black people every day, why not have a week and kill white people? In other words, white people, this government and that mayor were well aware of the fact that black people were dying every day in Los Angeles under gang violence. So if you're a gang member and you would normally be killing somebody, why not kill a white person? Do you think that somebody thinks that white people are better or above dying when they would kill their own kind?"

A satisfied look on his face, Gumbel addressed Breaux, "That's something quite apart from just saying 'go out and kill white people,' isn't it?" Breaux said that rap singers should express their views on a "more positive" way.

Gumbel finally got to the crux of the matter—that Clinton had shown a flare of independence not dared by the last two Democratic nominees, Walter Mondale and Michael Dukakis. "Sen. Breaux," he asked, "do you find it somehow annoying or curious that the Rev. Jesse Jackson has yet to endorse Bill Clinton?" [Interpreted: Gumbel finds it "annoying and curious" that Clinton isn't kowtowing to Jackson.]

No, Breaux said, he had no particular concern, repeating that Clinton is "not just another politician."

Gumbel tried three more times to get Breaux to grovel for Jackson's blessing. "All right, let me rephrase it then. How

136

much do you think Bill Clinton needs the endorsement of the Rev. Jesse Jackson and his support?. . . . You seem to make a distinction between the minority vote and the support of Jesse Jackson?. . . . Real quick: can he possibly win the kind of large black voter turnout that the Rev. Jesse Jackson potentially could deliver?''

Breaux wouldn't play Gumbel's game. No person speaks for 100 percent of any group of voters, he said, and Clinton wanted to appeal to non-traditional Democratic votes.

Gumbel thanked Sen. Breaux, but he didn't look very happy. Perhaps he saw that Jesse Jackson's era of petulant, coercive politics is passing, and that a bit of his own derivative prestige thus fades as well.

If so, good riddance. The *Today* anchor is a daily disgrace to his network, and an insult to viewers who don't share his nitwit view that it's OK to talk about blacks killing whites—just so long as the threats are ''in context.''

June 19, 1992

Panic-Promotion Misinformation About The Environment

On the eve of the Earth Summit in Rio de Janeiro, *The Washington Post* punched a hole in the global warming balloon with an excellent article by Boyce Rensberger pointing out that the alarmist claims that we are going to fry if we don't curb the emission of greenhouse gases are not supported by the empirical evidence. Rensberger pointed out that the climate scientists don't differ about what the data show. They agree that there is a greenhouse effect produced by the earth's atmosphere that has been keeping the planet warm for billions of years. They agree that some of the gases which contribute to this effect, notably carbon dioxide, have increased since the industrial revolution began some 200 years ago.

They also agree that the increase in the earth's mean surface temperature over the last hundred years of about one degree Fahrenheit is within the range of normal climate variability, but they then divide into two groups. One group believes that the warming is due to the increase in greenhouse gases in the atmosphere, not to natural causes. They cite the increase in the percentage of the carbon dioxide component of the atmosphere from about .00028 percent in 1800 to about .00036 percent today, warning that if the present rate of increase continues, it will lead to a heating of the globe unprecedented in human history.

Helen Caldicott, the Australian pediatrician who achieved fame in this country as a crusader against all things nuclear, is now running around the country warning that the planet may heat up 18 degrees Fahrenheit in the next 50 years. She fears that in ten years we might not be able to smell the roses and the trees may not come out in the spring. She calls on her audiences to give their lives to save the planet, urging them to

138

march on Washington and take over the White House and Congress.

Caldicott complains that the big corporations that she says control the United States are keeping her from getting on television to air her call to arms. Caldicott got plenty of media exposure back in the days when she was just an anti-American anti-nuclear nutcake. If the networks are refusing to give her time, it isn't because they are reluctant to panic the public about global warming. Even though Caldicott can get standing ovations from naive students, if her exaggerations were aired on national TV, they might give panic-mongering a bad name.

The networks prefer Michael Oppenheimer, the scientific spokesman for the Environmental Defense Fund. Oppenheimer has been all over the tube lately ladling out panic-promoting misinformation. On ABC's *This Week With David Brinkley* he said "there's no question" about the long-term warming trend continuing. He cited a White House report that said that there is a consensus among a broad range of scientists that the build-up of greenhouse gases will lead to a warming of the earth in the range of three degrees to eight degrees Fahrenheit over the next century. Oppenheimer said, "That would make the earth warmer than at any time in the history of the human species . . . That's a threat we need to act on now."

The same day, Rensberger in *The Washington Post* reported that climate scientists are divided into those who want immediate action to curb greenhouse gases and those who don't. He said: "Most of the scientists who specialize in the subject still can't figure out whether anything unusual is actually happening to Earth's climate . . . Scientists generally agree that it has been getting warmer over the last hundred years, but the average rate of change is no greater than in centuries past, and there is no consensus that human activity is the cause. And while there is no doubt that continued emissions of 'greenhouse gases' tend to aid warming, it is not clear that cutting back on emissions could do much to stop a natural trend, if that is what is happening."

Dr. Fred Singer, a scientist who opposes panicky action,

says the White House paper cited by Oppenheimer is a misrepresentation of the 1990 report of the Intergovernmental Panel on Climate Change (IPCC). This report observed that the future warming rate could accelerate and increase by as much as 5 degrees by the year 2100, but it did not claim that there was any consensus that this would occur. The IPCC report said: "It is not possible at this time to attribute all, or even a large part, of the observed global-mean warming to the enhanced greenhouse effect on the basis of the observational data currently available."

Why was Fred Singer allowed only a few seconds in the taped introductory segment of the Brinkley show while people like Michael Oppenheimer and his think-alike, Sen. Albert Gore, are featured guests? Rensberger supplied this answer, "They are the most visible because many are backed by large activist organizations and because the news media traditionally give alarm calls prominence."

Tom Murphy, the CapCities/ABC chairman, claims that ABC wants to give the public all the facts. He has said, "We would like to think we are discussing all these major issues of our time with all the scientific community, and we're trying to do the best we can." Try a little harder, Tom. You can do a lot better.

June 5, 1992

New York Times Critics Denounce PBS

In an editorial thundering with righteousness, *The New York Times* on April 20 denounced "Republican critics" and "Republican hostility" which it claimed threatens the liberals' cherished icon, public television. "Their complaints that public broadcasting is marred by 'liberal bias' have yet to be substantiated," the editorial said. "Senate Republicans say public television is too liberal, but they have failed to make their case."

Do *Times* editorial writers read their own newspaper? One of the most biting mainstream critics of public TV in recent years has been none other than the *Times'* own Walter Goodman. We suggest that *Times* editorialists might spend profitable time reading Goodman reviews before giving another knee-jerk endorsement of public TV. Here is a sampling of recent vintage:

—May 6, 1991, headline, "Documentaries That Lean Left." "[W]hen it comes to documentaries, it is difficult to argue that [PBS's] drift is anywhere but to port side. How come?"

—March 22, 1992, headline, "Pull the Plug on PBS?" "Neither the Corporation for Public Broadcasting nor the Public Broadcasting Service has ever come clean about the chronic bent to the left of their public affairs programs . . ."

—May 18, 1992, headline, "A Running Debate About Public TV." Goodman took issue with Bill Moyers' earnest claim in an ABC *Nightline* debate with George Will that PBS was not biased. Despite these denials, Goodman wrote, "at least in prime time, PBS documentaries on subjects like foreign policy, welfare, social issues and the environment have long had a pronounced slant." Goodman made plain that he felt that the "slant" was to the left.

There is much more. Indeed, Republican critics could eas-

141

ily make their case against public TV simply by quoting what Goodman and other *Times* critics have written about its bias in recent years. C.H. "Max" Freedman, a Brooklyn columnist and media analyst, gave us a seven-page compilation of excerpts from reviews in which *Times* critics detailed bias in PBS programming. The comments speak for themselves.

—Aug. 24, 1986, "Born in Flames," a documentary about lesbians. "Productions like this provide an argument for the abolition of Federal financing. Liberal apologists for public television pretend the programs don't exist. 'Born in Flames' is left-wing sludge . . ."

—July 1, 1986, "Mandela," a documentary about the South African politician. ". . . falls victim to its own reverence [for the Mandelas] . . . flouts the rules of reporting . . ."

—July 24, 1986, "Refugee Road," on Asian immigrants. ". . . misrepresents recent history . . . The United States is the oppressor and Southeast Asians are the oppressed . . . sees no difference between what is spurious and what is real."

—Oct. 6, 1986, "The Africans." ". . . as scholarship it runs on empty . . . stretches the notion of tendentiousness [and] condones racial war . . . a pretentious fraud."

—Oct. 6, 1987, "Vacation Nicaragua." ". . . gorgeously done propaganda. This is a Nicaragua that receives no Soviet military aid and has no Cuban advisers . . . should find its way into a museum as a classic in video propaganda."

—Nov. 27, 1989, "America's Century," on postwar America. Host Lewis Lapham "and most of his guests . . . speak mainly from the left [and see the Pentagon] as the Great Satan."

—Jan. 21, 1990, "A Confusing Decade, Its Roots and Its Legacy," on the 1950s. "The first hour . . . offers a picture of the 1950s that is straight out of the New Left canon: . . . anti-communist fanaticism, fear of atomic annihilation . . . takes the youth rebellion pretty much at its own assessment. . ."

—June 18, 1991, "POV" [Point of View] segment on AIDS: "skewed to the left."

—April 21, 1992, *Frontline* segment, "The Bank of

Crooks and Criminals." "Like the recent *Frontline* report on charges that supporters of Ronald Reagan delayed the release of American hostages before the 1980 elections, tonight's program suffers from the producers' evident wish to believe and to publicize more than they can prove."

Senate debate is to begin on June 2 on whether taxpayers should be soaked for carloads of money for the Corporation for Public Broadcasting—$310 million for fiscal 1994; $375 million for 1995; and $425 million for 1996.

Rather than dealing with the realities of bias, defenders of PBS such as *New York Times* editorial writers hide behind Big Bird's feathers. As a nonprofit organization, Accuracy in Media can't lobby. But we do offer advice to the senators demanding that PBS clean up its act: insert a dozen or so *New York Times* reviews of PBS programs into the Congressional Record and rest your case.

May 29, 1992

143

Did Recklessly Irresponsible TV Cause The Riots In L.A.?

We saw in the flames of Los Angeles the awful cost of convicting people of serious crimes in the media before they have their day in court. The nation was appalled in March 1991 to see on television the videotape of Los Angeles police officers clubbing and kicking a black man lying seemingly helpless on the ground. Even the most ardent supporters of the police found it difficult to defend those officers.

Four of the officers were suspended and charged with several felonies. Nearly every news report that mentioned the case was coupled with a reprise of that shocking videotape. The officers were tried and convicted in the minds of millions by what appeared to be unassailable evidence.

Thus the public felt a stunning shock on April 29, 1992 when the jury acquitted the officers except for one charge against one officer on which they failed to reach agreement. Immediately the TV screens were filled with comments from people whose knowledge of the evidence was limited to 30 seconds of videotape that they had seen so many times. They couldn't understand how jurors who had spent three months in court hearing the evidence and arguments presented by both sides could have arrived at a different verdict from their own.

Our media somehow never got around to addressing an important issue: Should criminal defendants be convicted on the basis of a snippet of televised film, or are they entitled to a trial where jurors have the opportunity to hear and evaluate all the evidence? Implicit in the jury's acquittal was a conclusion that our networks had not given the public the full story of what happened during King's arrest. We agree.

Jurors interviewed by the networks emphasized that there

was credible testimony that King aggressively resisted arrest when officers ordered him from his car after a high-speed chase down a freeway and then through residential streets. The jury saw the full amateur video, but no network, to our knowledge, has shown the entire tape. The defense used it to convince jurors that the actions of the police were purposeful and justified, which was not the impression viewers got on TV.

The excerpts shown on local and network television were generally 30 seconds or less. They showed a man being beaten but they didn't explain why. This bobtailed video is what convinced much of the nation of the officers' inexcusable brutality. Even prosecutor Terry White (who is black) acknowledged that the full tape could hurt King. "We knew that there were parts of the videotape that showed Mr. King in somewhat of what could be seen as aggressive movement towards the officers," White said on ABC's *Good Morning America* on April 30. Ironically, ABC at this point showed a film clip not of the "aggressive movement" but of police batons flailing at a seemingly helpless King.

White said the jurors "looked at a man who had led police on a chase, who didn't stop when the police tried to pull him over and he acted strangely once he got out of the car and didn't immediately follow their commands." Viewers of the tape didn't know that, nor were they told that two passengers in King's car promptly obeyed the instructions of the police but that the powerful King had repulsed the officers when they tried to handcuff him. They weren't told that he was then hit twice with a Taser stun-gun, which knocked him down but not out. Defense attorney Michael Stone told CNN that the tape showed King starting to get up. He said, "My perception is that if you run this tape in real time, you will see Mr. King moving as fast as any professional linebacker . . . Mr. King has already been Tasered twice when this starts. He has fought off the effects of 50,000 volts of electricity."

Harvard law professor Arthur Miller, who is legal commentator for ABC News, saw much of the trial on cable TV. He said on *Good Morning America* on April 30, "I think that a jury of 12 people, having heard all the evidence, might have

145

come to the conclusion that these officers were using reasonable force in the circumstances. I personally, having watched a good deal of the trial, thought that at least two of the officers would be acquitted."

Trial by video is the technological equivalent of lynching. Our system wisely provides for trial by jury, where citizens can hear *all* the evidence, not just a snippet selected by a TV news department and broadcast ad nauseum. It is chilling to see so many intelligent people trashing the system because it failed to produce the verdict trial by video led them to expect.

May 1, 1992

The New York Times Revives KAL 007 "Spy Plane" Lie

On February 21, 1992, *The New York Times* proudly distributed to readers a flier stating that the paper is now being printed with "new high-tech inks that are substantially less likely to rub off on your fingers." We congratulate the *Times* and new publisher Arthur O. Sulzberger, Jr. for resolving a problem that has infuriated readers for decades. Now we urge young Sulzberger to rid his paper of a far more serious stain blotching its news department.

We refer to the *Times'* blind obstinacy concerning the 1983 Soviet shootdown of a Korean civil airliner, KAL 007, with the deaths of 269 passengers. In an article that filled two thirds of a page on February 20, 1992 the *Times* revived the leftist myth that U.S. intelligence agencies connived in the flight of KAL 007. The article rested on research by Robert W. Allardyce, who has pushed KAL 007 conspiracy theories for at least seven years, and collaborator James Gollin. The *Times* reporter, retired aviation writer Richard Witkin, has shown an appetite for conspiracy theories as well.

Allardyce attempted to refute experts who say KAL 007 strayed off course on a flight from Anchorage to Seoul because the pilot mistakenly punched the wrong digits in keying flight coordinates into the navigational system. Witkin wrote that Allardyce "has gathered evidence that in his view" shows that KAL 007 "was on a deliberate flight path and did not stray accidentally into Soviet territory." Allardyce and Gollin "assumed" the reason for the overflight "had to do with intelligence collection."

Not until the 37th paragraph did Witkin give a tipoff as to the tainted evidence on which the thesis rested: "A keystone of the Allardyce-Gollin reconstruction is the Russian map of

147

the course the airliner supposedly flew from the time it was picked up on Russian radar until it vanished just west of Sakhalin. The most startling feature is a zig-zag, a 75-degree right turn for 65 miles to the north and then a 100-degree left turn to the southwest toward where the plane apparently started across Kamchatka."

The Times did not tell its readers that the Soviets themselves have disavowed the map. It was first displayed on September 9, 1983, at a press conference by Marshal Nikolai Ogarkov, the chief of staff, as part of a propaganda effort to deny Soviet criminality in the murders. Later, Marshal of Aviation Piotr Kirsanov sent a substantially different map to the International Civil Aviation Organization, one showing a straight-path course across Kamchatka and Sakhalin until the impact in the Sea of Japan. The official Soviet military magazine *Red Star* used the straight-path map in an article on KAL 007 on July 16, 1991.

The *Times* knew these facts, and ignored them.

On February 17, three days before the Witkin article was published, Nicholas Wade, science editor of the *Times*, telephoned James Oberg, a Texas space scientist who has written frequently on KAL 007. "I told him that the Allardyce theory was impossible—that the Soviets themselves had repudiated the Ogarkov map," Oberg said. He faxed Wade a copy of the Red Star map. "Since it knocked the props from under their story, they didn't use it—it didn't fit, so the *Times* didn't print it," Oberg added.

Oberg also briefed Wade on Allardyce's long campaign to blame U.S. intelligence for the Soviet murders. Allardyce and Gollin were major sources of *Shootdown*, a widely-discredited 1986 conspiracy book by R.W. Johnson, an Oxford don, and for a 1988 NBC "docudrama" of the same title. This work was done when Allardyce was a consultant for a far-left group, the Fund for Constitutional Government, funded by leftist benefactor Stewart Mott.

Uneasy about the conspiratorial tone of its docudrama script, NBC retained aviation expert Dr. Richard Gilbert, who concluded that "informed opinion in the air establishment regarded the Johnson-Allardyce theory . . . not only minority but as fanatic." To its discredit, NBC aired "Shootdown" anyway.

A glaring omission from *Times'* coverage of the KAL 007 tragedy is its silence on disclosures about the flight recorders—the so-called "black boxes"—which were on KAL 007. These recorders would show the course which the liner followed from the time it left Alaska until it was shot down. Former Soviet military men interviewed by Izvestiya in December 1990 and January 1991 stated that divers recovered black boxes from the crash site. This admission was repeated in a Red Star article on December 10, 1991, by Colonel V. Dudin, a member of the Soviet commission that investigated the shootdown.

February 21, 1992

[Note: The Russians subsequently delivered the black box tapes to the International Civil Aviation Organization (ICAO) for analysis. ICAO released its report on June 15, 1993. It found that the tapes proved that KAL 007 had overflown Soviet territory because of an navigational error that was not known to the crew until the time their plane was shot down. ICAO concluded that the plane had accidentally been left on a magnetic course setting for the autopilot rather than being switched to the inertial navigation system (INS) before it was beyond the range for the INS to capture the desired track. The result was that the plane maintained a constant magnetic heading that took it on a virtual straight line over Kamchatka and Sakhalin. The tapes showed that there was no mechanical problem and that the crew behaved normally for a civil aviation flight, unaware that they were off course, and not realizing that they were in danger until the rockets exploded.]

Media Didn't Tell Public That The Book *Roots* Was Fiction—Not Fact

Alex Haley, the author of the book *Roots*, which ABC converted into a very successful television miniseries in 1977, passed away last week at age 70. He was extravagantly eulogized as a historian who had accomplished a unique feat. It was said he had traced the genealogy of his ancestors back to their roots in Africa. Some of us whose ancestors came from European countries where reasonably good written records were kept would be unable to match Alex Haley's feat, unless those forbears were of sufficient prominence to have been the subject of biographies.

Alex Haley claimed that he had drawn upon stories about his ancestors that had been passed down orally from generation to generation. Of course, there are oral histories that have been handed down for many generations, but these are stories of great heroes, such as Ulysses in the *Iliad* and the *Odyssey*, whose inspiring deeds have been preserved in poetry and song. The lives of more humble folk are seldom exciting enough to capture the imagination of their children, much less their grandchildren.

So how did Alex Haley manage to tell the story of his forbears from the time Kunta Kinte was enslaved and shipped off to America in such absorbing detail? The answer is found partly in a lawsuit that was filed against him in 1978 by Harold Courlander, an author who charged that substantial parts of Haley's family history were actually taken from a book he had written called *The African*.

Courlander charged that over 80 passages in *Roots* were copied from *The African*. But his complaint went much further than that. He charged that the material that Haley copied "constituted the framework, life and substance of *Roots*." He said that Haley had copied the language, thoughts, attitudes, incidents, situations, plot and character of his book. He said it was doubtful that Alex Haley could have written *Roots* if he had not borrowed the ideas and words of *The African*, and that if he had, it would have been a very different book.

Courlander had written about a fictional slave named Hwesuhunu, who had grown up in Gambia. Like Haley's Kunta Kinte he had a strange dream, foreboding trouble, before he was captured and made a slave. On the slave ship, both were horribly afflicted with lice. Both had a companion on one side with whom they could communicate and a companion on the other side who said nothing and who died during the voyage.

The two characters were identical in their refusal to forget their African heritage and follow the course taken by most of the slaves in accepting their degraded status. This concept won praise for Courlander's novel when it was published in 1968. Ten years later it helped Alex Haley win a Pulitzer Prize and make a fortune. Alex Haley settled with Harold Courlander out of court, agreeing to pay him $650,000 and acknowledging his debt to Courlander's creativity. Normally, this would be a stain on an author's reputation that the media would not let anyone forget, but our media so loved Alex Haley and his *Roots* that they have neglected to mention that it was a work of fiction that was in large measure copied from another novel.

February 14, 1992

151

Who Is Lying?
Does It Matter?

Last October, Anita Hill charged that when she worked for Clarence Thomas ten years earlier, he had sexually harassed her by describing pornographic movies and asking who left pubic hair on his soft-drink can. Judge Thomas categorically denied her charges. His nomination to the Supreme Court hung on the question of who was telling the truth. The search for the answer dominated the news.

Now comes Gennifer Flowers, claiming to have had an affair with Governor Bill Clinton, the leading contender for the Democratic presidential nomination. The story was broken by the *Star*, a supermarket tabloid, and picked up by the *New York Post* on January 17. Gov. Clinton called it "an absolute, total lie." The only report about this on the network news that night was a brief mention on NBC of Clinton's denial. The next day, *The New York Times* dismissed it with a brief mention of Clinton's denial, and it kept on giving the story minimal coverage as it developed.

Abe Rosenthal, a *New York Times* columnist and former executive editor of the paper, congratulated the editors for their restraint, commenting, "Disdain for the poison-pen press and its emulators leapt deliciously from the page." Many people agree with Abe Rosenthal that the media have gone too far in making marital fidelity a test of a presidential candidates fitness for office. A *Washington Post/ABC News* poll released January 29 found that 54 percent of those polled felt that Clinton should withdraw from the race if it was found that he had lied in denying that he had an affair with Gennifer Flowers. An earlier *ABC News* poll found that 85 percent of those who felt Clinton should withdraw if Flowers' charges were proven correct were concerned about lying and only 5 percent were concerned about infidelity.

This indicates that in this case, as in the Thomas-Hill confrontation, the main issue with many of the voters is veracity. But in the Clinton-Flowers confrontation, most of our media seem to have decided that trying to ascertain which of the parties is telling the truth and which is lying is not their responsibility.

The *New York Post* is one of the few papers that went to the trouble of trying to check out the story. Others in the media made much of the fact that Miss Flowers had been paid for her story by the *Star*, picking up Governor Clinton's line that it was "trash for cash." But Gennifer Flowers had provided evidence backing up her claim—tapes of phone conversations with Governor Clinton. If Anita Hill had possessed comparable tapes, Clarence Thomas would be history. The tapes don't confirm all the details of Miss Flowers' claim, but the transcripts demonstrate to our satisfaction that they were more than casual acquaintances. At first doubts were expressed about their authenticity, but Gov. Clinton himself removed those doubts when he apologized for derogatory remarks the tapes showed that he had made about Governor Mario Cuomo and Senator Bob Kerrey.

Newsweek checked out Miss Flowers' story, and found seven false claims, such as her recollection that she had met Governor Clinton at a hotel in 1979 or 1980 when the hotel hadn't opened until 1982. None exposed a fatal weakness in the story. If *Newsweek* found any corroboration of the story, it didn't report it, but the *New York Post* did. For example, Miss Flowers claimed that she had lost a wealthy beau when she told him of her involvement with Governor Clinton. The *Post* found him. Finis Shelnutt, a wealthy stockbroker, confirmed her story. It also found a former co-worker at KARK-TV, where Miss Flowers worked when she first met the governor, who confirmed that she had frequently spoken of the affair.

Charlette Perry, an Arkansas state employee who had hoped to land the job that Gennifer Flowers was given last June after appealing to Governor Clinton, filed a grievance over the special treatment Miss Flowers was given. Ms. Perry charged that the job description had been changed to better fit the qualifications of the governor's good friend. She complained that this "allowed unqualified applicants to be considered, more particularly the person who was ultimately hired." A state grievance panel upheld her claim, but the Clinton appointee in charge of the office disregarded the finding. As soon as Miss Flowers ceased being the governor's good friend, she was fired for being absent from work for three days without leave.

In 1976, Wayne Hays, a veteran Democratic Congressman who wielded great power as chairman of the House Administration Committee, lost his seat because of the disclosure that he had put his girl friend, Elizabeth Ray, on his payroll as a secretary even though she couldn't type. It would seem that the discovery that Governor Clinton had done a similar favor for Gennifer Flowers might be newsworthy, but that and the evidence that the governor is lying are details that much of the the prestige media have overlooked in their eagerness to show that they were different from "the poison-pen press."

January 31, 1992

How Media Have Misled America About PCB Danger

A dubious chemical scare trumped up by years of media hysteria is costing taxpayers of New York State at least half a million dollars and causing a weeks-long disruption of life at a college campus.

The public affairs woman at the State University of New York/New Paltz sighed deeply over the telephone in describing her school's plight. "We got pretty paranoid around here when it happened," Karen L. Summerlin said of the PCB "contamination" that is forcing closing of her campus for more than a month. "It's getting to where you wonder if you should go outside and breathe in the morning."

The financial sting and inconvenience began when a car struck a power pole on Dec. 29, causing electrical transformers to overheat and explode, exposing 29 persons and five buildings to smoke-carried particles of polychlorinated biphenyls (PCBs).

State Health Department bureaucrats promptly chased students off the campus and announced that the new semester won't begin until February 3 at the earliest. Karen Summerlin said the cleanup would cost a minimum of $500,000. SUNY will also lose thousands of dollars in dorm and dining hall fees.

PCBs are a family of heat-resistant chemicals used for decades as coolants in electrical equipment. Their manufacture ended in 1978 when chemophobic bureaucrats put them on the carcinogenic suspect list. PCBs remain in place in older equipment such as that damaged at SUNY.

But was the SUNY scare necessary? As a front-page story in the January 7 *New York Times* by reporter Lisa W. Foderaro pointed out, "Although PCBs are known to cause cancer in animals, studies have yet to prove a definitive link between PCBs and cancer in humans.''

Unfortunately, Foderaro's careful—and accurate—assessment cannot offset media scare stories that constantly cite supposed dangers of PCBs. Typical was a story in *The Wall Street Journal* on March 12, 1991 by chronic chemophobe Frank Edward Allen, ''PCBs have been linked to liver damages and cancers.'' A March 11, 1991 Associated Press story said PCBs are ''suspected of causing cancer and birth defects.''

So what are the facts? Hundreds of industrial workers were exposed to high concentrations of PCBs on the job during the 1950s through 1970s. But, as Philip H. Abelson wrote in *Science* magazine last July 26, this exposure ''led to no known cases of cancer.'' However, lab researchers were able to induce cancers in rats by subjecting them to massive doses of PCBs. On this basis, the Environmental Protection Agency halted the manufacture of PCBs and ordered a ''cleanup'' that is expected to cost at least $100 billion.

Studies by the non-governmental Institute for Evaluating Health Risks (IEHR), with offices in Washington and Menlo Park, California, show that EPA's blanket condemnation of PCBs was in error. IEHR reconstructed the five rat tests which led to the EPA ban. It found that the only PCBs that caused excess tumors in the rats were those that were most highly chlorinated, i.e., PCBs with 60 percent chlorination.

The IEHR found that PCBs with levels of chlorination below 60 percent showed no ''statistically significant elevations of liver tumors'' in rats. These PCBs that were not shown to be carcinogenic by the EPA tests accounted for 88 percent of the those marketed. The IEHR study, released last July and signed by former EPA acting administrator John A. Moore, stated, ''The current cancer policy is clearly overstating the cancer risks associated with many exposures to PCBs in the environment.'' EPA's regulatory decisions on PCBs, Moore said, are causing ''a major economic impact for, at best, trivial public health gain.'' There is no evidence that even the 60 percent chlorination concentrations cause cancers in human. (As of this writing, cleanup crews had not estimated the concentration in the PCBs involved at SUNY.)

Dr. Bruce Ames, the famed biochemist at the University of California at Berkeley, is more blunt. Based on the average daily intake for humans, he has written, persons who drink wine face 23,000 times more risk of cancer than through exposure to PCBs.

But this scientific evidence is of no solace to SUNY. Miss Summerlin told us that the potential exposure of students heightened public concern. She pointed to the media hype over a state office building in Binghamton that spewed PCBs after catching fire a decade ago. More than $35 million in cleanup costs later, the building remains closed, and it is a highly visible symbol of "PCB danger" to New York bureaucrats. Like asbestos and dioxin, PCBs have been indicted as dangerous carcinogens on the basis of bad science.

So SUNY students remain on a forced holiday, unable to retrieve personal belongings from dorm rooms in the affected buildings. With New York State finances in enough of a shambles to scare Governor Mario Cuomo away from running for the presidency, taxpayers face a whopping cleanup bill—thanks to media hype about overdosed lab rats.

January 10, 1992

More Examples Of News People Lying

Benjamin C. Bradlee, the retired executive editor of *The Washington Post*, was recently given a big chunk of the Sunday *Post* to condemn lying by several of our recent presidents. Bradlee would have us believe that lying is particularly abhorrent to journalists in general and to him in particular.

In 1986, when the Iran-Contra scandal broke and *The Washington Post* was salivating over the prospect of getting its second presidential scalp, Ben told a friend, "This is the most fun we've had since Watergate." When that remark was reported, Ben was pressed to explain what he meant. He came up with this: "Newspaper people get particularly excited when people fail to tell the truth and therefore interfere with the process of reporting—when people fail to tell the truth to their superiors, when they fail to tell the truth to committees of Congress. It is this sense of excitement that I meant to convey." Sure, Ben. *Post* columnist Michael Kinsley was more candid. He wrote, "The fall of Reagan is a laughing matter . . . Dry those tears. Repeat after me. Ha. Ha. Ha."

Bradlee has never displayed joy, excitement, or even much interest in exposing journalists who interfere with the process of reporting by failing to tell the truth to their superiors and to the public. In 1978, the then national news editor of *The Washington Post*, Laurence Stern, lied about why he had refused to report what a Cambodian who had escaped from Pol Pot's killing fields had told a Washington news conference about the genocide the communists were carrying out in his country. Stern said the *Post* had already carried several similar stories about Cambodia. That was exposed as false. Instead of rebuking the editor who had lied to explain his coverup of the Cambodian holocaust, Bradlee attacked the person who exposed the editor's lie. He berated Stern's accuser, Reed Irvine, as "a miserable, carping, retromingent vigilante."

158

When Stern died a year later, he was fulsomely eulogized by Bradlee and others. The others included Teofila Acosta, Fidel Castro's top intelligence agent in the United States, who praised the deceased editor as "a good friend." *The Washington Post* established a fund in memory of Cuba's "good friend" Larry Stern, who had lied about why he wouldn't tell the *Post's* readers about the Communist killing fields in Cambodia.

Bob Woodward is another Bradlee protege who has found lying no obstacle to career advancement at the *Post*. Woodward and Bernstein's Watergate reporting earned them dishonorable mention in Sissela Bok's book, *Lying*. Their book, *The Final Days*, was so riddled with mendacious reporting that John Osborne, who covered the White House for the liberal *New Republic*, described it as "the worst job of nationally noted reporting that I've observed during 49 years in the business."

Woodward earned the sobriquet "Mortuary Bob" with his tale about interviewing the late William J. Casey shortly before he died. He told three conflicting versions of how he got into Casey's heavily guarded hospital room: (1) that he just walked by the door and Casey waved him to come in; (2) that he showed his press pass to the guards and was admitted; and (3) that someone helped him sneak in in a way that had to be kept secret lest the identity of the accomplice be detected.

Woodward claimed to have conversed with Casey, who was paralyzed and unable to speak intelligibly after his brain surgery. The *Post* didn't have enough confidence in Woodward's story to print it, but he included it in his book *Veil*. His claim that Casey had admitted knowing that profits from the Iranian arms sales were being diverted to the Nicaraguan resistance created a minor sensation that helped sell his book. Woodward's lies didn't bother Ben Bradlee. The *Post* would not report the evidence that his Casey story was fabricated. It even rejected a paid ad submitted by Accuracy in Media that did so. It spurned demands that Woodward be fired.

In his opus on lying, Bradlee acknowledged that newspapers sometimes lie, citing the case of Janet Cooke, the *Post* reporter who made up a story about a child heroin addict. He said, "That sort of lie must be dealt with head on . . .," not mentioning that he had ignored evidence that the story was fiction when the *Post* nominated it for a Pulitzer Prize. It was only when the story won a Pulitzer and the AP reported that Janet Cooke had falsified her resume that Bradlee faced the lie head on. He had no choice.

Two years ago, responding to journalists who favored advocacy over straight reporting, Bradlee said, "I don't think there's any danger in doing what you suggest. There's a minor danger in saying it, because as soon as you say, 'To hell with the news. I'm no longer interested in news, I'm interested in causes,' you've got a whole kooky constituency to respond to, which you can waste a lot of time on." The Bradlee message: it's okay to fudge the facts, but don't tell your readers and viewers.

November 22, 1991

How Doonesbury Cartoon Was Used To Spread A Lie

Mr. Donald Graham
Publisher, Washington Post
Dear Don:

You might be curious as to why Accuracy in Media has had an investigative cartoonist in the newsroom of *The Washington Post* the last several days, making sketches of various reporters and editors. Our cartoonist will be calling on you soon, hence this explanation.

We've received phone calls from a mental patient alleging the existence of a pedophilia ring in the *Post's* news department and Style Section. He wants out of the hospital to which he has been involuntarily committed for more than a decade. He says that as a high editor of *The Washington Post* dating back to Civil War days, he saw "shenanigans all over the news room that would blister the hooves off a taxi cab." (We are uncertain as to this metaphor; we pass it along as taken off the tape.)

Our source has other interesting stories. He was a personal assistant to Lenin in the 1920s. As Lenin told him just the other day in a long distance call from Anguilla, where he now lives, the collapse of communism resulted from the failure of the USSR to put the country's currency on a "cabbage standard"—one head of cabbage per ruble.

As Charlemagne's horse in a previous life, the source overheard General Robert E. Lee remark at Antietam that the battle would be lost unless General MacArthur got his M-1 tanks onto line in a hurry. When we remarked that he had his centuries, generals and technology juggled a bit, the source replied, "Credibility is the bane of truth. One must believe the thought, not the fact."

Great source, wouldn't you agree? We put him right up there with the two jailbirds who provided Gary Trudeau with his material for the "Doonesbury" cartoon series concerning Vice President Dan Quayle. If you read your own paper (we hope you do), you know that your own reporters looked at these charges, which came from jailbirds serving long prison sentences, and dismissed them as baseless.

So, too, did America's premier pit bull news show, *60 Minutes*. *The New York Times* on November 7 quoted *60 Minutes* executive producer Don Hewitt as saying one of these "sources" came to him in 1990. Hewitt told the *Times* that CBS reporter Morley Safer "twice watched as the accuser was given lie detector tests in an attempt to verify his assertions.

"The guy not only flunks the test,' Mr. Hewitt said, 'but then he breaks down and cries in front of Morley and says, "I made it up, trying to get out of jail."

Michael Wines of *The New York Times* on November 7 identified one of the "sources" making charges against Quayle as Brett Kimberlin, an inmate serving a 51-year-term in a Federal prison on drug-smuggling and bombing convictions. As Wines noted, on the eve of the 1988 presidential election, Kimberlin charged that he had sold marijuana to Quayle in the 1970s when he was a student at the Indiana University law school. Wines wrote that the charges were "not substantiated." Kimberlin could provide no proof of ever even having met Quayle.

The other "source" was identified in a November 13 story in the *Indianapolis Star*, whose reporters were permitted to examine the "Quayle file" of the local Drug Enforcement Administration office. To recap: a man named Charles Parker was arrested on suspicion of selling Quaaludes. In turn, he told agents that one of his customers, one Terry Carson, alleged he sold cocaine to both Quayle and to Senator Strom Thurmond, the South Carolina Republican. When questioned, Carson "admitted he told the story but said he made it up to impress Parker." He passed a polygraph test in which he confessed having fabricated the story.

So, Don, what do we have here? A nut charge is made against an elected official. News organizations such as *The Washington Post* and *60 Minutes* investigate and say the charge is absurd and refuse to put the information into print or on the air. Then a comic strip artist puts the lie into print in the form of "social commentary."

When we heard of this pending series, we wrote to you, on November 9, "As a grunt in Vietnam, and a foot cop in Washington, you proved your spunk." We suggested that "it's now time for a backbone test in your position as publisher." We asked, "Do you really intend to publish the Quayle nonsense in *The Washington Post?* There must come a time, Don, when a decent publisher must say, 'No more, the lies and smears have gone far enough, and they're not going to be published in my newspaper, in any form."

As the publisher of perhaps the most influential of the approximately 1,400 American newspapers which carry "Doonesbury," you had a chance to set an example for decent journalism. A good many other publishers spiked the series. By publishing the Doonesbury panels, you pushed the bounds of decent journalism a bit further into the mire. You also violated the standards by which decent people live.

Having set community standards for the press in Washington, we hope you won't object when our investigative cartoonist asks you for a brief posing session. Our artists wants you in half-profile—as if you are averting your eyes from something you know was wrong, but did not have the backbone to stop.

      Sincerely,
      REED IRVINE and JOE GOULDEN

November 15, 1991

How PBS Used A "Dirty Trick" To Make Uncle Sam Look Bad

The Americans who provide public broadcasting with $229.39 million tax dollars annually saw their money at work October 29, 1991 on a PBS *Frontline* program "The War We Left Behind." PBS suited up two of its heaviest leftists for the project, the husband/wife team of Andrew and Leslie Cockburn. After viewing an incessant series of pictures of starving children and destroyed homes, critic Walter Goodman of *The New York Times* felt compelled to stress the Cockburns' "political slant," and their "underlying animus" against an Administration that won a war they opposed.

The thrust of the Cockburn piece was "the devastating effect of the war on the people of Iraq." They claimed wanton destruction of civilian facilities such as electrical power plants. They claimed that "anywhere between 75,000 and 175,000 children could die due to the public health conditions that we caused." Douglas Broderick, of Catholic Relief Services, stated, "We have been having a disaster in slow motion for the last four months." The Cockburns blamed U.S. bombing for these conditions.

Yet accounts in *The New York Times* and *The Washington Post* put the blame for the misery squarely on Saddam Hussein. The same Broderick interviewed by the Cockburns detailed an entirely different story for *The New York Times* on November 2. He said the regime is blocking food distribution by foreign organizations in an effort to build international pressure to force the U.N. to lift economic sanctions and the U.S. to release frozen Iraqi assets. In the Basra area alone, Broderick said, 250 tons of food are being withheld, putting "at risk" 3,000 pregnant women.

Caryle Murphy of *The Washington Post* wrote on July 5

of an Iraqi strategy of accusing Washington of waging economic war. She found that this is the "message the government wishes to see carried by the Western press, which is being given unusually open access here in the hope that its reporting of economic hardships will generate sympathy in the West for the lifting or easing of sanctions." The Cockburns eagerly swallowed this propaganda line.

Alan Cowell of *The New York Times* reported on June 9 that the shortages aren't hurting Saddam loyalists in the military or the ruling Baath party. Imported foods, cars and high-ticket consumer items flow to the country's elite, Cowell wrote, while the regime deliberately keeps food from the masses.

Another Cowell article from Baghdad on June 10 reported that "residents here say electric power has returned from up to 16 hours a day, water runs from faucets, gas stations pump gas and, sometimes, even a telephone rings." Cowell described how engineers have cannibalized plants to restore much of the country's power plants. Unlike the Cockburns, Cowell reported "little evidence of what allied spokesmen called 'collateral damage' to places nearby," a finding repeated by Erika Munk in *The Nation* on May 6.

The *Frontline* segment suggests that the Cockburns formed their conclusion before doing their reporting—that they slanted facts to fit their politics.

Air Force Colonel John A. Warden III, a key architect of U.S. bombing policy, spoke with Andrew Cockburn for half an hour. Warden told us that the Cockburns ignored an important point he made. Fewer Iraqis died, either civilian or military, than in any other war in history in which one side suffered such a calamitous defeat. Planning from the outset was to minimize civilian casualties. The United States did not want to permanently alienate either the Iraqi people or the Arabic world. Warden feels—and he told Cockburn—that the strategy worked; that only "about 2,000 civilians, give or take a hundred," died in the bombing.

Predictably, the Cockburns tried to make an atrocity of the bombing of a communications bunker in Baghdad which Leslie Cockburn says killed over 200 women and children.

She called it a "mistake,' displaying what she said were "the original blueprints, scorched and waterlogged." She claimed they proved "what the Pentagon apparently did not know," that "before the war, this shelter was reserved for the exclusive use of civilians."

Warden disputed the word "mistake" and explained to Andrew Cockburn that the installation was a "very important" military target and "we just plain did not know that there were civilians in there." These remarks got on the air.

But the Cockburns censored the most important part of Warden's statement. Camouflage paint covered the bunker roof. Brent Sadler, who covered the war for Britain's ITN, transmitted close-up pictures of the roof that proved that. Under the Geneva Convention, a camouflaged building is a legitimate military target. Warden said that civilians must have entered and left the shelter at dusk and dawn, when they were invisible to U.S. reconnaissance.

PBS and *Frontline* executives knew what they were buying when they signed the Cockburns. Andrew's father, Claud Cockburn, was a longtime British communist who wrote for the communist press. Leslie did outlandish stories for PBS and CBS trying to link CIA and the Nicaraguan democratic resistance with drug trafficking. Andrew helped her write a book, *Out of Control*, outlining these fantasies. So this is how PBS misused some of your $229.39 million of tax money that public broadcasting received this year.

November 8, 1991

Media People Spread False Information About Asbestos Danger

One of the dirtiest little secrets in Washington journalism is the cozy relationship between the Environmental Protection Agency and reporters who write about environmental matters. Time and again we've seen media people reflexively accept anything said by EPA bureaucrats as scientific gospel. Even the EPA's recent embarrassing admissions of error on dioxin and asbestos have not shaken reporters' blind faith in the agency's infallibility.

An uncritical press protected EPA again on October 21 when the Fifth U.S. Circuit Court of Appeals issued a 57-page opinion blistering EPA for major procedural and scientific misconduct in banning nearly all asbestos products from the market. The opinion bristled with criticisms of EPA's "zeal to ban asbestos." EPA studies were "flawed . . . not promulgated on the basis of substantial evidence . . ." EPA "failed to muster substantial evidence . . ." Its economic review was "meaningless." The court found a "cavalier treatment of the EPA's duty to consider the economic effects of its decisions . . ."

The thrust of the court order was that EPA must hold further hearings before it can pursue its ban on such asbestos products as water pipe, insulation, auto brake linings and fireproof clothing. EPA claimed (but did not prove) that 148 to 202 lives might be saved, at a cost from $450 to $800 million.

We attended a press briefing at which officials of the Asbestos Information Association discussed the ruling. We expected some questions about an order that was tantamount to an indictment of a major Federal agency. Instead, we saw at first hand how the press protects its pet.

Reporter Michael Weisskopf from *The Washington Post*

didn't care about the court's tough language; all he demanded was that someone from industry show him where the opinion said asbestos was not dangerous. AIA attorney Edward W. Warren was patient. Whether asbestos was "safe" wasn't the point, he said. The court simply said that EPA had not made its case, and that the EPA had not considered restrictions less severe than a total ban.

The lead paragraph of Weisskopf's story noted that the court criticized EPA "for failing to take into account the health risks posed by substitutes and the high costs of prohibiting "the ubiquitous but deadly mineral." That was Weisskopf's description, not the court's. He devoted two paragraphs to the reaction of an EPA official who moaned that the ruling "calls into question our ability to regulate chemical-by-chemical in an efficient way." But his story was short on specific details on how the court found that EPA misbehaved in making a decision that would have ruined the asbestos industry.

The core of EPA's misconduct was its abuse of the Toxic Substance Control Act (or TSCA) under which asbestos was banned. TSCA requires that once a "reasonable basis" is established that a substance presents an "unreasonable risk of injury" to health or the environment, the EPA should "use the least burdensome regulation to achieve its goals of minimum reasonable risk." But EPA chose a "death penalty alternative" rather than considering less Draconian options.

In banning asbestos EPA showed regulatory stupidity. For instance, it commissioned a study by the American Society of Mechanical Engineers which concluded that many proposed substitutes for friction products, including replacement auto brakes, "are not and will not soon be available," and "may or may not assure safety." The substitutes "actually might cause more deaths than those asbestos deaths predicted by the EPA ... including cancer deaths from the other fibers used ... Many of EPA's own witnesses conceded on cross-examination that the non-asbestos fibrous substitutes also pose a cancer risk upon inhalation, yet the EPA failed to examine in more than a cursory fashion the toxicity of these alternatives."

EPA suggested polyvinyl chloride (PVC) and ductile iron as likely substitutes for asbestos pipes, although as the court noted, both "contain known carcinogens." Banning asbestos in pipes might save three lives in the next 13 years. But EPA conceded that the cancer risk from ductile iron pipe "could be comparable to the population cancer risk for production of A/C (asbestos containing) pipe." Suggesting PVC pipe as a substitute "is particularly inexplicable,' the court said, "as the EPA already is studying increasing the stringency of PVC regulation in separate rulemaking proceedings." In this proceeding, EPA estimates that the cancer risk from PVC plants "to be as high as 20 deaths per year . . . *far in excess of the fractions of a life that the asbestos pipe ban may save each year, by the EPA's own calculations.*" (The emphasis is the court's.)

Why don't our media exercise greater oversight over the rogue EPA? Former EPA press officer Jim Sibbison bragged in a 1984 magazine article how he used gullible reporters to spread scare stories. "One of the first things I learned," he said, "is that reporters take too much on faith what the government tells them." He added that EPA press releases stressed "the hazards of chemicals, employing words like 'cancer' and 'birth defects' to splash a little cold water in reporters' faces." The asbestos decision should be "a little cold water" of a different sort for reporters who still put credence in the EPA.

October 25, 1991

How A News Reporter "Came Within A Whisper" Of Defeating Clarence Thomas

Do circumstances ever exist when a news organization such as National Public Radio is justified in breaching a promise of confidentiality to a source who uses the media to smear a political opponent? NPR reporter Nina Totenberg was chosen by the cowards fighting Justice Clarence Thomas's nomination to air the flimsy sexual harassment charge made weeks earlier, in secret, by Anita Hill.

That these cowards demanded anonymity show they knew they were doing dirty work. We are disturbed at our media's hypocrisy in not pursuing the leaker's name. Arguments recently made before the U.S. Supreme Court by the nation's leading news organizations would justify NPR revealing its source. Here's the background:

In 1982, Dan Cohen, a public relations executive who was doing work for the Republicans, met with reporters for the *Minneapolis Star Tribune* and the *St. Paul Pioneer Press*. On a promise of confidentiality, he gave them derogatory material about the Democratic nominee for lieutenant governor. But editors of both papers overruled their own reporters. According to court papers, they felt that Republicans were trying to use them to take a "cheap shot" at a candidate. The editors asserted that Cohen's leak was itself "highly newsworthy" because it showed the tactics the GOP was using in the election. So the stories featured Cohen's name, and the fact that he was spreading dirt about the Democratic candidate.

Within hours Cohen was fired by his firm. He sued the papers, charging breach of contract. At trial he won $200,000 in actual damages and $500,000 in punitive damages, awards which were thrown out by the Minnesota Supreme Court. Cohen appealed to the U.S. Supreme Court.

A Who's Who of the media establishment supported the papers' contention that they were right in breaking their promise to protect the source. Briefs were filed by the American Newspaper Publishers Association, the American Society of Newspaper Editors, the Associated Press, the Gannett Co., the New York Times Co., and the Times Mirror Co. Although admitting that the papers' conduct was "far from orthodox," they argued that editors have the right to decide when the source of a leak is more important than the information leaked.

During oral arguments newspaper lawyer John French asserted that publishing Cohen's name "brought out the whole truth." Justice Thurgood Marshall, an absolutist in defending the First Amendment, asked whether the papers had also published their "broken promises" to Cohen. No, lawyer French admitted. "Now you're talking about truth," Marshall responded with what one observer called "evident distaste." Marshall continued, "You didn't publish all the truth." The court reinstated Cohen's case and sent it back to the Minnesota courts for a review of the damages due him.

What parallels can be drawn with NPR's refusal to reveal the name of the person who gave Totenberg a copy of an affidavit which Anita Hill had given to the FBI under a cloak of confidentiality? Her broadcast, along with a concurrent story in *Newsday*, started an emotional firestorm that gripped the nation's attention for a full week. But there was an element conspicuously missing from the story: the "who," the leaker who started the whole affair. Demands are heard for an investigation, but no one feels the Democratic majority is serious about finding the source.

Totenberg prides herself on being a scalp hunter. Two years ago, to borrow Mafia terminology, she "made her bones" by assassinating Supreme Court nominee Douglas Ginsburg. University of Virginia professor Larry Sabato reveals in his book *Feeding Frenzy* that a disgruntled former girl friend took revenge on Ginsburg by telling a public interest lawyer that the nominee had used marijuana years earlier. The information was leaked to Totenberg, whose story killed Ginsburg's nomination. Totenberg came within a whisker of killing Thomas as well. He was saved only by public disgust generated by televised hearings which permitted Americans to see the witnesses and make up their own minds, without having to rely upon TV anchors to tell them what was happening.

Totenberg now has a chance for another "kill." As Senator John Danforth, R.-Mo., pointedly said on the Senate floor the night of October 7, any Senator who leaked confidential FBI material to Totenberg faces expulsion. Will she take advantage of her chance to "bag" a sitting senator?

We argued earlier this year that the Minnesota papers were wrong in breaking their reporters' promise to Dan Cohen. We still think reporters should keep promises once they are made, but we don't see any of those who defended the release of Cohen's name suggesting that NPR release the leaker's name, even though that would be a big story. At Brown University last March, Michael Gartner, president of *NBC News*, was asked what he would do if the FBI offered him tapes showing marital infidelity by Dr. Martin Luther King. Gartner exclaimed, "There's the story: the FBI was peddling tapes of Dr. King. The story isn't what Dr. King was doing."

NPR could have had a big story by exposing the Senator or staffer who was peddling dirt on Clarence Thomas. Polls show the public want the leaker identified, but the media haven't shown much interest in it. We haven't even been able to get Michael Gartner to say, "There's the story. We're going after it."

October 18, 1991

An Example Of Why The U.S. Military Does Not Trust The U.S. Press

The New York newspaper *Newsday* and *ABC News* have taken a final dirty shot at the brave American troops who routed the Iraqi army by describing their military actions in a manner tantamount to accusations of war crimes. These news desk strategists apparently haven't learned that an important mission of combat commanders is to keep as many of our own troops alive as possible.

Anchorman Peter Jennings gave this summary of the *Newsday* story on ABC's *World News Tonight* on September 11: "We have learned something new today about the way the United States fought the war in the Persian Gulf. A New York newspaper, *Newsday*, has discovered that when U.S. forces broke through Iraqi front line trenches, their tanks, mounted with plowblades, deliberately buried thousands of Iraqi soldiers, some of whom were still alive, some still fighting. A Pentagon spokesman said today, "I don't mean to be flippant, but there is no nice way to kill somebody in war."

The *Newsday* story, which ran under an inflammatory headline in inch-high type that read "BURIED ALIVE," was written to maximize its shock value, giving the impression that our troops may have committed an atrocity. But readers who got past the first seven paragraphs at least discovered that the tanks were used to destroy Iraqi trenches and either kill or force the surrender of the troops defending them. Other tactics could have been used to achieve this objective. But getting past the trenches meant killing a lot of Iraqi soldiers and the commanders of the 1st Division wanted to do so in a way that didn't result in unnecessary deaths or injuries to American troops.

Had the 1st Division attacked on foot, without the use of

173

tanks or armored vehicles, we suppose Field Marshal Peter Jennings would have griped about the stupidity of "human wave assaults."

A follow-up story in *The Washington Post* on September 13 by Barton Gellman put the maneuver into much more accurate perspective. The unit involved, the 1st Infantry Division (Mechanized) realized that the desert sand in which the Iraqis had dug their trenches made it easy to destroy those trenches. Troops devised the tactic of running tanks fitted with plow blades along the line of trenches, collapsing them. Many Iraqi defenders were buried in the trenches. *Newsday* said it was estimated that there were over 8,000 Iraqi soldiers in the area and that over 2,000 surrendered. It quoted Colonel Anthony Moreno, one of the commanders of the tank force, as saying that for all he knew they could have killed thousands.

Jennings said that our forces "deliberately" buried thousands of Iraqi soldiers, some alive. This brief report focused on the horror of men being buried alive, but it said nothing about why this was done. *Newsday* at least mentioned the military justification. It quoted Colonel Lon Maggart as saying, "I know burying people like that sounds pretty nasty, but it would be even nastier if we had to put our troops in the trenches and clean them out with bayonets."

Colonel Maggart told *The Washington Post* that well-entrenched troops cannot normally be defeated without the attacking troops dismounting from their vehicles and engaging them. He said that a single Iraqi soldier could destroy a 5,000-gallon fuel truck with a rocket launched grenade. Those soldiers had to be rendered ineffective. Collapsing the trenches did that with no loss of American lives.

A spokesman for the 1st Division denied that thousands of Iraqis had been killed. He said several thousand had surrendered, accounting for the majority of the troops at the point where the Iraqi lines were breached.

Colonel Maggart said most people don't realize how violent ground combat is. He said the Iraqis in the trenches had more opportunity to surrender than did those who were killed by artillery, rockets or bombs from aircraft. To the combat soldier, the notion that he should risk his life to save enemy lives has very little appeal. The *Post's* Barton Gellman reported from Fort Riley, Kansas, the 1st Division's headquarters, that troops were baffled about press attention to the episode. "Given the option of having my guys shot and blown up," Maggart said, "I will tell you I would do it this way every time."

Why didn't *ABC News* send a crew to Fort Riley to get this sort of background before running a truncated rewrite of the *Newsday* story? We suggest that ABC is using its power to settle some old scores with the military. News people at this network and elsewhere complained loudly during the Gulf War that the military was unjustly excluding them from covering the battlefield. We know of no restrictions barring reporters from Fort Riley. Why didn't the outfit that boasts of being America's leading source of news show some professionalism and do the job right?

ABC chose to use the *Newsday* story as an opportunity to take a cheap shot at the American military, and in doing so it did a disservice to our troops in failing to give their side of this story. So another chapter is added to the thick book entitled *Why the U.S. Military Does Not Trust the U.S. Press*.

September 13, 1991

175

Confessions Of An *NBC-TV* Correspondent

Journalists react angrily when critics such as Accuracy in Media state that the people who work in our nation's newsrooms are mostly liberal/left. We thought that argument was settled a decade ago by surveys that showed that two-thirds of reporters and editors were liberal, and more 80 percent voted Democratic. Nonetheless, journalists continued to argue that biases don't influence their reporting, even though AIM has documented case after case of slanted news coverage for the last 22 years.

We are happy to report some confirmatory evidence from within the media itself. Martin Fletcher, a veteran correspondent for *NBC News*, in an amazing burst of candor recently confessed both that bias does affect the reporting and that TV news entertains more than it informs. You've seen a lot of Fletcher on NBC broadcasts in the past months from his vantage point as chief of bureau in Tel Aviv. NBC obviously trusts Fletcher's reporting, for his assignment is one of the most sensitive in network television. He covered the Israeli end of the Persian Gulf War, and he is the regular reporter on the ongoing Israeli-Arab conflict.

Earlier this summer Fletcher played host to a group of visiting young journalists in his Tel Aviv office. Among them was Andrew Gold, a reporter for the *Near East Report*, published by the American Israel Public Affairs Committee (AIPAC), the U.S. lobby for Israeli causes. During the free-wheeling conversation Fletcher talked about the intense media coverage of the *intifada*—the uprising by Palestinian youths against the Israeli occupation of the West Bank and the Gaza Strip.

"The press has this liberal bias," Fletcher told Gold. He added that journalists "care about the underdog more"—in this instance, the Palestinians. He went on to say that the

Palestinians manipulate the press by depicting themselves as "David" versus a powerful Israeli 'Goliath," a metaphor that Gold notes that Fletcher used in a 1988 report on the *intifada*.

Fletcher thus puts himself into camp with Karen DeYoung of *The Washington Post*, who told an audience at the leftist Institute for Policy Studies a few years back that she and other journalists reflexively consider leftist guerrillas "the good guys" in civil wars in Third World countries.

Martin Fletcher's candid comments on bias at *NBC News* and elsewhere are refreshing. The public would be better able to evaluate the news it is getting if it knew more about the journalists. When more critics than defenders of Judge Clarence Thomas are interviewed on ABC, CBS and NBC, the viewers should know that this reflects the bias of the network journalists, not the weight of public opinion.

In his interview with Andrew Gold of *Near East Report*, Fletcher "confirmed accusations" that *Today* show co-anchor Bryant Gumbel is "unfriendly towards Israel." Gold quotes Fletcher: "In private conversations, he's certainly very antagonistic toward Israel ... I don't think it should come across on the air, and in some cases it does." Fletcher did credit Gumbel for asking tougher questions than most morning show interviewers. "I think all of those morning show questions are really pathetic," he told Andrew Gold. "So it's all relative."

So how much faith should viewers put in network news? After all, polls show that nearly 70 percent of American adults rely upon TV news as their primary source of information. Fletcher suggests the public might be wasting its time.

"I don't think it's the job of the press to educate the public," Fletcher told Gold. "If you want to get an education, you really don't watch the network news...We do a terrible job covering foreign news."

The opening sentence of NBC's "News Operating Policies" comes out strongly against bias: "*NBC News* seeks to report and analyze accurately, clearly, and fairly, as an independent source of information essential to the public in a democratic society." We asked Fletcher's bosses at *NBC News* for comment on his statements. We got no response.

Alexander Cockburn is one journalist who never concealed his biases. Columnist George Will recently suggested that the Smithsonian Institution should save a glass space where Cockburn could be displayed as American journalism's last Stalinist. As communism collapsed in its motherland, even its erstwhile champion, Phil Donahue's buddy, Vladimir Pozner, became an anti-communist. But not Cockburn.

"Like any other 50-year-old," Cockburn laments in the September 16 issue of *The Nation*, "I felt sad." He explains, "The Soviet Union defeated Hitler and fascism. Without it, the Cuban Revolution would never have survived, nor the Vietnamese." He also states that the Brezhnev years "were a Golden Age for the Soviet working class." We'd like to hear Cockburn make that argument in Red Square. The man wouldn't escape with his hide intact.

We always knew Cockburn was a Stalinist, but being up front, he did a lot less damage than others who, flying the liberal flag, helped bring about the communist takeovers that imposed a Brezhnevian "golden age" on Cuba and Vietnam.

September 6, 1991

Ted Turner, Environmental Fanatic

Charles Alexander, the science editor of *Time*, Andrea Mitchell, Capitol Hill correspondent of *NBC News*, and Ben Bradlee, the recently retired executive editor of *The Washington Post* have all gone on record as saying that it's all right for news organizations to forget about straight, objective reporting in covering environmental issues. They approve of advocacy journalism, at least in reporting on the environment, meaning, to quote Bradlee, an approach that says, "To hell with the news, I'm no longer interested in news, I'm interested in causes."

This, as Bradlee explained, is because there are just some things that are so important that "you have to pay them special mind." If you need to suppress information such as the findings of the $537-million dollar NAPAP study of acid rain to get the Clean Air Act passed, you suppress, which is what *Time*, NBC and *The Washington Post* all did.

No one is more ardent on this score than Ted Turner, the founder, chairman and CEO of the Turner Broadcasting System. Last May, Turner gave vent to his strong emotional feelings about environmental issues in an address to EPA employees in Washington. Turner said he had been able to influence the networks to do a lot of environmental programming. There is no doubt that he has pushed environmental advocacy hard within his own company. Joel Westbrook, a TBS vice-president, commenting on "The New Range Wars," a program that was partially funded and aired by TBS, said "We know who we work for. Ted believes in shows like this. We don't air it because it makes money; we air it because we believe in the message. Hopefully, it does make money in the process." Ted Turner is the only network owner who can get away with that kind of abuse of power. Imagine the public furor that would be kicked up if General

Electric, were to "encourage" NBC, a GE subsidiary, to air money-losing documentaries to expose panics such as the apple scare, the dioxin scare and the acid rain scare that environmentalist promoted but which have been shown to be unjustified.

"The New Range Wars," which was partially underwritten by General Electric, was an excellent example of an effort to *promote* just such a scare. Its objective was to convince the viewers that grazing cattle on the public lands in the West was damaging the ranges and endangering wildlife. Objective experts say this is not true, that the condition of the ranges in question have improved greatly since the mid-1930s and that they benefit from cattle grazing as it is now practiced. Dick Davis, the president of Sportsman Productions, Inc., previewed the program and sent TBS a list of 25 things that needed to be fixed. All were ignored, including the recommendation that they not say that cattle grazing had forced bighorn sheep to find refuge in the mountains. The mountains are their natural habitat.

Advocacy journalism by definition suppresses or distorts the true facts. The advocates are so convinced of the correctness of their goal that the facts that get in the way are dismissed as irrelevant. Many of them see nothing wrong with fudging the truth, twisting the facts, if doing so will gain support for their cause. This was made clear when *60 Minutes* interviewed a spokesman for the Natural Resources Defense Council about the NAPAP study of acid rain. He said his organization had not paid much attention to this massive, ten-year scientific study because we already had all the facts we needed. What they wanted was action.

Ted Turner's emotionalism on these issues was evident in his address at the EPA. He said, "We thought that the way the stone-age man had lived for five to ten million years in balance with nature was bizarre, old-fashioned. More and more we are learning that that was the only way to live and to continue to live for extended periods of time because the way of life we are leading now is going to lead to death, death for humanity and near death for the planet." Perhaps this is why he has decided to stock bison on his Montana ranch. Are he and Jane Fonda planning to tear down the ranch house and move into a wigwam?

Turner told the EPA employees, "I don't like what we're doing to the national forests, cutting trees down at taxpayers' expense and destroying the forest, just so we can have a few jobs. That is like saying, Adolf Hitler trying to justify the Nazi concentration camps—it provided employment for people. Bullshit! I'm fanatical. A part of me is so angry that I want to take out a gun and do something about it . . . Even though in my heart I do get angry and frustrated, I have never done anything . . . and I want to go down and burn lumber mills in the middle of the night and spike trees, I don't do it. I just dream about it occasionally. I work within the system."

But Ted Turner is abusing the system—the Turner Broadcasting System. He has a duty as a holder of broadcast licenses to air all sides of controversial issues, but he can't bring himself to tell the other side of the story.

August 30, 1991

181

How Words Are Used To Distort The Truth

During the abortive military-KGB coup in the Soviet Union, *ABC News* engaged in semantic disinformation that displayed a long-standing media bias against conservatives and the collective villains it calls "right wing." *ABC News* couldn't bring itself to describe accurately the hardline communists who tried to overthrow President Mikhail Gorbachev.

Correspondent Mike Schneider talked about the timing of the coup, asking why "this was the time for right wingers to act." ABC Pentagon correspondent Bob Zelnick said that Soviet analysts had "recognized the possibility of a right-wing coup." Anchor Peter Jennings dropped one or the other of the words into his commentary with nagging frequency.

The talking-head Soviet experts the networks brought in were as careless with their terminology as were the newsmen. On ABC, Professor Robert Legvold of the Harriman Institute talked about "conservatives organizing a coup." Judith Kipner, a Soviet affairs scholar formerly with the American Enterprise Institute, a conservative think tank in Washington, went on CBS to blame the "right wing" for the overthrow of Gorbachev.

What a paradox! Conservatives and right-wingers are the Americans who stood up to communism for long hard years, arguing that freedom and private enterprise were superior to state dictatorship. It was wishy-washy liberals and left-wingers who kept whining about giving communism and the Soviet Union another chance. Well, our side won, and we enjoyed watching the Soviet people rejecting communism as a failed system.

Then the media turned language on its head by calling the military-KGB thugs "conservative" and "right wing." This media nonsense has been going on for months. We did a computer search of a media data bank to see how many times newspapers, magazines and wire services used the words "right-wing" and "conservative" within 15 words of the term "Soviet Union." The computer found more than 500 such entries from January through July, 1991.

Senator William Cohen, a Maine Republican, attempted a correction during a joint interview with Gary Hart, the former Colorado senator, on the *Larry King Live* show on CNN. "You keep saying right winger," Cohen protested. "But right winger doesn't mean in the Soviet Union what it means here."

Hart blithely replied, "A right winger is a right winger."

What nonsense. What Hart was really saying was that the media and the left use the term "right wing" as a code word which says, "These are the bad guys." The bias of semantics is pervasive. Part of the media's power in America lies in its ability to apply misleading labels to issues. Picking up on a Sandinista term, the media called the democratic resistance in Nicaragua the "contras," the Spanish word for "against," with its negative connotations. A single speech by Senator Ted Kennedy was enough to convert President Reagan's Strategic Defense Initiative (SDI) into "Star Wars," equating an important defense program with a video game or sci-fi movie.

The bias of semantics favors the left. We still find hardcore leftists identified as "progressive"—despite the fact that "progressive" is the self-descriptive term American communists used during the Stalinist era. *The New York Times, The Washington Post* and the Big Three networks call the Farabundo Marti National Liberation Front in El Salvador "leftist guerrillas," rather than communists or Marxists. We have a load of FMLN literature in the AIM office in which its leaders boast of being Marxist and communist.

Finally, the bias of semantics is infectious. People who should know better carelessly follow the media's usage. Even President Bush referred to the "right wing" opposing Gorbachev in a Kennebunkport press conference on the attempted coup. On ABC's *Good Morning America*, Deputy Secretary of State Lawrence S. Eagleburger, speaking of Gorbachev, stated, "The right-wing albatross he had hanging around his neck has been lifted."

Perhaps we need new political shorthand. The left/right classification dates to the French Revolution, when the revolutionary Jacobins sat on the left side of the aisle in the National Assembly, and the Monarchists on the right. The left wanted change in France, the right wanted to preserve the existing order.

But in the United States, "left" was long synonymous with sympathy towards the communist system that Boris Yeltsin is trying to destroy. This is a matter of historical record, through President Roosevelt's recognition of the USSR to the Henry Wallace "progressive' presidential campaign of 1948 and beyond, to the mushheads and apologists—and we include media people—who defended the Soviet system up to the time it collapsed.

When "right winger" Ronald Reagan came to Washington, he wanted to change, not preserve, the existing (Democratic/leftist) order; in a political sense, he was a modern Jacobin. Reagan also gave communism its final, fatal shove. The media's attempt to blame "right wingers" for trying to preserve communism with their coup abuses both semantics and the truth.

August 23, 1991

184

Another Bogus Environmental Scare

Laurence Tisch, the billionaire chairman and CEO of CBS, was angry the afternoon of June 13, 1991 when we met him in his palatial office in "Black Rock," the CBS corporate headquarters in Manhattan. Tisch spent the first part of our hour griping about high taxes and inflated government spending in New York. Tisch was so riled, in fact, that he said he had considered moving CBS out of New York. After hearing his hot tirade, we decided the time was ripe to alert Tisch to a major government waste story which his network had missed.

In April Dr. Vernon L. Houk, a high official of the Centers for Disease Control, admitted he erred in recommending the evacuation of Times Beach, Missouri in 1982, because traces of a dioxin had been found in the soil. Last April, Houk told an environmental conference at the University of Missouri that there is now convincing evidence that dioxin is not the potent carcinogen that it was thought to be in 1982. Asked if this meant that the $250 million cleanup of Times Beach and other dioxin-contaminated sites would continue, Houk replied there was little choice but to go ahead "because we've got the public so riled up."

The *St. Louis Post-Dispatch* reported Houk's turnabout under a front-page banner headline. The Associated Press moved a so-so story that was not given prominent play by the national media. NBC and Tisch's CBS, which had done a lot to get the public "riled up,' ignored it completely.

But Tisch sloughed off our suggestion that the Times Beach boondoggle would be a good story for *CBS News* and that putting it on *60 Minutes* might bring the costly, needless cleanup to a halt. Tell them yourselves, Tisch suggested. "Well," we told Tisch, "you're the guy that runs the store." We suggested that *CBS News* could halt the waste by "publicizing the facts, by educating the public." Tisch replied, "That's not our job."

Tisch was by no means alone in ignoring Dr. Houk's confession of error. Outside of Missouri, none of the big media seemed to think it was an important story. ABC was the only broadcast network to mention it even briefly. Appalled at this lack of interest in correcting a major environmental myth that had been exposed by an official who had helped get it started, we turned to *The Wall Street Journal*. The *Journal* frequently serves up important news on its editorial pages that others have overlooked or suppressed. It did so again in this case, publishing a column we supplied them on August 6 headlined, "The Dioxin Un-Scare—Where's the Press?" After detailing what Dr. Houk had said and why it was important to inform the public, the column concluded, "The media that got people riled up with scare stories about dioxin-tainted Agent Orange, Times Beach and paper-mill effluent have done little to 'unrile' them." We hoped this would inspire other media to get riled up about the Times Beach scandal— the costly cleanup that Dr. Houk now says is unnecessary.

Four months after the Houk speech and nine days after *The Wall Street Journal* column, *The New York Times* made the reversal on dioxin its front-page lead story on August 15. The headline read, "U.S. Officials Say Dangers of Dioxin Exaggerated." The story said that the chemical, "once thought to be much more hazardous than chain smoking, is now considered by some experts to be no more risky than spending a week sunbathing." Together with a sidebar on Dr. Houk, the two stories by Keith Schneider totaled 65 column inches—a major cannonade by America's newspaper of record.

The *Times* had not only recognized that the reversal on dioxin was newsworthy, but also that it had an obligation to educate its readers about the underlying facts. Along with *The Wall Street Journal*, it deserves commendation, but we can't say as much for the TV networks which are the main source of news for tens of millions of Americans. Tisch's CBS was the only network to air a report about dioxin on its morning program as a result of the *Times* story. ABC was the only one to report it on the evening news. NBC, which is in the news ratings cellar, was preoccupied with a long report about dinosaur bones and didn't cover it. ABC's Ned Potter began, "For years we've become used to the Federal government warning on the dangers of various chemical compounds such as Alar and dioxin. But it turns out that in some cases the fears may have been exaggerated."

After reporting Dr. Houk's reversal, Potter proceeded to interview Jacqueline Warren of the Natural Resources Defense Council, the group that started the bogus apple-Alar scare of 1989. Warren didn't concern herself with scientific evidence; she griped about alleged economic pressures on the EPA "to redefine the dioxin problem out of existence." Since bogus environmental scares bring in the funds to finance NRDC's $12 million annual budget, Warren may fear that her group will be "out of existence" once the public realizes how it has been conned over the years.

Come to think of it, that would be a good assignment for *60 Minutes*.

August 16, 1991

Boston Globe's Vendetta
To Destroy A Man Fails

As dean of the communications school at Boston University, Joachim Maitre was a painful bone in the craw of the far-leftists who dominate much of academia in the Boston area. A refugee from East Germany, Maitre hated communism, and he fought the detested ideology with words and ideas, first as a journalist, then as an educator. As dean he created a program to train Afghan journalists who could report honestly on their country's fight to expel Soviet invaders. He was vocal in his disgust at the Sandinista suppression of a free press in Nicaragua.

All these activities were anathema to Boston academia. Being vocally anti-communist is not "politically correct" for a teacher, and especially for one who trains journalists. The left prefers professors who produce future editors and reporters who are liberal ideologues rather than honest journalists. So the Boston leftists seethed, and they whetted their knives for Maitre—and they finally found their opportunity to slash him this summer because of a trivial glitch he made in a communication school commencement address.

Speaking ad lib from a sheaf of notes, Maitre used several passages from a magazine article written by Michael Medved, a PBS film critic. Maitre did not credit Medved, and hence he was technically guilty of plagiarism. The evidence is that the slip was inadvertent: Maitre had been so impressed by the article, first published in the Hillsdale College journal *Imprimis*, that he distributed it to associates, and kept reprints in his office to give to visitors. The article had also been reprinted in the *Reader's Digest*.

The Boston Globe learned of Maitre's error from a video tape of the commencement exercise which Boston University was selling to graduates. Maitre was out of the country and could not be reached to explain how the error occurred; nonetheless, the *Globe* commenced a savage assault that was tantamount to character assassination.

Over 12 days the *Globe* ran no less than 12 articles about "the Maitre case;" there were also an editorial, a cartoon, and four letters to the editor, all critical of Maitre. The stories and the editorial comment were unrelentingly harsh. Many of the denunciations came from anonymous sources who did not have the courage to put their names behind their smears. A teacher who had been fired by Maitre was quoted, "He is a phony and a liar." Another source (anonymous) compared Maitre to "the Nazis."

The *Globe* constantly pointed out that plagiarism is considered one of the most serious offenses in academia. But the *Globe's* treatment of Maitre was in sharp contrast to how the paper handled a far more serious case of plagiarism involving a scholar at the same Boston University—the Rev. Martin Luther King, Jr.

On November 9, 1990, *The Wall Street Journal* reported that researchers preparing Dr. King's papers for publication had discovered that substantial portions of his doctoral dissertation and other academic studies had been plagiarized. The "borrowing" was described as "heavy," far more serious than Maitre's use of some 500 words in a 20-minute off-the-cuff talk.

The *Globe* defended King, quoting scholars who did not feel the plagiarism would harm King's reputation. One justification offered was that King was bright enough to have written his dissertation without plagiarism. Perhaps—but had the plagiarism been caught at the time, King would not have received a doctorate. The story quickly vanished from the *Globe*. King's dishonesty was not mentioned by the *Globe* in its Maitre coverage.

Nor did the *Globe* mention another case of plagiarism, that of the late Howard Simons, former managing editor of *The Washington Post*, and later curator of the Nieman Fellowships at Harvard (in the Boston suburbs). In 1981, a reporter for the *Allentown* (Pa.) *Call-Chronicle* found that Simons had incorporated 557 words from an article by another *Post* editor into a lecture he delivered at Cedar Crest College in Allentown. Simons first denied the plagiarism and then tried to claim the article from which he had lifted words was actually a kind of joint product—although his name wasn't on it.

There was no campaign to force Simons to resign. His plagiarism was never mentioned by the *Post* or any papers except the *Allentown Call* and those that carry the Accuracy in Media column. The plagiarism did not prevent Simons from being appointed to the prestigious Harvard post.

Unlike Howard Simons, Maitre didn't offer lame excuses. He conceded he made a bad mistake, and he resigned his deanship. *The Boston Globe's* smear campaign gave BU President John Silber no choice but to accept Maitre's resignation (he remains a tenured professor of journalism).

The Boston Globe's vendetta wasn't against Maitre the accused plagiarist; it was against Maitre the unabashed enemy of communism. Maitre erred, and he was man enough to admit it. But *The Boston Globe's* campaign to destroy him went beyond the bounds of decent journalism.

July 19, 1991

How Slanted News Can Defeat A Supreme Court Nominee

Conservative activists met over lunch on July 2, the day after President Bush nominated Judge Clarence Thomas to the U. S. Supreme Court, to discuss how to protect the black conservative from being "Borked." This peculiarly Washington word came into the political vocabulary in 1987, when the media helped leftists smear another Supreme Court nominee, Robert Bork, as a Neanderthal who would stomp on human rights. Now conservatives expect a similar blitz against a black man who had the audacity to become a success on his own. One man remarked, "Bork was dead before he started—by the time the media got through painting the picture their leftist friends wanted, the poll figures were so bad that nobody in the Senate would stick their neck out for him."

The TV onslaught against Thomas actually already was underway when the conservatives lunched. Within hours of his appearance with President Bush in Kennebunkport, Thomas received a working over of the ferocity usually reserved for such pariahs as Saddam Hussein or Muammar Qaddafi. Let's look at the "Borking" scorecard of these networks the evening of July 1.

NBC Nightly News opened with a report by White House correspondent Jim Miklaszewski. After scenes of Bush's announcement, NBC brought on three persons to comment on the nomination: Eleanor Holmes Norton, a black civil rights activist who is now the non-voting representative in Congress from the District of Columbia; Judith Lichtman, a pro-abortion lawyer; and Representative John Lewis, a black Congressman from Atlanta. All opposed Thomas.

NBC followed with a biographical sketch narrated by legal correspondent Carl Stern, which had comments from two persons: Senator Howard Metzenbaum (D., Ohio), one of two Senators who voted against Thomas when he was named to the D.C. Federal Court of Appeals, and Nan Aron of the Alliance for Justice. Metzenbaum opposed Thomas; Aron was dubious but did not flatly reject him. Thomas talked about his legal philosophy in a film clip.

NBC's scorecard: Against Thomas, four; so-so but leaning against, one; for Thomas, two (only Bush and the nominee himself). Oddly, NBC chose not to air the most moving moment from Thomas's appearance with the President in Maine, when his voice choked as he thanked his grandparents, rural sharecroppers who raised him in a shack with no plumbing, for insisting that he get an education.

The CBS Evening News did show that scene, then correspondent Rita Braver produced "talking head" comments from Derrick Bell, a black Harvard law professor, who opposed Thomas; NAACP President Benjamin Hooks, who claimed neutrality but was hostile; Senator Orrin Hatch (R., Utah), firmly for Thomas; Senators Paul Simon (D. Ill.) and Metzenbaum, opposed; and Ralph Neas, head of the Leadership Conference on Civil Rights, opposed.

CBS's scorecard: Against Thomas, four; "neutral," one; and supportive, one. Braver suggested she felt the chief issue to be debated was abortion. She said, "The thing that has most people worried, though, is a statement he once made about what he called the unenumerated rights—the things like abortion that are not specifically mentioned in the Constitution. He once talked about how judges should not be roaming unfettered through the Constitution, and to some people that means they should not expand those rights, should not expand abortion."

Do most people in fact worry about a strict construction of the Constitution? Results of the last three presidential elections suggest otherwise; both Presidents Reagan and Bush ran on promises to appoint Supreme Court justices who would not stretch constitutional language to fit political goals. Thomas fits that definition.

ABC's *World News Tonight*, to its credit, balanced the commentary in a report by Jim Wooten—Metzenbaum and

Hooks against Judge Thomas, Hatch and Senator Dennis DeConcini (D., Ariz.) for.

Stern, the NBC correspondent, has shown through his Supreme Court reporting that he sides with the quota-mongers who oppose Thomas. Take his story of January 23, 1989, on a decision on contract "set-asides" for minority groups. Justice Sandra Day O'Connor, writing for the majority, said set-asides should apply only when minority firms can prove they suffered because of "past, intentional discrimination," and that strict racial quotas can be just as discriminatory as if whites had applied them to blacks.

Stern interviewed four persons for the story, all of whom deplored the decision. He called the decision "a severe setback to the civil rights movement." We queried Stern then as to why he didn't interview people supporting the decision—say, the plumbing contractor in Richmond, Virginia, whose firm brought the suit. Stern said the contractor wouldn't go on camera. He didn't explain why he didn't seek out other persons who oppose reverse discrimination. Stern and NBC were content to air a slanted story. The same slant continues on Thomas.

Judge Thomas's life is a modern Horatio Alger story. But two of our Big Three networks show that he is in for a siege of "Borking" before his confirmation.

July 12, 1991

Nightline's Attempt To "Get" William Casey Collapses

Ted Koppel departed from the usual *Nightline* format on June 20 to present a *60 Minutes* type investigative report on the "October Surprise" story. This is the allegation that the Reagan campaign in 1980 persuaded Iran to delay the release of the hostages until after the election.

ABC News had investigated the charge made by an Iranian arms dealer named Jamshid Hashemi that Reagan campaign manager William J. Casey had cut this deal with a representative of the Ayatollah Khomeini at meetings in Madrid at the end of July and during the second week of August 1980. By going through the records of the Hotel Plaza in Madrid, they were able to prove to their own satisfaction that Hashemi and his brother, Cyrus, were in Madrid at the time these meetings allegedly took place. Hashemi claimed that he and Cyrus had helped arrange the meetings and that they served as interpreters.

Having established that Hashemi was telling the truth about his own presence in Madrid, *Nightline* set out to determine if it was possible that Casey could have been there at the same time. They found what they thought were mysterious gaps in the record of Casey's activities for July 27-29 and the second week of August 1980. Jeff Greenfield, who does reports for *Nightline*, said that on the dates of the alleged meetings in Madrid, "There are no recorded appointments for Casey that his former secretary could find. More puzzling, there are no references to Casey in any of the newspapers or video logs that we searched. No interviews, no sightings . . . No record of any transactions, no meals, no appointments . . . None of his aides has any record of any meeting or conversation with Casey during that time."

194

Greenfield concluded, "In late July and mid-August William Casey's whereabouts cannot be confirmed, and both of those times correspond to those times that we know the Hashemi brothers were in Madrid." Was it possible, he asked, that Casey could have left the country? The answer was yes. He had found a story in *The New York Times* of July 30 that quoted a Reagan spokesman saying that Casey would take up a certain matter "when he returns today from a trip abroad."

Koppel did not claim that this proved that Casey had conspired to delay the release of the hostages, but he suggested that it was enough to justify an official investigation that could tell us "if some of the people who led this country during the 1980s stole an election and broke the law." He added that it might also tell us that they didn't.

Publicized by *ABC News* and much of the print media, this report revived the flagging campaign for an "October Surprise" Congressional investigation. Senator Al Gore jumped on the bandwagon, citing the *Nightline* story. Speaker Tom Foley commented, "There seems to be evidence that Mr. Casey may have been there." He promised a decision on whether an investigation would be held in a few weeks. *Time* magazine also came out in favor of an investigation, again citing the *Nightline* findings.

A snowball was beginning to roll, but it fell apart on the night of June 26 when Koppel gave a brief update on the story on *Nightline*. He said: "That report has produced some new information. We have spoken with several men who attended the Anglo-American Conference on the History of the Second World War. William Casey attended that conference at the Imperial War Museum in London. Indeed he delivered a paper on secret operations in France during the war. That was on the morning of July 29." They even showed a photograph of Casey at the reception on the evening of July 28.

This shattered *Nightline's* hypothesis that Casey had mysteriously disappeared for three days, July 27-29, on a secret trip abroad. The discovery that Casey was attending a conference in London proved what Casey's former secretary had told *Nightline*—that the only records she could find of

195

Casey's activities in 1980 were very incomplete. It was a mistake to read any significance into dates for which there was no record of his whereabouts.

But Ted Koppel wasn't willing to admit that finding Casey in London, not Madrid, had destroyed the credibility of his key witness. Knowing only that Casey was present at the reception on July 28, Koppel said, "That would still have allowed Casey time to meet in Madrid with the Iranians during the day of July 27 and earlier in the day on the 28th. Flying time from Madrid to London is approximately 90 minutes."

Koppel couldn't bring himself to eat crow and retract his call for an investigation. The media that were quick to report the cloud that *Nightline* had hung over William Casey failed to report that *Nightline's* key witness against Casey, Jamshid Hashemi, had been shot down, possibly ringing down the curtain on the "October Surprise."

July 5, 1991

Which Is More Important— Patriotism Or "The Story?"

During the Persian Gulf War we heard a lot of people ask whether the Cable News Network, had it existed during World War II, would have put itself at the service of Adolf Hitler as it did for Saddam Hussein of Iraq. We shared the outrage felt by many Americans over "Baghdad Pete" Arnett's uncritical recitation of Iraqi propaganda claims about civilian casualties.

Now we have the answer: CNN would have done Hitler's dirty work, just as it did for Saddam Hussein. Our authority for this remarkable disclosure is none other than Bill Headline, the Washington bureau chief of CNN, and before that a longtime producer and executive for CBS News.

After addressing an Accuracy in Media conference on War and the Media in Washington on April 26, Headline was asked, "Mr. Headline, it is December 13, 1941. A long arduous war is beginning. Hitler invites Peter Arnett to come to Berlin and be in Berlin for the duration of the war. Does CNN send Peter Arnett to Adolf Hitler's Nazi Germany to be managed by Joseph Goebbels for the duration of the war? Yes or no."

"Yes," replied Bill Headline. "You bet."

There was a collective gasp from the audience. The questioner, Dolf Droge, the chairman of the Council for the Defense of Freedom, could hardly believe his ears. He asked, "Have you checked that answer with Ted Turner?" Headline said he had not, but he was confident that Turner, whose Turner Broadcasting System owns CNN, would agree.

Headline was then asked if he thought it would have made any difference in the outcome of the war if a reporter for a U.S. network such as Peter Arnett had been allowed to broadcast from Nazi Germany during the war.

Headline, after a long pause, said, "That's such a different situation that I really need to give that a little bit of thought." He added, "I would do it from the standpoint of being able to report on what was happening in all main geographical locations affected by the war. Whether it would have an influence on the duration of the war, I don't know."

Earlier we had debated with Headline the wisdom and propriety of having correspondents report from behind enemy lines, given Arnett's broadcasts from Baghdad during the Gulf War. We stressed that Arnett had admitted that he had been used by Iraqi dictator Saddam Hussein to report on civilian casualties in order to show how our power "was being applied or misapplied."

Saddam Hussein hoped these broadcasts would influence public opinion abroad to oppose the war. We pointed out that a reporter in Germany during World War II would have found it much easier to report on civilian casualties caused by our bombing because it was far less accurate than it was in Iraq and we killed perhaps a million German civilians.

Arnett's reports gave the impression that civilian casualties from our bombing were very heavy. Headline didn't think that viewers got that impression, but General Norman Schwarzkopf himself made that complaint, saying his entire staff resented the implication that the Allied coalition was deliberately targeting innocent civilians when, in fact, every effort was being made to keep civilian casualties to a minimum.

Brent Sadler, the correspondent for Britain's Independent Television News who also reported from Baghdad during the war, told the Accuracy in Media conference that he believed that fewer than a thousand civilians were killed by our bombing of Iraq.

Sadler said most of these deaths came in a single episode, the bombing of a bunker which the Iraqis had put to use as a bomb shelter for civilians. He told the AIM conference that he saw few actual bodies other than victims of this bombing, and he was sure the Iraqis were not concealing civilian dead from the foreign correspondents. Quite the opposite. They took them as far away as 300 kilometers to see fresh cases of civilian damage caused by allied bombs.

Sadler also gave an interesting sidelight to his reporting on the bunker. Immediately after the bombing, Allied spokesmen reported in Saudi Arabia that their intelligence sources said the bunker was actually a command and control center and the roof was camouflaged.

Sadler's crew went up on the roof and told him they could see no camouflage. When he reported that there was no camouflage, his London editor asked him if he had seen the roof with his own eyes. When he admitted he hadn't, the editor said he would not air the report that there was no camouflage. Sadler said he went back and examined the roof himself. He said he had to scrape away 6 inches of debris. Beneath it he found the camouflage paint.

CNN did not exercise that kind of supervision over Peter Arnett. His reports were aired live, and they created the impression that our bombing was causing thousands of civilian deaths. That was false, but many people around the world believed it. If CNN had been able to do for Hitler what it did for Saddam Hussein, Nazi Germany might have won World War II.

May 3, 1991

Highly Critical Nancy Reagan Biography: Did It Belong On The Front Page?

Not too many years ago, staffers at *The New York Times* joked that the paper's "attribution" rule was so firm that the Weather Bureau had to be quoted as the authority for the fact that it rained in Manhattan. Standards change. The April 7 Sunday *Times* ran a long front-page article summarizing the sleazier parts of a biography of Nancy Reagan by Washington writer Kitty Kelley. The *Times* said the book "offers sensational claims that the Reagans practiced a morality very different from what they preached," including "allegations of scandalous sexual conduct."

To persons familiar with a paper that claims to publish only "All the News That's Fit to Print," the *Times* article put a stamp of respectability on the most sensational book of the decade. But the *Times* did not pursue two relevant questions: whether Kelley knew what she was writing about, and her own reputation for forthrightness.

One supposed bombshell is Kelley's claim that Mrs. Reagan conducted a long affair with singer Frank Sinatra, including White House trysts. Kelley's language is artful. She never flatly puts the First Lady and the crooner in bed. She uses an anonymous "member of Mrs. Reagan's White House staff" as the claimed source for a long paragraph about the three-hour meetings in the solarium: "We always knew better than to interrupt those private 'luncheons.' . . . You could feel the air charge when he was around here . . . She usually would arrange those 'luncheons' when the President was out of town . . . All calls were put on hold," even the President's.

During interviews with Bryant Gumbel of NBC's *Today* and *The Washington Post*, Kelley acted the innocent when asked if she claimed the relationship was sexual. "I only take

200

you up to the bedroom door of the White House, I don't take you inside," she told Gumbel. Since she had talked with neither Sinatra nor Mrs. Reagan she could not tell what happened next. (Kelley was bolder with Harry Smith of *CBS This Morning* on April 11, declaring flatly she thought they had an affair.)

Peculiarly, essentially the same passage appears—without suggestive quotation marks around the world "luncheon"— in Kelley's 1986 biography of Sinatra, with no insinuation of a sexual affair.

In instances where principals are now speaking out, many of Kelley's nastier stories rapidly dissipate. Kelley asserts that Mrs. Reagan refused to invite press secretary Jim Brady to the White House after he was wounded in the 1981 assassination attempt because "his slack-jawed presence and occasional wailing made her uncomfortable." Sarah Brady said in fact they visited the White House half a dozen times and Mrs. Reagan made them feel welcome. Sarah Brady cited dates supported by her engagements calendar.

Similarly, Kelley claims that Mrs. Reagan told White House aide Michael Deaver to leave his wife—an assertion Deaver told *The Washington Times* was "somebody else's version of real life." Barbara Bush dismisses as nonsense Kelley's claim about Mrs. Reagan passing along to someone else her Christmas gift of a wreath. "Trash and fiction," Mrs. Bush said.

Kelley is heavy on insinuation. She has a section about lesbianism at Smith College, which Mrs. Reagan attended in the 1940s, then drops in an unattributed passage that a "secret but romantic 'best friends' relationship developed between Nancy Davis and a classmate who later became an avowed lesbian." She quotes a long letter from homosexual activist Larry Kramer alleging that son Ron Reagan is gay ("we know our own") despite considerable contrary evidence.

Did Kelley really interview the 1,002 persons she claims in her source notes? She told *The Washington Post* that researchers did "about 15 percent" of her interviews, which suggests she did about 852 personally. Kelley is a hard worker. Nonetheless, this means she crammed an inordinate amount of work into the four years she spent on the book. Assuming she researched three years, she would have conducted 284 interviews a year—or more than one per work day, even counting travel and other research.

How authentic were the claimed "interviews?" Lou Cannon, now of *The Washington Post*, covered Ronald Reagan when he was California governor and President. He is listed as a Kelley interviewee. But on the NBC *Today* show on April 12, Cannon said flatly, "She didn't." We hear other denials also.

Kelley's own past contains the same sort of "deceptions" for which she criticizes Mrs. Reagan. At one time she claimed, falsely, to have been Gene McCarthy's press secretary during his 1968 presidential run. A *Washington Post* writer who was doing a profile of Kelley in 1989 uncovered a peculiar series of letters written to persons who could either boost or hurt Kelley. A documents expert said they came from Kelley's typewriter.

Is the Kelley biography authentic? Kelley writes on the first page that "two entries on Nancy Reagan's birth certificate are accurate—her sex and her color." We'll vouch for the accuracy of two things concerning Kelley's book: its title, and the name of the author.

April 12, 1991

Hollywood Movie Used
To Spread Big Lie

A new movie, "Guilty by Suspicion," starring Robert De Niro, is one more shot in a 40-year-old campaign on the part of the Left to convince us that the U.S. government carried out a reign of terror during the late 1940s and 1950s. Their propaganda has been so effective that to dispute the basic thesis is to endanger one's credibility. But those of us who lived through that era have a duty to expose the lies that are used to brainwash the younger generations. We find "Guilty by Suspicion" guilty of distortion.

In 1947 hearings before the House Committee on Un-American Activities, former communist Howard Rushmore testified that most Hollywood stars were "political morons" who could easily be duped into following a dictated line. "Guilty by Suspicion" demonstrates that Hollywood's political sophistication hasn't improved much in succeeding years.

The story is about a successful director, David Merrill, played by DeNiro, who was never a member of the Communist Party but who had attended a few party meetings in 1939. To keep working as a movie director, Merrill was told by his studio that he would have to "purge' himself by testifying before the House Un-American Activities Committee (HUAC). He was advised that this would involve identifying others who attended the meetings of the Communist Party or the front group. That he refuses to do, because he does not want to see innocent people, like himself, falsely accused of being Communists.

This is the big lie underlying the propaganda campaign: that the victims of the reign of terror were not Stalinists who were using their positions in an effort to spread the gospel of communism, but were innocent liberals like David Merrill. This was summarized in this statement shown on the screen at the conclusion of the film: "Thousands of lives were shattered and hundreds of careers destroyed by what came to be known as the Hollywood blacklist. People like David and Ruth Merrill faced terms in prison, suffered the loss of friends and possessions, and were denied their right to earn a living.''

The truth is that only ten Hollywood figures went to prison. These were the famous "Hollywood Ten," all Communist Party members who were subpoenaed by HUAC in 1947 and refused to answer any questions, citing the 1st Amendment as their defense. They were convicted of contempt of Congress and sent to jail. One of them, director Edward Dmytryk, broke with the Communist Party. After his release, he agreed to testify before HUAC and to identify other party members. He said in his book, *It's a Hell of a Life*, that the committee's investigators made one thing clear: "They did not want to hear a name mentioned unless his (or her) membership in the party was certain and verifiable.''

Moreover, Dmytryk said that after he and actor Larry Parks testified in public in the spring of 1951, the committee changed its procedures and permitted witnesses who were naming party members to do so in closed session. Even though "Guilty by Suspicion" is set in the period after Dmytryk testified, it tells us that HUAC was summoning witnesses and insisting that they testify in public and accuse others of being Communist Party members even though they had no basis for doing so.

The film flat-out lies when it suggests that the members of the committee were pressuring witnesses to accuse others of being party members in public to get publicity to further their careers. Ignoring the careful work done by the committee investigators, it shows a Congressman at a hearing saying, "We know they're out there, but I'll be damned if I know how we're supposed to find them guilty. It'd be a lot easier if you wore some kind of identification like a pin or bumper sticker. Then we wouldn't have to sit here and go through all this.''

An even more egregious distortion is showing the FBI relentlessly tailing David Merrill wherever he goes, apparently only because he has refused to testify voluntarily before HUAC. Unable to work in the movie industry, he is reduced to working in a friend's store in New York. The film shows the FBI agents tailing him asking the store owner to let them know if he changes jobs. The FBI didn't have agents to waste on such absurd tasks.

The communists are unhappy about this film. They wanted it to be more accurate, to show that those who were subpoenaed by HUAC were party members. They want to be vindicated, but most Americans, especially now that communism is in total disgrace throughout the world, might not agree that Stalin's Hollywood lackeys were harshly treated in being exposed for what they were. And so Hollywood perpetuates the fiction that our government targeted non-communists and exposed them to constant FBI surveillance and public humiliation just because they would not accuse others of being communists.

It does not want to acknowledge that there was a serious Stalinist infiltration of the movie industry in the 1930s and 1940s, that the Stalinists were blacklisting anti-communist writers, actors and directors, and that Ronald Reagan, Gary Cooper, Adolphe Menjou, Morrie Ryskind and other anti-communists performed a valuable service in fighting this incubus.

April 5, 1991

A Snow Job About Grand Canyon Haze

Journalists, who pride themselves on being skeptical of anything the government says, seem to suspend their skepticism when it comes to the Environmental Protection Agency. On issues such as acid rain and asbestos, EPA has been forced to admit that it put its imprimatur on scientific nonsense. Yet most of the media play the patsy's role for EPA bureaucrats.

A good recent example is the flap over whether the Navajo Generating Station (NGS), a power plant in Arizona some 80 miles from the Grand Canyon, should be forced to spend $2 billion to reduce the sulfur dioxide in its emissions. An environmental piece on NBC's *Today* show on March 18 by correspondent Roger O'Neil demonstrates how a zealous correspondent swallowed EPA's position while ignoring credible counter evidence.

O'Neil opened by stating an inarguable premise: "If a picture is worth a thousand words, then the view of the Grand Canyon after a winter storm is worth a whole roll of film." O'Neil said that EPA was about "to force the Canyon's biggest polluter, a power plant, to clean up." (O'Neil didn't mention forest fires and Los Angeles smog, two major canyon haze culprits.)

O'Neil recited, as if undisputed fact, an EPA contention that at the canyon "most of the haze" comes from the Navajo Generating Station (NGS), and that this justified requiring the NGS to cut sulfur dioxide emissions by 70 percent. He continued, "But at a public hearing in Phoenix the public said it wants more, a 95 percent clean up." O'Neil had talking-head interviews with an EPA bureaucrat and two National Park Service officials, all of whom wanted drastic action to eliminate the haze that sometimes hangs over the Grand Canyon. The NGS was not given an opportunity to tell its side of the story.

Completely absent from O'Neil's report was any suggestion that (a) the EPA-financed study blaming NGS for Grand Canyon pollution was so flawed that some participating scientists refused to sign it; and that (b) a more thorough, and recent, study disputed the contention that NGS emissions were largely responsible for the Grand Canyon haze.

The irony is that NGS has the reputation of being one of the nation's cleaner power plants, one never cited for pollution violations. Built at a cost of $650 million, $200 million of which was for environmental protection, it was completed in 1976. NGS burns coal with one of the lowest sulfur content used by any generating plant in America, 0.5 percent. But it is conspicuous, with 750-foot stacks (the better to disperse pollutants) and it is only 80 miles northeast of the Grand Canyon.

In 1987, the EPA and National Park Service conducted a test called WHITEX to determine where the NGS emissions were going. This involved putting a tracer gas into the plume from NGS. Since the prevailing winds were from the southeast, the test was designed primarily to detect gases north and east of the power plant. Surprisingly, the tracer gas also showed up at the Grand Canyon's Hopi Point. Although the test was not designed to determine how much of the emissions were reaching the Grand Canyon, the EPA and National Park Service concluded that the NSG was the main cause of the winter haze.

Scientists such as Dr. Jerry L. Shapiro refused to sign off on this conclusion, arguing that the design did not justify the use that was being made of the experiment. Shapiro headed a study designed specifically to measure the emissions reaching the canyon. Done under NGS auspices, it monitored 26 receptor sites at the Grand Canyon for 81 days. The conclusion was that neither test provided data "that could be used to quantify the impact of plant emissions on Grand Canyon haze."

The sulfur dioxide emitted by the NSG has to be converted into sulfates to create haze. To produce sulfates that would have a significant impact on visibility, the relative humidity would have to be more than 70 percent, a rarity for the Grand

Canyon. The few times when humidity was that high, and NGS emissions were in or near the canyon, sulfate formation was often limited by the absence of such oxidizing agents as hydrogen peroxide. During the infrequent occasions when the levels of humidity and oxidizing agents were high enough to form sulfates, visibility was already obscured by fog, clouds or darkness.

The WHITEX group claimed visibility changes of 4 percent contrast, or "perceptible," on 100 days; 10 percent, "quite noticeable," on 58 days; and 20 percent, or "very apparent," on 21 days. NGS's estimates were "perceptible" for eight days, "quite noticeable" for two days—and these during winter months, when tourist traffic is low.

Shapiro stated, "The biggest single factor in visibility impairment is humidity. When visibility is poor, and you can't see the other side of the canyon, it has nothing to do with the Navajo Generating Station." Yet the EPA and the National Park Service want to force NGS customers to pay for $2 billion in changes that might or might not give a small number of tourists a slightly better Grand Canyon vista. NBC correspondent Andrea Mitchell has said that NBC has crossed the line from straight reporting to advocacy on environmental issues. Roger O'Neil's report is a good example of that.

March 22, 1991

The Phony *60 Minutes* Amalgam Fillings Scare

We have a story suggestion for *60 Minutes*. How about exposing a gang that tries to convince people on national TV that they have a good way of both preventing and curing arthritis and multiple sclerosis. They disregard warnings that there is no sound epidemiological evidence or controlled clinical trials to back up their claims. But using a few impressive testimonials from people who have experienced miraculous cures, they persuade people all over the country to spend hundreds of dollars to seek relief from their pain and suffering.

Can't you just see Mike Wallace eviscerating these charlatans who are willing to hold out false hopes and stampede pain-wracked invalids into spending money many of them can ill afford on a miracle cure for arthritis, colitis, multiple sclerosis, skin rashes, and other disabling ailments? Well, Mike wouldn't have to go far to interview his targets. All he would have to do is interview Morley Safer, his colleague on *60 Minutes*, and Patti Hassler, the producer of a *60 Minutes* segment titled "Is There Poison in Your Mouth?" that aired December 16, 1990.

The program was designed to push the claim of some dentists and doctors that the amalgam dental fillings that nearly all of us have in our mouths are dangerous to our health because they contain mercury. They say that mercury vapor, released in minute quantities when we chew with our amalgam-filled teeth, is poisoning us. The overwhelming majority of dentists and doctors disagree. The American Dental Association strongly disagrees. It points out that amalgam has been used safely for 150 years. Dr. Enid Neidle of Columbia University says that only 50 cases of allergy to amalgam fillings have been documented in medical literature in 60 years.

The ADA feels so strongly about the safety of amalgam that it considers it unethical for dentists to advise patients to have their amalgam fillings replaced with other materials except for cosmetic reasons. It has even acted to revoke the licenses of dentists who advise patients to have their fillings replaced, since this is viewed as dental work that enriches the dentist without benefiting the patient.

60 Minutes gave the ADA an opportunity to present its views on this issue through Dr. Heber Simmons, but Dr. Simmons was up against the usual *60 Minutes* stacked deck. He appeared on the program as the lone defender of amalgam. Arrayed against him were two dentists and an allergist-dermatologist who were very forceful critics of amalgam fillings. They were supported by four patients who had experienced remarkable improvements in their health after having their fillings removed. Totally absent were any interviews with doctors or scientists defending amalgam except for the ADA spokesman. Although there are plenty of people who have gone to the expense and trouble of having amalgam fillings removed without seeing any improvement in their health, not one of them appeared on the *60 Minutes* program.

The star of the CBS show was Nancy Yost, an attractive young woman from San Jose, Calif., who had been diagnosed as having multiple sclerosis and had to use a cane to walk. The day after she had five fillings removed she threw away her cane and went dancing. Dr. Peter Seland, who runs a multiple sclerosis clinic, criticized CBS for raising false hopes. He said that many people have similar but temporary remissions from almost any form of treatment for multiple sclerosis if they believe in it. Two weeks before the *60 Minutes* program aired, the National Multiple Sclerosis Society issued a statement saying that its medical advisory board had concluded "that there is no sound epidemiological evidence which relates mercury amalgam fillings to MS and no sound clinical evidence, gained through controlled clinical trials, which suggests that replacement of dental amalgams leads to any improvement in MS." Anticipating the kind of anecdotal evidence that *60 Minutes* relied upon so heavily to make its case, the society said, "Reports of remissions resulting from amalgam removal appear to be anecdotal and cannot be separated from placebo effect or spontaneous changes in disease.

There are many people with MS who do not have such fillings and others with MS who have had amalgam fillings replaced with no demonstrated benefit."

60 Minutes ignored that warning. Instead, it concluded with Morley Safer asking the anti-amalgam allergist if he was advising everyone "to go out and have your fillings removed." The doctor replied, "Absolutely, absolutely." Morley Safer then remarked that not everyone agreed with that advice and that consultations were advisable. As a result, dentists were reported to have been deluged with inquiries. Dr. James L. Adams of Los Gatos, Calif., was quoted as saying he had to take his phone off the hook to get some sleep and that he has at least 30 new patients awaiting appointments. "The television show was wonderful," he told the *San Francisco Examiner.*

December 21, 1990

Why Apple Growers Are Suing *60 Minutes* and CBS

When a television show such as CBS's *60 Minutes* does a report, its producers and correspondents have absolute power to dictate what gets on the air. Viewers are shown only what the TV people want them to see—truth and objectivity all too often are sacrificed in the name of journalistic drama. And even when it is demonstrated that a network has erred, no law says it must air a retraction. CBS, ABC and NBC all have their own rules that say that errors must be corrected, but this requirement is frequently flouted.

But it now looks as if America's most arrogant network, CBS, is going to have to try to prove in court the wild charges its *60 Minutes* program made in 1989 concerning Alar, a growth regulator that was used by many growers of red apples until it was forced off the market by the hysteria generated largely by *60 Minutes*. Using a scientifically flawed report put together by the Natural Resources Defense Council (NRDC), a radical environmentalist group, *60 Minutes* told its millions of viewers that Alar was the most potent cancer-causing agent in our food supply. Correspondent Ed Bradley added emphasis to that charge by making it against the background of a big red apple emblazoned with a skull and crossbones. Even if one didn't listen to what Bradley was saying, that graphic sent a clear message: apples are poison, not the healthful fruit that keeps the doctor away. Children were said to be especially at risk. The broadcast caused wide public panic. Mothers poured apple juice down the drain and bypassed apples in supermarkets.

What *60 Minutes* did not tell viewers that Sunday evening was that three weeks earlier, the Environmental Protection Agency had issued a press release announcing the results of the rodent tests it had ordered to determine if Alar was a carcinogen. The release said the tests had shown that Alar was "statistically negative for cancer response." In other words, even when Alar was fed to laboratory mice in massive doses over a long period of time it could not be shown to induce cancer.

Immediately after the Alar program aired, Accuracy in Media told the *60 Minutes* executive producer, Don Hewitt, about the EPA statement and faxed him a copy at his request. We thought that under CBS's own rules, *60 Minutes* would promptly correct its error. It aired a second program on Alar in May, but instead of correcting the original error, it repeated it, saying ten times that Alar was a carcinogen or potential carcinogen. CBS was saying, in effect, that it wasn't going to let facts interfere with its dramatic scare story—even if mom-and-pop apple growers throughout the country were ruined by its sensationalism.

Now CBS is going to have to defend its Alar broadcast in a forum where both sides have their say—a court of law. A group of 11 apple growers in Washington state has filed a class action suit against CBS, the NRDC and the public relations firm that orchestrated the anti-Alar publicity campaign, Fenton Communications. The complaint, which was filed in Yakima County (Washington) Superior Court on November 28, charges the defendants with product disparagement, interference with business expectations and unfair or deceptive trade practices. The plaintiffs say the class they represent consists of approximately 4,700 individuals or business entities that owned red apples that were in storage in the state of Washington at the time the *60 Minutes* program aired and who grew red apples in the 1989 growing season "which were devalued as a result of the communication or publication of the false, misleading and scientifically unreliable statements of the defendants concerning red apples."

The complaint charges that the defendants were responsible for "false, misleading and scientifically unreliable statements about red apples, with reckless disregard of the truth or falsity of such statements." They are accused of violating Washington's Unfair Business Practices Act, and the plaintiffs seek actual damages, which have been estimated as high as $150 million for Washington's apple growers.

The apple growers face a tough challenge. The famed New York lawyer, Floyd Abrams, who frequently represents media companies in libel cases, says that under the law governing product disparagement, the plaintiffs will have to prove that CBS lied. Abrams says, "That is a very difficult burden." But if the growers succeed in getting their case before a jury in Yakima County, it will be CBS that will have the difficult burden of proving that it didn't lie when it said that Alar, a non-carcinogen, was the most potent cancer-causing agent in the food supply and when it labeled that beautiful red apple with a skull & crossbones.

November 30, 1990

Famous TV Anchor Makes A Remarkable Admission

During his years as anchor of the *CBS Evening News,* Walter Cronkite pretended to be an objective reporter who did not let his political bias affect what he put on the air. Now Cronkite has made an admission that won't be surprising to those of us who have harbored suspicions about his claimed "objectivity." Cronkite states that in the spring of 1968, he encouraged Senator Bobby Kennedy to run against incumbent Lyndon Johnson for the Democratic presidential nomination.

You might recall those turbulent months. Lyndon Johnson's presidency was in trouble. The media had managed to convince the American public that the Vietcong and North Vietnamese won a victory during their Tet offensive earlier in the year, even though just the opposite was true.

Cronkite himself suddenly became a vocal foe of Administration policies—and given his prominence as an anchorman, his views carried disproportionate weight. He made a two-week "fact-finding trip" to Vietnam and then on February 27 aired a widely-discussed documentary urging that the United States should get out of the war. "To say that we are closer to victory today is to believe in the face of the evidence. . . . optimists who have been wrong in the past," Cronkite said. "It is increasingly clear to this reporter that the only rational way out would be to negotiate—not as victims, but as an honorable people who lived up to their pledge to victory and democracy and did the best they could."

In a subsequent radio interview with CBS colleague Eric Sevareid, Cronkite turned military strategist in discussing the beleaguered outpost of Khe Sanh. He stated, "I found very few people out there who really believe . . . Khe Sanh could be held if the North Vietnamese are determined to take it." He called Khe Sanh a symbol of "administrative intransigence and military miscalculation."

Because of Cronkite's stature, his get-out advice had great impact on public opinion, and the Johnson Administration saw support for the war rapidly evaporating. Another senator, Eugene McCarthy, had already challenged Johnson for the nomination, and made a surprisingly strong showing in the New Hampshire primary election. Realizing that the President could be denied nomination, Kennedy was agonizing more or less publicly about whether to run himself. It was in this context that he invited Cronkite to an off-the-record luncheon at a Senate dining room in Washington.

Cronkite described the meeting in a recent talk at Harvard University, excerpts of which *The New York Times* published on its op-ed page on November 17, 1990.

During the private talk Cronkite heard Bobby Kennedy talk about Vietnam, and concluded that "his strong views . . . happened to coincide with my own." So Cronkite said he told Kennedy, "If you feel so strongly on the subject, it seems to me you certainly ought to run for the presidency." They sparred a bit over the pros and the cons, and then Cronkite said Kennedy told him, "I want you to run for the Senate in New York." Cronkite quickly declined the suggestion.

Cronkite professed to have "a long held principle in refusing even to entertain the idea of running for office." He continued, "Should one who has achieved national fame as a presumably impartial news person ever run, the public is going to have every reason to question whether that person has been tailoring the news to build a political platform. The burden of credibility is already heavy enough without that extra load," Cronkite continued.

As Cronkite tells the story, word of his private talk with Kennedy quickly leaked to President Johnson, who complained to CBS president Frank Stanton. What Cronkite did not mention in his Harvard talk was revealed later by a man who worked on the White House staff at the time: that the CBS anchorman told Kennedy that his program would be at the senator's disposal if he should run.

Johnson's anger at Cronkite's secret machinations was understandable. In addition to being anchorman, Cronkite carried the title of managing editor of the *CBS Evening News*.

Why should the nation's leading news anchorman be meeting secretly with a senator and urging him to challenge a sitting president? Like it or not, Cronkite's sympathy for Bobby Kennedy—and his anti-war views—threatened the fairness of anything the *CBS Evening News* said about either the war or the presidential election.

Aside from being called on the carpet by Frank Stanton, Cronkite suffered no in-house disciplining for his role as a secret advisor to Bobby Kennedy. CBS left him in his anchor's chair for coverage of the 1968 election, including the tumultuous Democratic national convention in Chicago. And in retirement he serves on the CBS board of directors.

Cronkite told a *New York Times* interviewer in early 1989 that as an anchor he had never disguised his sentiments about politics in general but that on TV he had "tried absolutely to hew to the middle of the road and not show any prejudice or bias in any way." Now we learn from his own words that deep in his heart, Walter Cronkite was a closet Kennedyite. So much for media objectivity.

November 23, 1990

Hypocrisy At
The Washington Post

The Washington Post is widely regarded as one of the most liberal papers in the United States. Katharine Graham, the principal owner and chairman of the board of The Washington Post Company, persists in denying that there is any liberal bias at the *Post*. Mrs. Graham says the paper is "independent," not liberal. She has adamantly rejected suggestions that the *Post* should try to find and hire some conservative reporters and editors to balance what readers have long perceived to be an overwhelming preponderance of liberal Democrats on the editorial staff.

At The Washington Post Company's annual shareholders meeting last May, Kay Graham denied that the staff was liberal, saying, "We have a very professional centrist staff in my view." She described executive editor Benjamin C. Bradlee as "apolitical," adding, "I don't know what he is." She said, "Len Downie (the managing editor) is the most centrist person and the fairest and decentest person you can imagine, and I would say the same thing about the assistant managing editors."

Kay Graham's vision that her paper was staffed by centrists was in sharp conflict with a column that its ombudsman, Richard Harwood, had just published. He said the Post had "trivialized" the recent huge pro-life rally in Washington, giving it only a small story in the local news section of the paper. He noted that a year earlier a comparable abortion rights rally had been the lead story on page one, and that more than 15 columns of space had been devoted to it. Pro-abortion bias explained the difference in treatment, Harwood said, noting that "most centrist" Len Downie believed that "journalists here not only are not part of the anti-abortion movement, but don't know anyone who is." Harwood concluded, "Journalists are pigeonholed fairly by the social scientists as 'liberal Democrats.'"

Kay Graham's vision was rudely shattered when *The City Paper*, a Washington weekly, decided to check the voter registration of 49 top Post editors, reporters and columnists. The results, published in its October 26, 1990 edition, revealed that only one registered Republican could be found, sports columnist Tony Kornheiser. An embarrassed Kornheiser explained that he wasn't a real Republican. He said he and his wife had flipped a coin to decide which should register as a Republican and which as a Democrat. They wanted to be on both lists in order to get mailings from both.

The City Paper identified 25 registered Democrats, including the "apolitical" Ben Bradlee and assistant managing editors Bob Woodward and Milton Coleman. It discovered 5 registered as independents and 10, including Len Downie, who were not registered to vote. One, columnist Colman McCarthy, explained that he doesn't vote because he's a pacifist. The remaining 9 lived in Virginia where voters are not required to register by party. Some of those whose party preference could not be found in the records were interviewed. None would admit to being a Republican sympathizer. Several are known from their work or their appearances on TV to be liberal.

Given its overwhelming domination by liberals, it was not surprising to find the *Post* hypocritically attacking Joseph Farah, the new editor of *The Sacramento Union*, for making his paper "unabashedly conservative." Among Farah's unforgivable offenses: labeling the National Organization for Women (NOW) a "radical feminist group" and decreeing that homosexuals not be referred to as "gays." The *Union* for many years had a conservative editorial policy, but the management made no effort to influence news coverage, and its news staff was dominated by liberals. In that respect it was very much like *The Washington Post* and the Union's local liberal rival, *The Sacramento Bee*.

Farah, a former editor of the now-defunct *Los Angeles Herald-Examiner*, says he is trying to get the news staff to change its ways and report more objectively. He makes no apology for putting a story about a large anti-abortion rally in Sacramento on page one under a headline reading, "16,600

Stand Proud Against Abortion." He pointed out that the *Bee* showed its pro-abortion bias by burying the story, just as *The Washington Post* had buried the story of the big pro-life rally last April. Farah says that the *Bee's* biases prevent it from exposing the corruption of the liberal establishment. He intends to see that the *Union* does that. He wants the paper to give conservatives and their causes an even break. To the liberal journalists, that is heresy, but it should be a refreshing change for the people of Sacramento.

October 26, 1990

Verdict Without Trial

To anyone who paused for a moment of rational thought, the item in *The Dartmouth Review* had the earmarks of a cruel hoax—the sabotage of a publication that infuriates leftists because it tries to nudge them out of the pseudo-intellectual sludge that covers most American campuses.

Someone with access to the *Review's* computerized printing system messed around with a small type "credo" published on the paper's editorial page. The usual quotation, from Theodore Roosevelt, was replaced by a quotation from Hitler's *Mein Kampf*, "I believe that today that I am acting in the sense of the Almighty Creator: By warding off the Jews, I am fighting for the Lord's work."

When horrified editors learned of the substitution, they managed to find and destroy 10,000 of the 13,000 copy print run. But they were too late: liberals who viscerally hate *The Dartmouth Review* were already forming their lynch mob, led by Dr. James Freedman, the college president. In a curious display of intellectual incuriosity, Freedman did not bother to talk to anyone on the paper before denouncing it for "an act of moral cowardice" and "vicious hatred." Through a college press agent, Freedman also said, "No one [sic] on the campus believes it was an accident."

Freedman's bias can be understood; he is the archetype of liberals who build Berlin Walls around their minds to shut out dissenting ideas. For instance, several years ago another generation of *Review* editors questioned whether a curriculum that costs students about $20,000 a year should include a professor who taught his classes in jargon that was a blend of obscenities and incomprehensible street talk. Freedman assembled a kangaroo court that expelled the students; they won reinstatement in a more sane proceeding. Freedman's hatred of the *Review* is evident.

But why did the press so eagerly bash the *Review*? Why no curiosity to pursue what was to us the more interesting angle—who slipped the Hitler quotation into the paper, and how and why?

The *Review* has about 40 staff members; there is no control on access to its office. The pages are produced on an Apple MacIntosh computer, which most students know how to operate. The offending passage was in a different type face from what is used on the standing Teddy Roosevelt quote, suggesting that the person who inserted it was not overly familiar with *Review* printing procedures. The paper is physically printed at a commercial plant not connected with the *Review*.

No source was given for the Hitler quote. But in short order, the Student Assembly, which is at perpetual war with the *Review,* managed to report that it came from Chapter Two of Volume One of *Mein Kampf.*

The Washington Post was extraordinarily lazy in its reporting. Michael Specter's first-day story devoted 700 words to statements that the quote was consistent with the paper's past performance. He gave only 100 words to editors' assertions that they were victims of a cruel hoax.

Indeed, Specter was hoodwinked himself while on campus. To illustrate his charge the Review is homophobic, he included a direct quote from someone he identified as Hugo Restall, "the executive editor of the paper." Problem: Restall is off-campus this semester, working in New York for *The National Review*. He never talked with Specter, which the *Post* admitted (although without apology).

Given this experience, shouldn't the *Post* have paid more attention to the editors' hoax claim? A follow story by Christopher Daly was even more slanted. He devoted 640 words to *Review*-bashing, and only 25 in its defense.

Ironically, a New York City Jewish paper, *The Forward,* treated the *Review* and its young staffers with the fairness they deserved. It ran an editorial in which it pointed out that an illustrious Dartmouth alumnus, Judge Lawrence Silberman, had previously likened Dartmouth's treatment of the Review to McCarthyism. *The Forward* allowed Kevin Pritchett, the *Review* editor, a thousand words to tell his side of the story— something no other paper, and especially *The Washington Post,* has matched.

Forward readers learned that the *Review* had distributed an explanation, apology and disavowal of the Hitler quote to everyone on campus, posted it on every campus building and published it in a full page ad in the campus daily.

Richard Cohen, the liberal op-ed columnist for *The Washington Post,* seemed grudgingly embarrassed by his paper's performance. He said that the "right-wing brats at the loathsome *Dartmouth Review* may be getting a raw deal." It was not clear to Cohen that anyone connected with the paper had anything to do with publishing the quote. "In other words," Cohen wrote, "we have a mystery."

But not a mystery that *Washington Post* reporters made any effort to resolve. The *Post's* performance points up the need for "alternative" media everywhere, in big cities as well as on campuses such as Dartmouth.

October 12, 1990

A Mike Wallace
You Won't Like

CBS correspondent Mike Wallace seems to have a bad hangup about the American military. At the sight of a U.S. uniform, he goes into critical spasms that can only be diagonosed as acute anti-Samism, as in Uncle Sam. His most recent seizure—of many—came on a *60 Minutes* segment on September 30 concerning civilian casualties in Panama during the U.S. invasion last December.

Actually, this was a double-dip error for CBS. On January 3 the *CBS Evening News* reported that a slum district called "El Chorillo" was destroyed the night of the invasion, with 12,000 to 15,000 people losing their homes. CBS blamed the destruction on the U.S. assault force.

But five days earlier *The New York Times* had run a long story quoting El Chorillo residents, including priests, as saying that General Manuel Noriega's thugs deliberately started the fires that burned the district the morning after the U.S. attack on his nearby headquarters. The *Times* headline read, "Residents Say Force Loyal to Noriega Set Fire to Neighborhood in Reprisal."

The Washington Post had a similar story the next day, on December 29, headlined "Homes Destroyed by Noriega's Men, Residents Say." Both papers reported that Noriega was angry with El Chorillo residents because they voted against his candidate in 1989 elections. The *Times* said Noriega's Dignity Battalions told residents, "If I go, El Chorillo goes with me."

We pointed out this error to CBS President Laurence Tisch, but there was no correction. However, we were surprised to see Wallace repeat the error on *60 Minutes* as "evidence" that civilian deaths caused by Operation Just Cause were far higher than the 202 confirmed by the Pentagon.

Wallace, who narrated the segment, reported correctly

that Noriega's headquarters came under heavy fire by U.S. gunships. He continued, "When the sun came up after that grisly night before, El Chorillo was still burning out of control. Reports had already begun to circulate that hundreds of civilians had been killed and thousands wounded in El Chorillo." These casualty figures are highly exaggerated, according to the Pentagon, but the question is: Who was responsible for burning El Chorillo?

CBS producer Charles Thompson told us he was aware of the *Times* and *Post* stories that Noriega's thugs had torched El Chorillo, but after viewing some 10 hours of U.S. military film he was convinced that our gunships started the fire. He also attached great weight to an Army memo—Wallace called it "secret"—saying the destruction was "the result of our ops."

We have that memo. It was never secret. It is not an investigative report. It is a memo of a phone call between a major in the Pentagon and a claims officer in Panama who was reporting what another claims officer had told him. The memo said an estimate of 1,000 civilian casualties was about right—a sentence Wallace used to bolster his charge that the Pentagon greatly underestimated the number of civilians. (The Pentagon says the 202 figure came from the Panamanian equivalent of the coroner's office.)

Wallace didn't mention another sentence in the memo. It blamed other civilian casualties on "shop owners shooting looters, Dignity Battalions shooting Noriega opponents, neighborhood protection/vigilante groups shooting Dignity Battalion members, and stray rounds from US-PDF firefights."

If *60 Minutes* had evidence that the residents of El Chorillo who told the *Post* and the *Times* that Noriega's men burned down their homes were wrong, it should have presented it. Instead, Wallace chose to bash Uncle Sam.

This outburst came only a few days after Wallace took a passing cheap shot at General William C. Westmoreland, in an attempt to pump credibility into CBS's mendacious 1982 documentary, "The Uncounted Enemy: A Vietnam Deception," which claimed Westmoreland conspired with intelli-

225

gence officers to give false enemy strength figures to President Johnson and the public. Westmoreland sued, then settled out of court. In a retrospective broadcast, Wallace said that "after a thorough internal review" CBS "remains firmly behind the broadcast."

Wallace fuzzed the truth. Burton Benjamin, a brave CBS executive who did the internal investigation, actually found that Wallace and company committed 11 violations of network guidelines. They chose witnesses to support the show's false thesis and ignored others. The Benjamin Report is famed as one of the most stinging self-criticisms ever in network TV. Why would Wallace dare make such a statement? He counted on two things: a short public memory, and his knowledge that Westmoreland won't take CBS to court again.

Wallace also displayed his anti-Samism during a discussion on ethics that aired last year on PBS. The moderator posed a hypothetical question. If a reporter was with an enemy patrol that was about to ambush a column of U.S. troops, should he shout a warning, or simply "cover the story?"

Wallace thought the story was more important than saving Americans from being shot to death. Asked by the interviewer, "Don't you have a higher duty to save lives?" Mike Wallace replied, "No, you do not have a higher duty. No, no, no." This man's anti-Samism seems incurable.

October 5, 1990

When Media Silence Is Censorship

On August 23 *The New York Times* ran a glowing 57-inch article depicting Congressman Joe Moakley, a Boston Democrat, as the conscience of the Congress concerning El Salvador. Reporter Clifford Krauss praised Moakley's "personal crusade" against continued aid because of the killings of six Catholic priests there last November. He cited Moakley's "plucky style" and said his blue-collar background gave him special credibility as a critic of the Administration's policy towards communist guerrillas. A subhead read, "One man's deeply held beliefs may affect foreign policy."

But neither Krauss nor any other reporter was around on September 5, when Moakley made an extraordinarily tough House speech denouncing the Farabundo Marti National Liberation Front (FMLN). Moakley flatly blamed FMLN obstinance for the failure of peace talks that have been been underway since May.

Moakley called an FMLN proposal for dismantling the El Salvadoran military "particularly extreme and unrealistic" and said it "provided no opportunity for the United Nations mediator to bring the two sides closer together." Moakley continued, "I also condemn, in the strongest possible terms, FMLN threats of another military offensive. The Salvadoran people are sick of war, and sick of people who talk of nothing but war."

In our view this statement by Moakley—a leading House dove on the war—was bombshell news. A consistent critic of the government of President Alfredo Cristiani, he was foremost among Democrats demanding that previous free elections be ignored and that the decade-long conflict be ended by negotiations with the FMLN communist terrorists. Now he condemned the FMLN.

Many Salvadorans, especially military officials, opposed

227

talking with the FMLN. They did not want to give legitimacy to terrorists who scorned elections and butchered hundreds of civilians and public officials. But Moakley and other doves insisted on negotiations, threatening to cut U.S. aid.

Now that the FMLN has sabotaged peace talks, where are the media that have been lavish in coverage of supposed "death squads" and other brutalities for which they blame the El Salvadoran military? We hear only silence.

Nor have the media reported other significant news coming out of El Salvador during the summer. At least twice FMLN terror squads assaulted President Cristiani's home in San Salvador, bent on killing the president. The FMLN's clandestine Radio Venceremos has broadcast repeated threats to mount another military offensive. "FMLN guns will again sound with fury," a spokesmen said on August 29. It boasts almost daily of FMLN attacks on military and government installations. FMLN land mines continue to blow the legs off farm people—many of them women and children.

Another story ignored by the U.S. media concerns the continued flow of arms into El Salvador from caches in Nicaragua. The most recent episode came on August 27, when Honduran customs officials at the Nicaraguan border stopped a Volkswagen minibus with a Belgian license plate driven by a 32-year-old French woman, Eve Florence de Maziere. A false floor concealed compartments holding a deadly trove of munitions: 229 shells for 81mm. mortars; and more than 100 individually packaged propellant charges, plus instruction manuals. The van also carried detailed maps of two Salvadoran military garrisons and correspondence and instructions for FMLN members.

Honduran newspapers quoted military spokesmen as saying de Maziere seemed to be an experienced smuggler. She carried six separate ID's on which her pictures differed noticeably and two bottles of ink used for falsifying documents. Her documents suggested she had made the run from Nicaragua to El Salvador at least six times. She lives in Mexico City.

These events should be no secret to U.S. correspondents in San Salvador, or to their editors in New York and Washington. They are covered and discussed in the El Salvadoran media. De Maziere's arrest was front-page news in three Honduran papers—*Tiempo, La Prensa,* and *La Tribuna.* The latter carried a front-page photograph showing three long rows of propellant charges laid out on the highway alongside her van.

The media's silence—censorship, if you will—deprives the American public of a full range of information on a conflict that has been a national issue for a decade. By ignoring the FMLN's dark side, the U.S. media consistently make the Salvadoran government the "heavy" in the war.

A prime example of selective coverage came the morning of September 14 when the Committee in Solidarity With the People of Salvador—the FMLN's U.S. political arm, although the press never calls it that—staged a minute but noisy demonstration outside the U.S. Capitol to protest continued U.S. aid. The scruffy bunch yelled the "Stop the War!" slogan heard uncountable times during the war. The event was about as newsworthy as a sunrise.

Nonetheless, a CNN crew moved around the periphery, busily filming a non-story while the important events in El Salvador go unreported.

September 14, 1990
[*Note: On May 23, 1993 an explosion in Managua led to the discovery of a huge underground arsenal of sophisticated weapons and explosives. Many of the arms were reported to belong to the El Salvadoran FMLN, which apologized to the UN for having lied in reporting that it had destroyed all weapons under its control in compliance with the cease-fire agreement. This proved that the FMLN's arms had been delivered via Nicaragua, but this story was also ignored by most of the media.*]

The 10-Year $537 Million Acid Rain Study They Didn't Want You To Know About

At an environmental conference last year, Charles Alexander, the science editor of *Time* magazine, said that *Time* had crossed the boundary from news reporting to advocacy on environmental issues. NBC's Andrea Mitchell said that was true of the networks as well, and Ben Bradlee, executive editor of *The Washington Post*, chimed in, saying that he had no problem with that but it was a mistake to say it publicly. Bradlee warned that when you say, "To hell with the news, I'm no longer interested in news, I'm interested in causes," you may find yourself under attack from "a kooky constituency."

That "kooky constituency" includes responsible scientists who believe that public policy decisions should be based on solid facts, not on unproven hypotheses and emotion-driven fears and fads. Unfortunately, there are lots of Alexanders, Mitchells and Bradlees who are willing to mount their white chargers and crusade for the latter. There is a shortage of journalists who have the will or the wit to oppose and expose their errors.

This was demonstrated when a "preliminary draft" report of the National Acid Precipitation Assessment Program (NAPAP) on acid rain was released on September 5, 1990. Based on a 10-year study that cost the taxpayers $537 million, this report pulled the rug from under the fearmongers in the environmental movement who have been predicting disaster if we don't take costly measures to curb acid rain. The media have done much to convince the public that emissions from coal-burning power plants are making the rain so acid that it is killing crops, forests and fish in the northeastern states and Canada, destroying buildings and endangering human health.

As a result, bills sailed through both the House and Senate last spring requiring that by the year 2000 annual emissions of sulfur dioxide be 10 million tons lower than they were in 1980. This is to be done by placing tough new controls on more than 300 electric power plants. Senator Daniel Patrick Moynihan (D-NY), tried in vain to get his colleagues to pay attention to the findings of NAPAP before passing this legislation. Its studies had already shown that the impact of acid rain on lakes, trees and humans had been enormously exaggerated, which the new report confirms.

This report gingerly tackles the question of what should be done about the problem. It estimates that in the absence of any new legislation, there will be a moderate increase in sulfur dioxide emissions over the next 15 years, after which there will be a sharp decline as old power plants are replaced by plants with new clean technology. It estimates that by the year 2030, even without any new controls, the level of emissions will be nearly the same as the goal set by the new legislation.

NAPAP estimates the additional cost of achieving this goal via the new legislation at $2.7 billion to $4 billion annually. The cost would have to be covered by higher rates for electricity. The new controls will bring about a shift from the high-sulfur Eastern coal to low-sulfur Western coal. This will have a serious impact on employment and the economy of the Eastern coal-producing states. It estimates that over the entire period, the negative effect on GNP will be greater than the direct cost of the emission controls.

The NAPAP report refrains from prescribing what should be done, but it shows that the benefits to be derived from the imposition of the new controls are trivial in comparison with the costs. It sees little or no benefit in terms of direct health effects, no benefit to crops and no significant benefit to forests. It says that new controls would reduce the acidity of some lakes and streams, increasing the benefits to trout anglers by an estimated $7 billion to $13.6 million in 2010 and $0.7 billion to $3.3 million in 2030. Earlier NAPAP studies noted that liming the watersheds of the acidic lakes in the northeast could lower their acidity at a cost of only a few million dollars per year.

J. Lawrence Kulp, former director of NAPAP, commented that it would be stupid to saddle consumers with billions of dollars in higher energy costs for such trivial benefits.

How was this victory for responsible science reported? CBS covered it in two sentences, saying, "A 10-year government study of acid rain, out today, finds no evidence that acid rain caused widespread damage to forests, lakes or streams across the country." The second sentence described the negative reaction of environmentalists. *The New York Times* devoted a full column to the report but put it back on page 24 under the misleading headline, "Acid Rain Report Confirms Concern." ABC, NBC, CNN, *The Washington Post* and *The Wall Street Journal* didn't even mention it. *The Washington Times* used three-paragraphs from an inaccurate and misleading AP story.

It isn't surprising that the advocacy environmental journalists spiked or misreported the story, but it is sad that those reporters and editors who honor the truth missed another chance to combat a costly and enduring myth.

September 7, 1990

The "Big Lie" About El Salvador Deaths

Propaganda about atrocities is a potent weapon in warfare. When the Belgians and British were trying to get the United States into World War I, despite the reluctance of President Woodrow Wilson, a mammoth "White Paper" claimed that the Germans had slaughtered women and children in barbaric fashion. Wilson had the sense to ignore the broadside (history later proved it was largely fabricated) and he eventually went to war for other reasons. But the big lie espoused in the "White Paper" caused him some nervous political moments because of its impact on public opinion.

The American leftists working for a communist takeover of El Salvador are using a contemporary version of the same atrocity lie in their efforts to force the United States to stop sending aid to that beleaguered country. They have claimed loudly—and without challenge—that "70,000 persons" have died in the decade-long conflict between the government and the Farabundo Marti National Liberation Front (FMLN). The leftists typically claim that the "majority have been civilians killed by the military or death squads," as Rep. Barbara Boxer (D- CA) stated during House debate on an aid bill in May.

Our media repeat the 70,000 figure without attribution; it has come to be a written-in-stone number intended to convince the public that something awful is being done in El Salvador with our tax dollars.

So how valid is the 70,000 figure?

The El Salvadoran military reported in early August on an exhaustive study of deaths since 1981. It says flatly the 70,000 figure is fabricated. The actual death toll since the FMLN began its terrorist campaign is put at 32,536, including 20,463 FMLN members killed in combat. The military itself lost 7,118 dead.

As to civilians, the military puts the death toll at 4,935—

233

many innocent victims of FMLN terror. In its efforts to disrupt the freely elected government of President Alfredo Cristiani, the FMLN has slaughtered mayors and other public officials. One recent victim was a former president of the bar association, a man with no political involvement. Few of these FMLN murders are reported by American correspondents.

So where does the far-left get the 70,000 figure? The primary source is a self-styled "human rights group" named Americas Watch, based in New York City. Americas Watch says its periodic reports "rely extensively on information gathered by Tutela Legal," associated with the Catholic Archdiocese of San Salvador.

However, a new study of Tutela Legal's methodology shows that much of its material is bogus. The report, "Politics of Death: The Manipulation of Human Rights Data in El Salvador," was written by Bruce Jones, a freelance journalist who has been working in El Salvador. Jones became suspicious of Tutela Legal because the group's predecessor, Socorro Juridico, had been disbanded by the Episcopal (governing) Conference of the Catholic Church for "creating confusion by adopting clear unilateral positions" and distorting facts for "political ends or group interests," i.e., the FMLN.

Curious about Tutela Legal's monthly reports, Jones compared them with the daily action reports circulated by the armed forces press office (COPREFA). He readily discovered that Tutela Legal took the COPREFA bulletins and, with liberal use of pejorative language, transformed FMLN guerrillas killed in combat into "victims of political violence" who were "victims of indiscriminate attacks." Of the 83 events of "political violence" listed by Tutela Legal during December-January, 90 percent "were first described" in COPREFA bulletins. Tutela Legal did very little independent research.

Internal evidence in the reports suggests the distortions are deliberate. In explaining deaths of soldiers, Tutela Legal will use language such as the following:

"Two soldiers, not identified, killed during a firefight between elements of the guerrilla and troops of the 1st Military Detachment in the proximity of the hamlet area of Aldea

Vieja, jurisdiction of San Jose Las Flores, Department of Chalatenango, 19-20 January 1990."

But in another section of the same report, under the heading of "Victims of Political Violence," the incident is described: "Three unknown victims of an indiscriminate attack by troops of the 1st Military Detachment during a military operation realized in the proximity of the hamlet area of Aldea Vieja, jurisdiction of San Jose Las Flores, Department of Chalatenango, 19-20 January 1990. . . ."

Often Radio Venceremos, the FMLN's clandestine radio, boasted of actions against the army which resulted in guerrilla casualties which Tutela Legal listed as "political victims." In essence, the FMLN gave the lie to Tutela Legal—but no U.S. correspondent in San Salvador had the wit or energy to spot the deception.

Accuracy in Media has made Jones' report available to major newspaper bureaus in Washington. To date no paper except the *Washington Inquirer* has published a line about his findings, nor of the Salvadoran military's study about the actual death toll. Our media would rather parrot the big lie about 70,000 deaths.

August 17, 1990

The *CBS* "Scoop" That Put U.S. Military At Risk

The afternoon of Tuesday, August 7, 1990 *CBS News* decided getting a scoop was more important than not endangering the U.S. military men being rushed to Saudi Arabia to fend off a threatened Iraqi invasion.

David Martin, the network's Pentagon correspondent, went live before a national TV audience at 3:33 P.M. "Frankly," he said, "we're reporting this after considerable debate about whether to report in advance on a troop movement. But all day we've been getting calls from local television stations around air bases . . . that are seeing troops and aircraft moving about that we did not think it was at all likely that the U.S. would be able to keep this secret as long as the Pentagon would like it to be secret."

So Martin aired the report about U.S. troops being deployed. CBS executive Joseph Peyronnin told *The Wall Street Journal*, "On balance, we felt this was such an important story that the American public deserved to know." Such was the judgment call at CBS. But a television network is on shaky moral ground when it publicizes the movement of American troops into a possible combat situation.

The consensus of press accounts is that President Bush decided to move troops into Saudi Arabia on Sunday afternoon. But the Administration withheld any public statements for two reasons. First, and most important, it did not want to prompt Iraqi President Saddam Hussein to make a blitzkrieg attack into Saudi Arabia before the U.S. forces were in place. Second, delicate negotiations were still underway with the Saudis, who were nervous about siding with the U.S. in an Arab versus Arab conflict.

CBS's disclosure thus revealed a key part of President Bush's strategy 17 hours earlier than the White House desired. As events turned out, the disclosure did not cost any lives. But several Pentagon officials with whom we talked expressed concern. One flag-rank officer stated, "The issue is responsibility. CBS and all news organizations knew we were in a delicate situation and dealing with a man of unpredictable temperament [Hussein]."

"This is not an instance where we were trying to cover up anything. In the course of events, the news would have come out. I asked my wife that night whether the so-called 'right to know' is worth the life of a single paratrooper in the 82d Airborne."

CBS's argument that "everyone already knew" is hollow. Reporters such as Martin have easy access to top-level officials, even in a time of crisis. Given the open nature of U.S. society, persons who live in proximity to military bases are soon aware of unusual troop activity. U.S. intelligence agencies assume that the Soviets keep deep-cover "spotters" around strategic installations to act as eyes-and-ears during times of crisis.

Fort Bragg, near Fayetteville, N.C., is especially visible. Bob Roule, managing editor of the *Dunn Daily Record*, near Fort Bragg, tells us that a shopping mall is located at the end of the runway of Seymour Johnson Air Force Base, one of the two bases used by the 82d Airborne, so heavy traffic is noticed immediately. "Local people work on the base, and husbands tell wives things," Roule said. He says that based on what the paper had learned during the day on August 7 "we probably would have run a story about the activity at the base—but only after getting official confirmation about what was going on." CBS's disclosure made the decision moot.

Bill Wright, veteran city editor of the *Fayetteville Observer*, says that in instances involving troop movements, "If they don't want to announce it, we cooperate. We try to go along with them." The *Observer* used Associated Press copy on CBS's "scoop."

CBS's action seems to typify the publish-and-damn-the-consequences attitude of our modern media. Seymour Hersh, who won a Pulitzer Prize for his exposure of the My Lai massacre in Vietnam, was candid about the new standards when he spoke to the Conservative Political Action Conference in

1987. Hersh said that if he had learned the D-Day date for the Normandy invasion while covering World War II, he would have published it.

Two other prominent journalists have publicly declared the same attitude. ABC's Ted Koppel said on a *Viewpoint* broadcast on January 19, 1984, that he got an advance tip about the planned U.S. invasion of Grenada; had he been able to confirm the story, he would have run it. And Joanne Omang of *The Washington Post* said the same year that she would not have hesitated a minute—that she would have rushed into print.

Given this cavalier attitude towards military security, should the media be surprised at the Pentagon's reluctance to trust correspondents with sensitive details of planned operations? CBS got a scoop; it could have easily gotten American blood on its hands by putting its judgment over that of the President of the United States on a sensitive military operation.

August 10, 1990

Shame On *ABC News!*

ABC News has been at the top of the ratings for the evening news programs of late, but its millions of viewers ought to consider changing channels. Its reporting on Fidel Castro's big party to celebrate the 37th anniversary of his failed 1953 attack on the Moncada Barracks was disgraceful.

Anchorman Peter Jennings introduced the report with a blooper that compares unfavorably with President Bush's advancing the anniversary of Pearl Harbor three months. Jennings moved the anniversary of communist takeover of Cuba ahead by six years when he said, "Cuba today celebrates the anniversary of the revolution that gave it communism 37 years ago."

This sloppy error was nothing compared to the misleading report that followed. ABC correspondent John Martin, covering Castro's big party in Havana, began by acknowledging that communism is "in poor health" in Cuba. He noted that the Soviets are cutting back on oil shipments and moving toward demanding payment in hard currencies, something the Eastern European countries are already doing.

Martin said the Cuban people are "bracing for electric power shortages" and that "shoppers can't find dairy products or some medicines." He added, "They line up for cans of Soviet sardines and Chinese fruit."

ABC News would not want you to think that these inconveniences bother the Cuban people in the least. Martin brought on Francisco Blanco, who had "returned proudly last week from military service in Angola." Blanco asserted, "We are satisfied with the system and will defend it to the last drop of our blood."

Martin then assured his viewers that Fidel Castro was solving these problems, saying, "Castro has disarmed potential adversaries. He's built new trade contacts across the hemisphere. He's reconciled with the churches here at home." He later added, "They (the Cubans) are expanding

239

tourism, building new hotels and promoting nightclubs with lavish musical spectacles. With new tourist money they are replacing East German computers with cheaper Asian models, phasing out Eastern bloc buses with vehicles from Japan and Sweden."

Martin also told us that "foreign analysts are impressed with his control of the army and the strength of the Communist Party." The analyst turned out to be William Leogrande, a longtime admirer of Castro and erstwhile adviser to the defeated Sandinista regime in Nicaragua. Leogrande predictably doubted that the collapse of communism in Eastern Europe would be repeated in Cuba. He said a sudden elimination of Soviet aid would be "destabilizing," but he didn't think that was in the cards. He thought the Soviets would reduce aid over five or ten years.

Martin's report overlooked the big news out of Cuba in recent weeks—Cubans seeking to flee the country by taking asylum in foreign embassies and the measures Castro took to keep this trickle from becoming a torrent. This was the main focus of the *CBS News* report on the July 26 anniversary. CBS reporter Juan Vasquez showed how Castro goons who had gotten into the Czech embassy by pretending to be asylum seekers had beaten up the real refugees and wrecked the place. He told how the same tactic had been tried at the Spanish embassy, putting the relationship with Spain, Cuba's principal Western creditor, in danger. Vasquez reported that with "breadlines proliferating, Soviet aid drying up, the economy stagnant, the last thing Castro needs is a fight with Spain."

NBC's Brad Willis reported that Castro was facing his greatest crisis, as the Cuban people "scrambled for dwindling supplies of essential goods," from bread to plastic baby pacifiers, their tempers growing shorter. Willis said, "It's a bleak future for the next generation here. With the collapse of communism worldwide, the Cuban people are isolated, still clinging to the ideology of a revolution that's out of step with the times."

CNN interviewed Gustavo Arcos, a former Castro ally, who risked his life by telling CNN's correspondent that the "system of terror and hardship is driving young people to flee this country any way they can, even at the risk of their lives.'' It noted that foreign embassies are now barricaded to keep Cubans out. Noting that Cubans have to line up for hours to get a bus to go to work and that it is estimated that on average they spend over two and a half hours a day lining up to buy food, CNN said, ''After 31 years of line-ups, the Cuban revolution is fighting for its life.'' It predicted, ''Worse austerity lies ahead.''

Cuba is short of a lot more than Soviet sardines, Chinese fruit, dairy products and some medicines. Everyone except *ABC News* seems to have noticed that. *ABC Radio* employs a reporter in Cuba named Lionel Martin, an American who went there in the 1960s to help the revolution. This report didn't have his name on it, but ABC ought to check for fingerprints.

July 27, 1990

Blame It On America

American left-wingers have been seriously embarrassed by the exposés of communist atrocities, corruption and monumental failures that have been pouring out of Eastern Europe since the collapse of most of the communist regimes there. The carefully cultivated image of communists as honest humanitarians dedicated to helping the poor and downtrodden has been thoroughly demolished.

But our domestic leftists are fighting back. Unable to defend the messes that have been uncovered in the former communist states, they have been trying to focus attention on the alleged sins and crimes of the United States. This probably explains the sudden flurry of stories in our media blaming the United States for the killing of many thousands of Communists in Indonesia in 1965, mainly by the Indonesian army. In May 1990, *The Washington Post* and several other papers ran a long story with this lead, "U.S. officials 25 years ago supplied the names of thousands of members of the Indonesian Communist Party to the army in Jakarta, which at the time was hunting down the leftists and killing them in a crackdown branded as one of the century's worst massacres, former U.S. diplomats and CIA officials say." The story was written by Kathy Kadane, who works for a small news service that specializes in supplying local papers with news about the activities of their Senators and Congressmen.

Boston Globe columnist Randolph Ryan followed with a column in which he said, "The Japanese emperor apologizes to Koreans for having 'inflicted unbearable suffering and sorrow.' Germans try to atone for the Holocaust. Soviet leaders rue the slaughter of Polish officers, and admit the invasion of Afghanistan was wrong. Fortunately, being American means never having to say you're sorry." Ryan said Kadane had found that embassy and CIA officials had prepared "a death list of 4,000-5,000 top (Communist) party officials and then gave it to the Indonesian army."

The *People's Daily World,* the Communist Party paper, said "the State Department and the CIA didn't actually slaughter thousands of Indonesians whom they suspected of being Communists or being associated with Communists" but, it said, "The blood is on their hands."

The leftist weekly, *In These Times,* wrote that "the U.S. role in the Indonesian army's 1965 massacre of an estimated 500,000 Indonesian Communist Party members and sympathizers had political reverberations far beyond (Indonesia)."

The New Yorker of July 2, 1990 said Ms. Kadane had "concluded that the U.S. government played a significant role in one of the worst massacres of the century," and said "credible estimates put the death toll at more than a million." Noting that the "Soviet surrender in the Cold War" was being treated as "proof of the untarnished morality of the United States," it concluded: "The unhappy truth is that in the history of the Cold War there is more than enough shame for both sides; the graveyards of Indonesia as well as Afghanistan, of El Salvador as well as Romania, are evidence of that."

Stephen S. Rosenfeld, deputy editorial page editor of *The Washington Post,* added a new twist in a signed column on July 13. He brought up the charge made by a left-wing historian, Gabriel Kolko, that the U.S. had even been behind the murder of six Indonesian army generals that he describes as "a pretext" for wiping out the Indonesian Communist Party. Rosenfeld said he wished a more mainstream historians would sift the evidence and provide an independent account of what transpired.

Prof. H. W. Brands of Texas A&M had published just such an article in the *Journal of American History* last December. It was based on declassified secret State Department and CIA documents that showed that both agencies were taken by surprise by the murder of the six generals on October 1, 1965 in an attempted coup that was intended to deliver the army to Communist control. Brand concluded, "The United States did not overthrow Sukarno, and it was not responsible for the hundreds of thousands of deaths involved in the liquidation of the PKI (Communist Party)." After reading the article, Rosenfeld wrote a second column, in which he said the question was closed as far as he was concerned.

But what about that "death list?" The officials who knew anything about the list strongly reject that characterization. Robert Martens, the embassy political officer responsible for analyzing and reporting on left-wing organizations, had routinely culled the names of party officials from the press. He shared this unclassified information with the Indonesian government at the request of a senior official. He said he felt it necessary to provide the people who were standing up to the communists with "the means to understand what was happening."

Tapes of his lengthy interview show that Martens made this clear to Kadane. He also emphasized that no one, including the Indonesian government, knew how many people had been killed, and he cited evidence that the figures had been enormously exaggerated. While he deplored the killing, he emphasized that the defeat of communism in Indonesia had changed the course of history significantly. Ms. Kadane feigned interest in all this, but all she wrote about was the blame-America smear.

July 20, 1990

"A Reverend Of Racism And A Minister Of Hate"

The New York bureau chief of *The Washington Post* has blasted his colleagues in the New York media for giving too much attention to "professional provocateurs" like the Reverend Al Sharpton. Howard Kurtz, in an article in the *Post* and during an appearance on CNN's *Larry King Live*, charged that the New York media have fueled racial tensions by covering Sharpton and his controversial statements. "There's tension in New York," he said. "That doesn't mean we have to cover those who would pour gasoline on the embers."

Appearing on the same show, Roy Innis, chairman of the Congress of Racial Equality, complained that the New York media fail to cover the views of blacks who are more conservative. He said, "If Sharpton says on a particular day, 'The city is going to burn,' immediately after that have some sensible people express their equally dramatic and eloquent points of view."

Kurtz described Sharpton as a "savvy guy, a media manipulator who knows how to deliver that inflammatory sound bite that television is so addicted to, the juicy quotes that reporters love." He also said that reporters are "lazy," that they find it easier to cover a Sharpton news conference than seek out opposing views. He said that while papers such as the *New York Post* gave considerable attention to Sharpton's provocative statements warning of racial violence, the New York media "paid scant attention" to revelations that this "Brooklyn preacher-without-a-congregation" has paid young blacks $5 to attend his rallies. Kurtz said the revelations came out of Sharpton's trial on fraud and grand larceny.

The Washington Post bureau chief argued that Sharpton and attorneys Alton Maddox Jr. and Vernon Mason should be

245

viewed by the media as "discredited," because of their roles in promoting the false claim in 1988 that Tawana Brawley was raped by a group of white men. Kurtz said, "But I have yet to read a news story that begins, 'The indicted Reverend Al Sharpton, who pays people to appear at his demonstrations and once publicized the false claims of Tawana Brawley, said today. . .' " He hailed as "revolutionary" the recent decision by *The New Jersey Herald & News* of Passaic, N.J., not to publish "reverend of racism and a minister of hate."

Innis said that six months before a Grand Jury came to the conclusion that the Tawana Brawley story was a hoax, he had issued his own report disputing the allegations. But he said his report was covered only by *The New York City Tribune* and a columnist. He added, "None of the major television or radio stations or major papers carried my investigation."

Innis said that while the media seem to cover anything with a racial angle to it, black-on-black crime is largely ignored. He said, "You have black kids being murdered every day by black hoodlums. You have black mothers who are grieving in loneliness every day, every week. Why can't you focus on that?" The greatest conflict, he said, is intra-racial, not inter-racial.

June 6, 1990

The CIA And S&Ls:
Tracing A Media Myth

A new conspiracy theory has the far left in a tizzy—that the CIA helped start the savings and loan crisis by looting savings institutions to finance the democratic resistance in Nicaragua and other covert operations.

The linchpin of the theory is a rambling, often murky series of articles in *The Houston Post* which, as reporter Pete Brewton asserts, "suggests that the CIA may have used part of the proceeds from S&L fraud to help pay for covert operations."

Leftist journalists such as Christopher Hitchens, Washington columnist for *The Nation*, are pushing the CIA-S&L conspiracy theory hard in an attempt to puff fire from the dead ashes of the Iran-Contra scandal. On the *Donahue* show on May 29, Hitchens demanded that the press "examine the diagram of the private economies these people were running to raise an illegal fund without the knowledge of Congress. See how they . . . were laundering the money . . . through the Savings & Loans." Hitchens said *The Houston Post* "has done a wonderful series on how the CIA was using the Savings & Loans to launder money." Hitchens' insinuation was that if the media would bestir itself, revelations from a CIA-S&L scandal would revive Iran-Contra.

Donahue followed up by inviting Brewton to be on his show. The program was taped on June 1, and AIM was represented in the audience. We had analyzed Brewton's work, and we wanted to show why the media aren't enthusiastic about his stories. Contrary to Brewton's printed claim, he does not report a single instance where S&L money went to the CIA, for covert operations or anything else.

Brewton conceded as much when we interviewed him before the program. Despite the work he has put into his articles, some of which stretch over more than two columns, he

247

has yet to find a "smoking pistol." "Frankly," he said, "I can't prove that the CIA ever got a dime of S&L money."

Several articles center on Houston developer Robert L. Corson, who is called "an associate of reputed organized crime figures and an alleged Central Intelligence Agency operative." Brewton offers no supporting evidence other than to quote "one former CIA operative" (unnamed) who claims that Corson used to carry money from one country to another for the agency. Corson denies any agency connection; nonetheless, the Post continues to call him an "operative."

One article claimed that Houston federal prosecutor John Smith said his investigation of banking and S&L problems involved the CIA. The agency wrote Congress, "Smith states that he told *The Houston Post* reporter that there is no connection between the CIA and the ongoing banking investigation. The reporter appears to have neglected to include this part of Smith's statement in the article."

Two of Brewton's named sources are men that journalists found unreliable. One was a publicity seeker named Richard Brenneke who had claimed to have been a CIA employee, and provided a forged document to prove it. Two Congressional committees and the Tower Commission found his stories about involvement in the Iran arms affair not credible. Brenneke is a source for Brewton's statement that the CIA "raised money for covert operations" through schemes to "siphon funds from financial institutions." (Brenneke was completely discredited in 1991 when *The Village Voice*, a New York weekly that had previously trusted him revealed that his own records proved that he had fabricated stories about his presence at alleged "October Surprise" meetings.)

Another Brewton source, Eugene Wheaton, received $20,000 for helping Washington's Christic Institute in its outrageous lawsuit against Generals John K. Singlaub and Richard Secord and others involved with the democratic resistance in Nicaragua. A Miami judge dismissed the Christic suit as baseless. He ordered the group to pay $1 million for legal costs of the defendants. Brewton's articles don't mention Wheaton's association with the Christics, identifying him only as a "former Pentagon criminal investigator."

Christic fingerprints are elsewhere on the CIA-S&L theory. A recent fund-raising letter (in an envelope emblazoned "S&L Loans and Cocaine Profits") states, "More than 18 months ago, sources for the *Post* articles contacted us with information about a series of mysterious S&L transactions." That is the same period Brewton began his research. The letter offers a reprint of the *Post* articles to anyone who contributes $50 or more.

The offer surprised Brewton. He states that although the Christics offered him information, "I found them untrustworthy." He expressed surprise that Wheaton had been on the Christic payroll, although the affiliation has been publicized.

We told Donahue's staff they had an obligation to air this side of the story on their program. They refused to include an AIM representative on the panel, but they promised to let us question Brewton from the audience. Donahue personally repeated this promise during the program, but he delayed keeping that promise until 10 seconds before the program ended, when there was not enough time to complete the question, much less get Pete Brewton's answer.

June 1, 1990

249

Media Fail To Report
Costly Congressional Bills

During the late-night session on May 23, 1990 when the House of Representatives passed its version of the multi-billion dollar Clean Air Act, Representative John Dingell, the chairman of the House Committee on Energy and Commerce, was heard muttering, "I hope we're doing the right thing. I hope we're doing the right thing."

The Michigan Democrat, who was understandably concerned about the impact of the legislation on the automobile industry, had reluctantly supported the bill. He explained what had happened in these words, "The President led. The public wanted it. And the House responded." Indeed it did. Only 21 Congressmen, five Democrats and 16 Republicans voted against the bill, which cleared the House after only one day of debate.

John Dingell was beset by doubts, and well he should be. President Bush threatened to veto the bill if the cost of the mandated changes to consumers and business exceeded $21 billion. No one really knows what the actual costs will be in terms of higher prices, higher electric bills and lost jobs. The benefit estimates are even more problematical. Public support was mobilized by scare stories about global warming and acid rain, stories based on theories and suppositions that empirical evidence has either refuted or failed to confirm. The EPA estimated that one group of toxic chemicals that are to be regulated by the act might cause 1,700 to 2,500 cancer deaths a year. A Harvard professor of public health believes a more realistic estimate is between zero and 1,000.

How can the average American expect to know the economic costs and impact of such complicated legislation? Our media aren't helping. We see a disturbing tendency at work in Washington. Congress decides to cope with an issue—such as clean air—which comes under the rubric "God, mother and apple pie." Since everyone favors clean air, why should the media bother with niggling questions?

Given media inattention, Congress can be likened to a restaurant that offers a menu of attractively described dishes, but doesn't list any prices. Only when the waiter presents the bill does the diner learn what he has spent. And the American taxpayer is about to be handed substantial bills for recent Congressional actions.

A day before its action on the Clean Air Act, the House overwhelmingly endorsed a disability rights bill that could affect everything from requiring hand controls on rental cars to whether a law firm could be legally forced to hire a blind lawyer and provide someone to read for him.

We learned those "for-examples" from a long story in *The Washington Post* on May 25—three days *after* the House vote. But while the bill was being discussed ("debated" is too generous a term) on the House floor, the media were content to report only that Congress was about to do something beneficial to millions of handicapped Americans. A column-long *New York Times* story on May 15, the day the debate started, called the act "the most far-reaching civil rights bill in more than a quarter-century." The story didn't mention some costly specifics such as the requirement that all buses in the country must be equipped with wheelchair lifts at a cost of $15,000 to $20,000 each.

Are these lifts needed? In Seattle, some 80 percent of the buses are so equipped. There is one user per bus every other day. In New York, 50 percent equipped, there is one user per day for each 19 buses. The American Public Transportation Association estimates the nationwide cost to modify buses, rail and subway cars at $20.7 billion.

The Clean Air Act is also slipping by with inadequate media attention. During the Earth Day propaganda fest earlier this spring the TV networks trotted out carloads of environmentalists to rail against the awful things being done to nature in an industrialized society. During one period Paul Ehrlich was on NBC's *Today* show so often we wondered if he would become an anchor. All this hoopla was intended to drum up support for the CAA.

251

The House passed the CAA after 10:00 p.m. on May 23, too late for the evening news shows (although CBS briefly mentioned the debate). The morning shows on May 24 had reports of varying quality: a brief overview on ABC; a somewhat longer piece on CBS; and an interview by NBC's Bryant Gumbel with a fellow from Chrysler who claimed that CAA would boost auto prices from $300 to $500.

Two of the three evening network TV news shows on May 24 didn't even mention the passage of the act, but NBC did air a report discussing its economic impact. Only *The Wall Street Journal* discussed the cost in depth, devoting over a page and a half to a the impact of this complicated legislation that is going to have a lot of customers screaming when they are presented with the bill.

May 25, 1990

Entertainment Tonight
Smears FBI

Entertainment Tonight, the popular daily half-hour TV program about the world of entertainment, has apparently been infiltrated by liberal/leftists who are using the program to promote their hidden political objectives. The program frequently airs puff pieces about leftist Hollywood activists. Recently it dredged up an 11-year old story about Jean Seberg, a now largely forgotten actress who died in 1979. The media eagerly picked up a charge made by Seberg's former husband that she had been driven to suicide by FBI harassment nine years earlier.

That charge was amplified a week later when the media prominently proclaimed that the FBI had admitted that in 1970 it had planted rumors that Seberg was pregnant and that the father was a member of the radical Black Panther Party. It was said that this rumor, published in the *Los Angeles Times* and *Newsweek*, had so upset Seberg that she gave birth prematurely. The baby died, and all this was said to have made her suicidal. Editorial writers and columnists accepted the story as true and heaped condemnation on the FBI.

A year later, Accuracy in Media obtained the FBI's Seberg file under a Freedom of Information request. The file revealed that the FBI had wiretap evidence indicating that Seberg believed the father of her child to be an official of the Black Panther Party. An agent in Los Angeles had suggested giving this information to gossip columnists, but Washington vetoed the proposal. The FBI had not admitted planting the rumor and there was no evidence that it had done so. Knowledge of Seberg's romantic involvement with Black Pathers was not exclusive to the FBI. That was one reason her former husband left her.

In addition, the FBI file showed that Seberg was on drugs while she was pregnant and had been warned by her doctor

253

that she was risking a miscarriage. It also showed that her reaction to the publication of the rumor about the identity of the baby's father was not what had been described by the media. She had told her Black Panther friends that she hoped to sue and win a lot of money, some of which she promised to give to the Black Panther Party.

The evidence was sufficiently clear that *The Washington Post* ran an editorial to set the record straight, acknowledging the facts as we have described them. *The New York Times* ran a corrective story, as did *NBC News*. All of this was made available to *Entertainment Tonight* by Ray Wannall, a retired FBI official who was interviewed on camera for 20 minutes.

But when the program aired, Wannall's interview was reduced to one sentence in which he explained why the FBI had Seberg under surveillance—because of her support of the violent Black Panthers. The original false story about the FBI planting gossip about her baby and causing the premature birth was revived. The false story that the FBI had admitted planting the story was conveyed by showing the old newspaper headlines. The retractions were not mentioned. The story said she turned to drugs and alcohol after the baby's death, concealing the fact that her use of drugs and alcohol contributed to her baby's death. *Entertainment Tonight* didn't want these facts to interfere with its objective—to smear the FBI.

May 24, 1990

New York Media Black Out Black Racism

When a Texas jury convicted three policemen on May 3, 1990 of killing a black prisoner in a small town jail, *The New York Times* ran the verdict on page one. Reporter Robert Suro wrote that the "case provoked sharp racial tensions in the region."

But the *Times* news staff ignored another racial struggle only a short subway ride from its Manhattan news room—the months-long siege of Korean grocery owners in Brooklyn, led by an avowed black racist who has said publicly that he is "anti-white." The racist, Sonny Carson, leads pickets around the Korean-owned stores; their leaflets say, "Don't shop with people who don't look like us." Koreans working at the store are called "monkey," "blood-sucking vampires," and worse, by menacing crowds led by Carson.

The unwillingness of the New York media to address the Brooklyn situation epitomizes a seemingly growing double standard by the press in reporting on issues involving blacks and other minorities.

To the *Times'* credit, it did make oblique reference to Brooklyn in an editorial on April 18 which dealt with rising black racism around the country. The focus was on an alderman in Milwaukee who is urging fellow blacks to arm themselves with rifles and pistols as a "self-defense corps" to fight against whites. The *Times* devoted only a single sentence to its local crisis, that a "black neighborhood is boycotting a Korean grocery for allegedly abusing his black customers." It did not mention Carson.

During the 1989 mayoralty campaign, Carson worked for candidate David Dinkins. He made remarks some persons interpreted as being anti-Semitic. Confronted, Carson said the persons were mistaken—he was not just anti-Semitic, he said, he was "anti-white." The *Times* reported his remark. Dinkins

255

dropped Carson from his campaign staff and publicly disavowed him. Dinkins is now mayor.

Eric Breindel, who edits the editorial page of the *New York Post*, is one journalist who has decried the Brooklyn black racism in print. In a column on April 26, he asked, "Are the media so fearful of addressing a manifestation of black racism that they're willing to ignore this grotesque an undertaking? That in itself seems racist—after all, the operative assumption has to be that coverage of the boycott will offend blacks."

The media's double-standard was a sub-theme of a recent Washington conference, "Second Thoughts About Race in America." The organizers were David Horowitz and Peter Collier, former leftist gurus and editors of *Ramparts* magazine, who now are in the vanguard of apostate radicals exposing the hypocrisy of causes they espoused in the 1960s and 1970s. Breindel, a panelist, related the Brooklyn incident as an example of media double-standards. He wondered what attention the press would have paid the boycott had it been whites assaulting a black-owned store with racial epithets and placards.

Joe Klein, political writer for *New York* magazine, told of covering the Boston busing dispute in the 1960s and discovering that black parents were equally adamant as whites in opposing the court-ordered scheme. But the liberal *Boston Globe* ignored the black objections and pushed busing heartily, in what Klein called a "combination of cowardice and cheerleading." Admitting that blacks detested busing was "too painful" for the *Globe* to report, Klein asserted.

What current racial stories are the media ignoring in fear of offending "black sensitivities?" Abigail Thernstrom, an author and a visiting lecturer at Boston College, ticked off a litany of stories we have not seen on the networks or in the national dailies:

—The professor at a Michigan university, a demographer, whose research upset black students; he was "harassed" so much he withdrew from classroom work and now does research solely.

—The scheme by Tom Hayden, a California assemblyman, that would guarantee the graduation of any minority student who entered a state university, regardless of academic performance. Hayden's measure was introduced after affirmative action admissions failed to increase significantly the number of minorities who graduate from California colleges. Preferential treatment of blacks and minorities, in admissions, grading and scholarship funds, is alienating whites in California and elsewhere, Thernstrom asserted.

—The decision by Massachusetts educators to cancel an academic proficiency test for high-schoolers after preliminary figures showed half or more would flunk.

At the end of the Second Thoughts conference, *Village Voice* columnist Stanley Crouch said that media paternalism towards blacks is in itself a form of racism, and one which he said fellow blacks should deplore. Whites who condone—or ignore—silly actions by or on behalf of blacks are saying, in effect, "Let them have their beating-the-drums festival." Crouch says blacks are mature enough for non-preferential media attention.

May 4, 1990

What *NBC Nightly News* Didn't Tell

El Norte, a provincial Mexican newspaper, has scooped the U.S. media with the first-ever public opinion poll done inside Cuba. And American reporters are ignoring the astounding finding that two-thirds of the Cuban people feel Fidel Castro has turned their country into a dictatorship. A similar percentage says they are "desperate to leave."

The poll, admittedly unscientific by professional public opinion standards, supports reports that Castro's grip on his countrymen's respect is skidding badly in his revolution's 31st year.

It also challenges the accuracy of what Americans were told on the *NBC Nightly News* by correspondent Ed Rabel on March 30. After on-camera interviews with several students, Rabel declared, "Cubans devoted to Castro far outnumber opponents."

Rabel did his polling by taking a camera crew to the University of Havana (Castro is class of '50), gathering students around him, and asking what they thought of the revolution. We think this is a rather nutty method of sampling public opinion in a land of omnipresent secret police and block committees. Unsurprisingly, all Rabel interviewees whooped it up for Fidel. "We have the best leader in the world, Fidel Castro," one earnest student said. "We love him, that's all . . . socialism or death, that's our future."

One of the Cubans interviewed by *El Norte* told why Cubans hesitate to speak freely anywhere—much less before American TV cameras: "When Fidel speaks in the street, there is a policeman for every five persons, and if they see you criticizing or disagreeing with the speech, you're in trouble."

Rabel's reporting is refuted by the much more thorough— if unusual—poll taken by four reporters from *El Norte*, the flagship paper of a Northern Mexico chain based in Monterey. During March, the reporters posed as tourists and "roamed the streets of Havana for a week, questioning Cubans about their political and economic opinions, their views on education and the family."

Each reporter interviewed 100 persons over age 18, for a total of 400, "inserting predetermined questions into their conversations." As *El Norte* stated, the poll does not have the usual statistical margin of error of three percent: "To endeavor to conduct a poll in a country whose very population statistics are unknown and which does not even have maps is virtually impossible." But *El Norte* said the findings provide "a basis of reference for defining how Cubans view Fidel Castro, their system of government, and their quality of life."

El Norte published its findings on March 20-23. The paper is available to U.S. correspondents in Mexico City. But we have seen no U.S. attention given to a poll *El Norte* calls the "first of its kind behind the 'Cane Curtain.' "

Although Rabel conceded that "many young people freely complain" about the lack of consumer goods, he found no parallel to the student discontent that helped topple communist governments in East Europe. He quoted the proverbial "unnamed diplomats" who buttressed this opinion.

El Norte did not specifically ask whether Cubans want Castro out of office. But the dictator's low marks are self-evident. Only 26 percent of Cubans consider him a "hero;" 43 percent said he is not a hero now, "but used to be." An astounding 63 percent of Cubans said they are not happy in their country.

Castro's dictatorship, in addition to generating hunger for food and freedom, has destroyed many families. Family unity is threatened because of the number of young people fleeing; several interviewees estimated the number at 25 daily. *El Norte* quoted a mother, "How can I be happy if two of my children escaped last year and I know nothing about them? My husband wants us to try to get to Miami in tires to go look for them."

Although a vast majority of Havana residents hear Castro's speeches live, 45 percent of them do so involuntarily to keep their jobs. Nor do they believe Castro, for they hear the same themes repeatedly. *El Norte* quoted one Habanero, "We have to go and applaud everything he says." Many considered him more of a "TV star" (because of his frequent televised harangues) than a leader.

On the positive side, 60 percent felt Castro's greatest accomplishment was education for all. Nonetheless, 68 percent did not like what they were studying, and 50 percent said they did not have enough to eat. And although Castro claims to have "purified" Cuba, the poll found that 94 percent of the people feel there are social classes; 96 percent acknowledged racism; and 87 percent knew of female prostitution.

El Norte reported that "four percent spontaneously offered up a very Cuban expression of scorn: 'He's a no-good SOB.'" Americans didn't hear that assessment from NBC's Rabel.

April 27, 1990

How A TV Station
Destroyed A Man

Journalistic fairness and basic human decency dictate that a reporter who does a story that can destroy a person's career give him a chance to respond before the report is printed or broadcast. A television station in San Antonio, Texas ignored this basic professional rule—a breach of conduct that resulted in a whopping $29 million libel verdict by a jury.

The case involved Dr. Sudhir Srivastava, who in 1985 was one of the busiest and most highly-regarded heart surgeons in San Antonio. A native of India, Srivastava enjoyed referrals from more than 60 physicians who trusted him to do life-saving and life-prolonging operations on their patients. Dr. Srivastava was so good at his profession, in fact, that he aroused professional jealousies of other persons in the San Antonio medical community.

Dr. Srivastava's career came to an abrupt halt in February 1985 when KENS-TV, a CBS affiliate in San Antonio, aired a four-part series accusing him of doing unnecessary surgeries for profit, often killing patients. The surgeon was depicted as a high-roller businessman who drove a $200,000 Rolls Royce and cared more about real estate deals than his patients. The series featured emotional interviews with family members of patients who allegedly died as a result of Dr. Srivastava's malpractice. One segment had a graveyard as a backdrop. There were surreptitious photos of Srivastava driving his Rolls Royce, and walking through an airport.

The hard core of news was that governing boards of several San Antonio hospitals were challenging the doctor's privileges to practice in their institutions. What the TV station did not point out was that Srivastava was engaged in bitter personal disputes with the very persons trying to drive him out of his practice.

KENS-TV also had confidential medical records that the

doctor's secretary stole from his office. Trial testimony suggested she was angry because Srivastava had fired her boy friend from one of his business enterprises. Giving medical records to an outside person violates Texas criminal law.

KENS-TV made a basic journalistic error in presenting its expose: Although the station worked on the story for almost three months, not until late in the afternoon of the day before the series aired did its reporter call Dr. Srivastava and ask for an interview. Srivastava was out of town. So the explosive series was telecast without his having a chance to answer the charges made against him, and to explain that he was the target of professional enemies.

When the series aired, Srivastava's $400,000 a year practice evaporated. KENS-TV so damaged his reputation that he had to move to another Texas town to try to rebuild his life.

The doctor sued for libel and told his story to a San Antonio jury. When put to the test of truth, the TV charges proved false. The Texas State Board of Medical Examiners reviewed each of the patient deaths and found no misconduct by Srivastava. A jury heard "outtakes" of a conversation in which a KENS-TV producer told a family not to tell the doctor the series was in progress—that they intended to "sneak up" on Srivastava. Other doctors had told KENS-TV that two of the patients who died were hopeless cases when Srivastava tried desperately to save them; none of these favorable comments got on the air.

Joe Goulden, of Accuracy in Media, testifying as a media expert witness, said KENS-TV violated both professional and ethical standards of journalism. Had Gonzalez seen fit to interview Srivastava, he said, he could have had an even more interesting story, one about vicious infighting in the San Antonio medical community. Instead, Gonzalez and KENS-TV chose to air what was essentially a hatchet job on the surgeon.

The jury apparently agreed with this assessment. It awarded Dr. Srivastava $29 million in damages—$11.5 million for loss of earnings, plus $17.5 million in punitive damages—one of the highest libel verdicts ever. The jury ruled that KENS-TV "acted with knowledge of falsity and with reckless disregard of the truth or falsity of the subject matter.'' KENS-TV says it will appeal.

Dr. Srivastava has his good name back. But nothing will heal the anguish caused him by slipshod television reporting.

During the trial the doctor said, ''Had the television reporter been decent enough to give me the chance to respond to these charges before putting them on the air, this suit would not have been necessary. The TV station accused me of 'malpractice.' Why don't journalists follow their own professional standards? They are quick to jump all over lawyers and doctors for 'malpractice.' Well, what they did to me was also 'malpractice.' ''

April 20, 1990

Does Agent Orange, Used In Vietnam, Cause Cancer? Which Network Do You Watch?

The Centers for Disease Control (CDC) recently released a long-awaited report on their search for some evidence that the spraying of Agent Orange in Vietnam during the war was causing cancer in Vietnam veterans. The findings were an unequivocal verdict of "not guilty" for the much maligned defoliant that had saved the lives of many American and South Vietnamese soldiers.

Not everyone welcomed this good news. Some veterans who were hoping to get the government to compensate them for their ailments were displeased, and the American Legion and Vietnam Veterans of America sided with them. The theory that Agent Orange caused cancer and other serious health problems in Vietnam veterans has been enthusiastically embraced by chemophobic and anti-Vietnam journalists for years. They weren't happy to have the rug pulled from under them by the CDC.

Maybe that explains the strange way ABC News reported this story. On ABC's *World News Tonight*, Peter Jennings introduced the report with a headline reading "AGENT ORANGE" behind him. The O in Orange was a skull and crossbones. In case anyone missed that message, Jennings said, "Some of the American servicemen who served in Vietnam still believe that Agent Orange is killing them." Correspondent George Strait then took over, saying, "After the war, many soldiers who were exposed to this *deadly* spray and came down with a number of rare cancers claimed Agent Orange was the cause. The government study released today concluded that Vietnam vets were 50 percent more likely to

264

develop lymphoma, a cancer of the lymph glands, but that there was no evidence that the lymphoma was caused by Agent Orange."

By definition, very few people develop rare cancers, so the statement that many soldiers exposed to Agent Orange did so gives the impression that they developed more rare cancers than those who were never exposed. This was reinforced by the statement that the government study had found Vietnam vets 50 percent more likely to develop lymphoma (actually, non-Hodgkins lymphoma). The statement that the CDC found no evidence that the cancer was caused by Agent Orange would not, by itself, allay suspicions in the minds of the viewers that Agent Orange could be the cause. That suspicion was bound to be strengthened when Strait next reported that the government had decided to pay compensation of more than $20 million a year to Vietnam veterans afflicted with this cancer. To help insure a guilty verdict, ABC quoted a spokesman for a veterans organization who claimed that there was lots of scientific evidence incriminating Agent Orange.

Strait noted that 34,000 veterans who claimed they had been harmed by Agent Orange would get no compensation, and that the administration was not backing bills in Congress that would provide compensation for them. "As far as the administration is concerned," he said, "the fight about Agent Orange is over."

ABC completely ignored the most important information in the CDC report. The CDC found that Vietnam veterans were no more susceptible to five of the six types of cancer studied than were men of comparable age who had not served in the Vietnam area. The one exception was non-Hodgkins lymphoma. The CDC had a very good reason for saying that the higher risk of this cancer among Vietnam veterans was not related to Agent Orange, but ABC neglected to mention it.

The study revealed that the men who had the highest rates of this cancer were naval personnel who had served on ships off the coast of Vietnam who were never exposed to Agent Orange. On the other hand, the veterans with the lowest rate of non-Hodgkins lymphoma were those who had served in the III Corps area, where the spraying of Agent Orange was the

265

heaviest. In other words, there was an inverse correlation between the likelihood of having been exposed to Agent Orange and the risk of contracting this particular cancer! The CDC could not explain why the sailors had a higher risk of getting lymphoma, but it was sure that it had nothing to do with exposure to Agent Orange.

Then why did the Department of Veterans Affairs decide to compensate those veterans who have lymphoma if Agent Orange is clearly not to blame? Secretary Edward J. Derwinski emphasized that this was not a decision based on scientific evidence. ABC News didn't report that either.

Over at NBC, Tom Brokaw's lead was that the CDC had concluded that there was no evidence linking Agent Orange to cancer in Vietnam veterans. Instead of labeling the herbicide as "deadly," correspondent Robert Hager pointed out that the government had never linked it to any ailments except a few cases of skin disease. He reported the higher risk of non-Hodgkins lymphoma among Vietnam veterans, but it was not the centerpiece of his report. He pointed out that the risk was higher among the veterans who were the least likely to have been exposed to Agent Orange.

NBC reported the news straight. ABC did not.

April 13, 1990

How The Media "Got" Judge Bork

Retired Judge Robert H. Bork says in his book, *The Tempting of America*, that during the confirmation battle over his nomination to the U.S. Supreme Court, he became so sick of the press coverage that he asked his wife "not to hand me anything but the sports pages."

Bork's nomination was defeated in the U.S. Senate after liberal-left groups such as the ACLU and People for the American Way mounted an assault against it. He said in a recent interview that the coverage by the network news programs of his nomination and other issues is even worse than the print media. "It's quite obvious," Bork said, "that a lot of it is heavily biased in its news reporting. Not all of the media. But the three network news programs are quite biased, with a liberal slant on news reporting."

The Tempting of America has been the subject of much commentary. But Judge Bork's critical comments on media coverage of his confirmation battle have not received much attention. Yet he said that the coverage of his confirmation battle did not turn him against the media. He said, "I've always been critical of the media." Bork, who stepped down from the U.S. Court of Appeals, spoke at a dinner sponsored by Accuracy in Media in 1989, where he was presented as a victim of the media. At that time, Bork joked that watching the three network evening news programs was like reading *The Washington Post* three times. But his book is deadly serious, and he complains that coverage of him in *The New York Times*, *The Washington Post* and the three network news programs "was almost unrelievedly hostile."

The judge notes that an analysis of "tag lines" or summary remarks on network news stories by the Center for Media and Public Affairs found that "my nomination held the record for bias among all issues whose reporting the Center had monitored: 100 percent negative on all three networks." Bork said the Center's analysis of judgments and comments issued by news sources in 232 television news and *Washington Post* stories found that 63 percent were negative and 37 percent positive. The sources themselves, Bork says, were 4 to 1 negative in *The Washington Post* and 6 to 1 in the network news shows. Of the network programs, he says, CBS was the worst, at 8 to 1 against Bork.

Bork strongly suggests that the media deliberately ignored some of those favorable to his nomination. He says, "It was not that so few defenders, or none, were available. Newspapers and television decide whom to ask and whose opinions to carry." And this coverage, he suggests, reflected media hostility to his nomination. Bork quotes an unnamed journalist as saying that "when a reporter wants to express his opinion in a news story, he goes to a source who agrees with him for a statement."

His book details the campaign waged against him by such groups as People for the American Way, founded by Hollywood producer Norman Lear, which "mailed memoranda to editorial writers at nearly 1,700 newspapers" and ran radio and print ads against his nomination. But the judge, as he fully admits, did not fight back in the media. That was a key mistake.

March 26, 1990

What's Wrong With Dan Rather? Plenty!

With his ratings in a free-fall, arrogant anchor Dan Rather of the *CBS Evening News* seems finally to be reaping the bitter public harvest of his notorious "ambush interview" of George Bush during the 1988 presidential election. Climaxing a two-month skid, Rather trailed the archrival ABC's *World News Tonight* by 1.8 rating points the week ending March 9, 1990—equaling the biggest gap ever in the ratings race, 11.5 to 9.7. CBS deadlocked with *NBC Nightly News* for second (or last) place. Each rating point equates to 921,000 viewers.

Not since the week ending January 7 has Rather ranked first among the big three networks. Since then, Rather has spiraled steadily downward, with ABC placing first nine weeks in a row (and 22 of the last 23). Resurgent NBC, a perennial third the last several years, seems set to wrest second place from CBS on a regular basis.

What's wrong with Rather? The anchor is notorious for his prickly on-air personality, and his penchant for such publicized stunts as walking off the set for six minutes to protest a tennis match delaying his news broadcast, but circumstantial evidence suggests Dan's troubles now run deeper than eccentricity.

"Did Rather-Bush Tiff Help Sink CBS Anchor?" the *Los Angeles Times* asked January 6 in a headline over an article by TV writer Rick du Brow. And Kay Gardella of the *Daily News* asked on March 9, "Is it conceivable that Rather is finally feeling a backlash from his celebrated combative interview a couple of years ago with then presidential candidate George Bush?" The references are to the now-infamous episode when Rather lured the Vice President into an on-camera interview on the pretext he was doing a political profile.

Instead, the segment opened with a pejorative film clip trying to implicate Bush in the Iran-Nicaragua arms deal.

Rather abandoned any pretense of objectivity, arguing at one point, "The question is, you've made us hypocrites in the face of the world." He continued, "There are clearly some unanswered questions remaining. Are you willing to go to a news conference before the Iowa caucuses, answer questions from all comers . . . ?

"I've been to 86 news conferences since March," Bush replied.

"I gather that the answer is no," Rather said. "Thank you very much for being with us, Mr. Vice President." He curtly ended the interview after having badgered the Vice President for nine minutes.

Roger Ailes, Bush's media adviser, felt "CBS decided to take George Bush out of the race, period," with the attack interview. Accuracy in Media demanded that CBS can Dan because the interview violated *CBS News* guidelines that state, "In approaching individuals or organizations for interviews or coverage, misrepresentation should be avoided." CBS sacked producer Richard Cohen but left Rather at his desk, apparently excusing the anchor's pit-bull behavior in deference to his then number one rating. Now Rather cannot hide behind his ratings.

Newsweek's "Periscope" suggests the first person to feel the axe over the bad ratings could be David Burke, the one-time Ted Kennedy aide who is now president of *CBS News*. Burke is already under fire for his botched handling of the Andy Rooney affair. *Newsweek* cites what might be Rather's best job protection—the expense of firing an anchor whose "contract runs until 1994 and will soon be worth roughly $4 million a year. And there's no one in sight to take Rather's chair—at CBS anyway."

Meanwhile, a new rash of "Rather stories" from former colleagues nibble at the anchor's credibility. Peggy Noonan, in her book *Present at the Revolution*, on her speech-writing days in the Reagan White House, recounts a conversation with Rather when she wrote his radio commentaries. The topic was the professional tradition at *CBS News*, started by the late Edward Murrow.

Noonan writes that Rather scoffed. "Listen," he said,

"this place has all the tradition of a discount shoe store." We suggest the comment says more about Rather than about the network that pays his megabuck salary.

In another new book, *Happy Talk*, former CBS legal correspondent Fred Graham pictures Rather as an ambitious driving newsman—and also something of a phony. Graham tells of the night Rather spiced an election broadcast with a series of down-home Texas sayings (a candidate's lead being "as shaky as cafeteria jello"). Rather left a scrap of paper on his desk. It was a memo from a Texas friend listing the colorful sayings which Rather had "spontaneously" reeled off.

Graham describes correspondent Lem Tucker standing in a studio as Rather prepared to broadcast a bulletin on a breaking story. The announcement was delayed, and Rather sweltered under the bright lights. Tucker's producer called him to finish a story. "You've seen Dan Rather before. What are you doing, looking at Dan Rather?" the producer asked.

As Graham writes: " 'Don't you understand,' Tucker exclaimed excitedly, 'that this guy, sometime, someplace, somewhere, is going to go stark raving mad! If it happens when he's around me, I don't want to miss it!' "

March 16, 1990

The Outrageous Lies In "Born On The Fourth Of July"

Oliver Stone's film "Born on the Fourth of July" was described as the gut-wrenching story of the transformation of Ron Kovic from a gung-ho marine to a disillusioned, paraplegic Vietnam veteran who ended up opposing the war. The movie was so powerful that some thought it could propel Kovic into a run for Congress against Republican Bob Dornan of California. But some in the media were reluctant to address the question of the film's accuracy.

Kovic has said the film is the story of his life, and director Oliver Stone has said he did not alter any of the facts. But doubts about the movie surfaced in January 1990 when a group of residents of Syracuse, New York, said the film was an unfair and inaccurate depiction of their city police. The film says that a 1970 student strike at Syracuse following the invasion of Cambodia was broken up by city police who brutalized the protesters. But New York State Senator Nancy Larraine Hoffman, a Democrat, said that she was there participating in the strike and that it was never disrupted by the police and that the police showed remarkable restraint and sensitivity. Bernard Busch, then a member of the police department, said, "we were never even called on campus."

The film clearly identifies the Syracuse police as engaging in brutality. And Busch says that he has been approached by people who have seen the film and who chastise him because they know he was a policeman at the time. One person told him, "I didn't know policemen did things like that." Well, they didn't. And if the film is going to lie about the incident at Syracuse, movie goers should be left wondering what else the film has lied about. Diana West of *The Washington Times* started wondering about that, and reported her findings in the

February 23, 1990 issue of the paper. She said her analysis shows that there has been a "willful twisting of fact to refashion history into the dramatic and political points the moviemakers hope to make."

Phil Shuman of KNBC in Los Angeles discovered that one of the dramatic scenes in the movie never occurred. This is when Kovic travels to a place called Venus, Georgia, to tell the parents of a son killed in Vietnam that he, Kovic, had accidently shot him. The parents, who believe their son died heroically, are obviously crushed. Shuman asked Kovic about the scene, and says that Kovic admitted it was only a nightmare he had been having. Stone then decided to put the nightmare into the film and make it seem real.

Other scenes have also been distorted, including Kovic's appearance on the floor of the 1972 Republican convention. The movie says that Kovic and other disabled veterans disrupted the convention and were then roughed up outside. Kovic was shown being thrown from his wheelchair. But other witnesses say that Kovic and the others were peacefully escorted from the convention hall.

Diana West's investigation showed there are sharp discrepancies between the movie, Kovic's book and the historical record. In doing her article for the *Times*, she found that Kovic, Stone and the movie's publicist didn't want to clear them up.

March 14, 1990

How Peter Jennings' Bias Tripped Him Up

"We begin tonight with some facts and figures from Nicaragua that are going to surprise some Americans," Peter Jennings said to open ABC's *World News Tonight* on February 20, 1990. "This Sunday, when the people of Nicaragua vote in their first free election in a decade, they will most likely elect as president the man Washington loves to hate."

Jennings reported that a poll jointly sponsored by *ABC News* and *The Washington Post* found dictator Daniel Ortega leading opposition UNO candidate Violeta Chamorro by a margin of 48 to 32 percent.

ABC's "facts and figures," of course, turned out to be the biggest polling goof since analysts helped Thomas E. Dewey put together a cabinet in advance of his "victory" over Harry Truman in the 1948 presidential election.

Jennings had the partial grace to admit the day after the election that the prediction was "terribly wrong." He laughed off the error by quoting a claimed saying about an inscrutable, mythical Mayan god: "It wears a mask, it never lies, but never tells the truth." Jennings' implication was that ABC and the *Post* should not be blamed for the error because the persons polled lied.

There is more to the story than Jennings told viewers. In a dictatorship such as Nicaragua, citizens are understandably wary about admitting opposition to the government. Jennings minimized this handicap when he reported on the poll on February 20: "A couple of other notes about our Nicaraguan poll. We designed the questions. The poll was conducted by the Washington pollsters Belden and Russonello, who have a lot of experience in Latin America. It wasn't a phone poll. All the respondents wrote down their answers, in secrecy, and apparently with great enthusiasm."

Jennings' description is highly misleading. The actual

274

face-to-face polling was done for Belden and Russonello by a Nicaraguan organization, INOP-Itztani, whose director is a man named Marvin Ortega. *The Washington Post*, ABC's poll co-sponsor, revealed Marvin Ortega's background in backhanded fashion on February 21, when it led the paper with the "Ortega Leads" story. But the *Post* waited until paragraph 32 of a 39-paragraph story to tell readers that a pro-Sandinista did the polling.

According to the *Post*, Ortega was a Sandinista guerrilla and served their government as a statistician. The *Post* claimed that Ortega's work "is well-regarded by academic researchers and private pollsters in the United States," although it did not name them. It also claimed—again, no names—that Ortega is "considered a leftist critic of the Sandinistas by foreign journalists in Nicaragua."

The *Post* story noted that 16 percent of the 925 persons polled would state no choice, "suggesting that Chamorro supporters may have been reluctant to express their preference . . . . a signal that the race may be closer" than the ABC/Post poll suggested. But Jennings of ABC made no such hedge— he reported the poll as a flat-out prediction of a Sandinista victory.

Actually, we smelled something suspicious in the poll the day it was released. We lifted an eyebrow at the "finding" that 59 percent had a favorable impression of Ortega, that more than half "approved of the job he has done as president," and that 63 percent said conditions have gotten better, not worse, or had not changed since the Sandinistas came to power. The "satisfaction" figures made us doubt the poll's validity.

Were Nicaraguans that enthusiastic about an inflation rate of 33,700 percent in 1988 and a 30 percent unemployment rate? Fifteen percent of the population fled Nicaragua during the Sandinista decade, itself a damning referendum on Ortega. Shops are bare of consumer goods; currency is worthless. Anti-communist reporters in Managua, such as Peter La Barbera, formerly of the *Washington Inquirer* and *The Washington Times*, told us Nicaraguans trusted neither pollsters nor U.S. reporters. He predicted a Chamorro win.

Why would ABC give prominent credence to tainted polling figures? Media antipathy towards Latin freedom dies hard. A major theme of Ted Koppel's *Nightline* two days before the vote was how the predicted Sandinista victory would change U.S. policy. Koppel's unstated premise was that Washington was wrong in supporting the armed democratic resistance.

Lindsey Gruson of *The New York Times* credited the peace plan promoted by President Oscar Arias of Costa Rica. "The plan appears to have achieved by peaceful democratic means what years of United States military and economic pressure could not," Gruson wrote on Feb. 27.

Does Gruson really think the Sandinistas held elections in a spirit of political altruism? They promised free elections immediately after seizing power in 1979—a pledge they kept only after Washington held their nose to the economic and military grindstone.

March 2, 1990

Media Ignore South African Leader Mandela's Marxism, Violence

In an artsy film segment climaxing an ABC *Nightline* special from South Africa on February 15, 1990 Winnie Mandela danced across the screen, exuberant hands waving, while the leftist American folksinger Tracy Chapman moaned throatily, "Let us all be free, free, free. . ." There were swift images of black and white children holding hands—the other whites depicted were dour-faced, as if disapproving freedom.

ABC News did not tarnish its image of Nelson Mandela's wife by quoting her zest for "necklacing," in which African National Congress goons cut off an opponent's hands, drape a tire filled with gasoline around his neck, and set it afire. Winnie Mandela said on April 13, 1986, "Together, hand in hand, with our boxes of matches and our necklaces, we shall liberate this country." Some 172 "lynchings by fire" occurred in three months that spring.

Nightline typifies the gush of unquestioning adulation the American media gave Nelson Mandela the week of his release from a jail where he served 27 years for attempting violent overthrow of the government.

The media coverup for Mandela and his ANC is two-fold. The media are keeping quiet about control of the ANC by the South African Communist Party (SACP) and about ANC's publicly stated intentions of using violence to convert South Africa into a one-party Marxist-Leninst dictatorship.

On February 11, the day of Mandela's release, the communists blatantly draped their hammer-and-sickle flag over the podium from which he spoke. Network commentators did not mention its presence; CBS aired mostly tight shots of Mandela's face, keeping the red flag out of viewer range.

In his remarks Mandela saluted the Communist Party for

its "sterling contribution to the struggle for democracy," praising its leaders as patriots. *The New York Times* devoted one sentence to this, deep in its story. *The Washington Post* story ignored it altogether. Neither paper ran a picture of the communist flag. However, the Post on February 17 published a photo showing fringe rightists brandishing a Nazi swastika, implying that conservatives opposing Mandela are Hitlerites.

At least 16 of the 30 members of the ANC executive committee were identified as communists in biographical data released by William J. Casey, director of central intelligence, on July 30, 1986. That was published in the *Congressional Record* the next day; hence it has been available to the media for years.

Numerous policy statements over the years have linked the ANC and the South African Communist Party (SACP). ANC head Oliver Tambo said in 1981, "Ours (the ANC and the SACP) is not merely a paper alliance . . . it is a living organism that has grown out of struggle." Concerning violence, Johnny Makatini, the ANC's "secretary of education," told *The New York Times* on October 9, 1986, "If there were only four million of us (black South Africans) left (out of 17 million) after the revolution, that would be better than the present situation." Oliver Tambo told the *London Sunday Times* (September 8, 1985), "White residential areas are the next target in the battle against apartheid."

The New York Times is unconcerned about Mandela's endorsing guerrilla warfare and nationalization of mines and industry. As Christopher Wren reported on February 16, Mandela "emphasized that those were existing policies of the African National Congress, which he supported but was not initiating."

What sort of government does the ANC want? Lithuanian-born Joe Slovo is the only white in the ANC hierarchy; intelligence sources consider him "Moscow's man" in the ANC. In an ANC policy statement published in the February 14 issue of *The Guardian*, Slovo strongly endorsed Marxism for South Africa. "We believe that Marxism clearly projects a system anchored in deep-seated democracy and the rights of the individual that can only be truly attained when society as a

278

whole assumes control and direction of all its riches and resources," Slovo said. "The bulk of humanity's resources will never be used for the good of humanity until they are in public ownership and under democratic (sic) control," Slovo added.

But *The Washington Post* quoted a BBC broadcast that suggested Slovo had abandoned the Marxist belief in state ownership of the means of production and ignored what Slovo wrote in the communist paper.

Slovo dismissed failures of socialism in Eastern Europe as flaws of leadership, not philosophy. Although he paid lip-service to multi-party rule, he said that not all one-party states "turned out to be authoritarian; indeed some of them are headed by the most humane leaders." He praised "the role they have played in preventing tribal, ethnic and regional fragmentation. . . ."

To *Washington Post* columnist Haynes Johnson, Mandela "suggests the greatness" of Martin Luther King. Johnson and the rest of the media should take a closer look at the man— and the policies—they want to foist on South Africa.

February 17, 1990

NBC's Environmentalist Slip Is Showing

NBC News correspondent Andrea Mitchell made a statement in the fall of 1989 that indicated that the networks had crossed the line from news to advocacy on environmental issues. Betty Hudson, NBC's vice president for public relations, said Mitchell did not mean that NBC was embracing advocacy in the sense of favoring a particular position. She noted that Mitchell had also stated that "the media's role was to inform and educate, not to lead people into battle." That, she said, was NBC's position.

Let's compare that position with NBC's conduct. NBC's *Today* show hired Paul Ehrlich, one of the nation's foremost radical environmentalists, to do a regular series titled "Assignment Earth." Ehrlich aired a report on January 9 that clearly set out to "lead people into battle" on an environmental issue.

Ehrlich was introduced with the statement that he was going to report "on how man is destroying the entire ecological system with something that appears completely harmless." He told the NBC audience that "our dependence on the cow has devastated the world environment," explaining, "Every year, thousands of square miles of rain forest from Brazil to Mexico are burned to create temporary pasture land for cattle that end up on the 'fast food' grills of the United States and Europe." He said that cows were creating "desert wastelands" in Africa and India.

"But," Ehrlich proclaimed, "nowhere has the damage from cattle been more severe or more uncritically accepted than on the public lands of the American West." He claimed that because of cattle grazing, "the ecological face of the West was changed forever," that "rich, fertile grassland" had been turned into "this barren, eroded moonscape." He concluded, "Hundreds of thousands of square miles had been turned into severe desert, but the West had been made safe for cattle."

All of this was designed to get the emotional juices of the viewers flowing as they were shown scenes of a range supposedly destroyed by greedy ranchers interested only in making money by despoiling the land. Next came Ehrlich's proposed solution. He showed a ranch where the land, he said, had been despoiled by grazing cattle. He claimed that it had been restored to health by the National Audubon Society after the cattle were removed. He said, "Scientists have measured fantastic improvements in the amount and variety of grasses. Deer have returned in large herds, and the world plants and insects is flourishing."

This was followed by a call to battle. Ehrlich declared: "Since most of the range lands of the arid west are public lands, owned by you and me, their fate is in our hands . . . the fees paid by ranchers are less than it costs to maintain the bureaucrats who have so dismally failed to protect them. Pulling cattle off the range would be a controversial bitter pill for ranchers to swallow. But if we ever expect to restore the grasslands and wildlife of the southwest, that is precisely what we need to do. . . ."

The program infuriated cattlemen, who felt betrayed by NBC. The Arizona Cattlemen's Association said that it had presented "a totally biased, inaccurate and sensationalized picture." They were particularly offended by NBC's failure to use material that had been provided to them showing that generally excellent conditions prevailed on the Western ranges. The Utah Cattlemen's Association demanded that NBC apologize to the ranchers and reprimand Ehrlich for the airing of misleading and inaccurate information. The National Cattlemen's Association denounced Ehrlich's presentation as "highly inaccurate, misleading and lacking in objectivity and fairness." They charged Ehrlich with eight factual errors. They noted that academic experts say that American rangelands are in the best condition they have been in the past 100 years and are, on average, still improving. They give some credit for this to the 1934 legislation that governs the management and protection of vacant public lands, passed with the support of the cattlemen.

They charged that Ehrlich deceived the viewers with his citation of the Audubon ranch as evidence of the improvements that would result from halting cattle grazing. They cited a published study showing that there is no significant difference between the vegetative cover of the Audubon range and an adjacent range where cattle have been grazed annually. The cattlemen contend that intelligent use of grazing is the best tool to enrich wildlife habitat, water quality and regeneration of the land.

NBC, which Betty Hudson says, is devoted to informing and educating the public, not advocating particular positions or leading the public into battle, has not even replied to these angry letters. It has not aired the cattlemen's side of the story, much less given them an apology.

In signing Paul Ehrlich, NBC proved that Andrea Mitchell was right in saying that they had crossed the line into advocacy. In failing to respond to the cattlemen, NBC is thumbing its nose at those who think that journalists have a duty to be accurate and fair.

February 9, 1990

"Tell The Truth! Tell The Truth!"

In March 1982, when 1.5 million Salvadorans streamed to the polls in that country's first free elections in 50 years, the American reporters were stunned when the voters shook their fists at them and cried, "Tell the truth, tell the truth!"

This has been El Salvador's *cri d' coeur* ever since, but it is one that the reporters covering El Salvador have consistently disregarded. The brave Salvadorans, who have been struggling for a decade to keep their country from falling to the communists, still find themselves victimized by reporting that tilts to the terrorist side.

We discussed this recently with Douglas Mine, who covers El Salvador for the Associated Press. Mr. Mine said that things have changed over the last ten years. He said, "We have gone through two Ronald Reagan administrations. Most of the young journalists who come down here aren't even liberal Democrats. A lot of them consider themselves conservative."

We asked if that included Lindsey Gruson, who represents the very influential *New York Times* in El Salvador and who formerly wrote for *Rolling Stone*. The answer was no. How about Chris Norton of the *Christian Science Monitor*, who also writes for a left-wing publication called *In These Times*. Mine readily admitted Norton was not conservative. Then there is Ronnie Lovler, who covers Central America for CNN. Ronnie is married to a Nicaraguan who is known to be a militant Sandinista. Mine agreed she was not conservative.

Pressed to name one conservative, Mine came up with the names of two reporters that he didn't think were liberal, Andres Oppenheimer of *The Miami Herald* and Julia Preston of *The Washington Post*. Julia Preston began her journalistic career with the leftist Pacific News Service. Her reporting on the arrest, trial and execution of Gen. Arnaldo Ochoa in Cuba

283

last summer followed the line put out by the Castro regime. Oppenheimer is also a liberal, according to our Miami sources. Score: liberals 5, conservatives 0.

It is easy to show that the liberal views of the reporters influence what they report and how they report it. In 1989 the FMLN used terrorism to try to wreck the elections, to try to murder officials from the president of the country down to village mayors and to plant an occupying force of 3,000 terrorists in homes in working-class neighborhoods, causing many civilian deaths in the fighting that ensued. In that year the supposedly objective Associated Press distributed only 17 stories in which the words "terrorist" or "terrorism" appeared within ten words of "FMLN." In the same period, the AP distributed 94 stories in which "death squads" appeared within ten words of "ARENA," the name of the party that won the presidential election in March.

The case of Jennifer Casolo, the young American "churchworker" who was caught with an arsenal of munitions buried in the garden of her house in El Salvador last year, provides a good specific illustration of how the bias of the reporter affects how he covers a story.

The evidence that Casolo collaborated with the terrorists in maintaining this munitions dump is very strong. Her garden had a high wall around it, and access was only through the house. The police were directed to the house by the man who delivered the munitions, Fausto Gallardo, a confessed member of the "People's Revolutionary Army" (ERP), one of the most violent components of the FMLN. Gallardo identified the occupant of the house as an American. Another captured terrorist, Ruth Aguilar Marroquin, identified Casolo as a member of the ERP. She said she had seen Casolo conferring with her unit commander. Personal papers, photos and other material belonging to Casolo were found buried with the materiel. These personal papers revealed Casolo to be a "radical" who sympathized with the FMLN. They included a note written to Casolo in Spanish and signed "David" that appears to refer to a terrorist operation.

None of this has been reported by Doug Mine, who accepts as plausible Casolo's claim that the materiel was buried in her garden without her knowledge. Asked why anyone would do that, he said, "I don't consider it my job to either pronounce on the innocence or guilt of Jennifer Casolo." Mine, like most of the American reporters in El Salvador, has not interviewed either of the two terrorists who tied Casolo to the arms and to the People's Revolutionary Army. He has not examined the documents found buried with the arms. He professes not to know what she means when she calls herself "radical." It is little wonder that many of those who depend on the reports from the AP believe that the wicked Salvadoran government tried to frame that nice little churchworker, Jennifer Casolo.

January 26, 1990

U.S. Media Weep
While Panama Cheers

Alexander Cockburn is a true-red, second-generation British Marxist who writes for the left-wing magazine *The Nation*—and for some odd reason, *The Wall Street Journal*. Once a month Cockburn appears on the *Journal's* op-ed page, possibly to raise the hackles of capitalist readers. Unfortunately for accurate journalism, Cockburn's ideology often outspeeds his facts.

On December 28, 1989 Cockburn's *Journal* column criticized the highly successful U.S. operation to restore democracy to Panama. Cockburn complained, "One has to read the dispatches long and hard to find the news that some 25,000 Panamanians are now homeless, their shanties destroyed in the U.S. bombardment of General Noriega's headquarters."

For a person of Cockburn's anti-American bent, truth is not nearly so interesting as fantasy. Inaccurate reporting botched the "homes destruction" story the first days of the operation. By the time corrected versions appeared, Cockburn and fellow press leftists had their slant—of a malign United States deliberately destroying homes of the innocent Panamanian poor. That is not what happened.

Initial coverage in *The Washington Post* was typical. When U.S. forces went into Panama on December 20, the *Post* reported prominently on page one that thousands of persons had fled the combat areas and were homeless. The *Post* specifically cited shanty dwellers in the Chorillo neighborhood, near Noriega's military headquarters.

The *Post* claimed that many of these homes had been hit by artillery and gunfire and burned. On December 23, next to a photo of refugees, the *Post* reported that in Chorillo alone, "28,000 were left homeless by the fighting."

Other papers, notably the *Los Angeles Times* and *The New York Times*, reported much the same version—that Chorillo

286

had been engulfed by fire as a result of the fighting that occurred when U.S. troops attacked Noriega's headquarters. Cockburn logically saw one or more of these reports; somehow he wanted even more attention focused on the tragedy.

Washington Post columnist Richard Cohen had the same gripe. "Nobody has paid much attention to the ghastly number of Panamanian dead, an estimated 300 people, or the leveling of whole neighborhoods," he wrote on December 30. Doug Tunnell reported on *CBS News* on January 3 that "officials said 12 to 15 thousand Panamanians were left homeless by fighting there."

Then *The New York Times* and *The Washington Post* took a closer look at Chorillo. They discovered the fires had not been caused by the fighting, but by Noriega's goons, for revenge. Noriega was angered because Chorillo residents voted against him in the May presidential elections, and then cheered the attempted October coup.

Noriega was said to have vowed, "If I go, El Chorillo goes with me." Members of his ill-named "Dignity Battalions" ("Dig Bats," to the U.S. military) were seen starting fires with grenades and gasoline the morning after his headquarters fell. The *Post* put the number who lost their homes at 3,000—not the 25,000 mentioned earlier.

The New York Times' Tom Wicker led media fretters nervous about "this latest show of U.S. dominance" and feared Noriega "might become a sort of martyr among the many Latins who fear and/or hate the "Colossus of the North." (December 22).

Similarly, talk show host Phil Donahue decried the intervention in harsh terms on Jan. 9 in a discussion with six White House correspondents—banging the table at one point to show how a mighty U.S. crushed Panama; he, too, lamented the death and destruction. But neither Donahue nor Wicker consulted with the persons most directly concerned: the Panamanian people.

A *CBS News* poll reported on January 5 found 92 percent of Panamanian adults surveyed approved of President Bush sending in troops; 64 percent "strongly approved." Another media worry was how long troops would stay in Panama, implying they should leave promptly. But the CBS poll found that 78 percent of Panamanians wanted them to stay six months "or as long as necessary."

Phil Donahue had trouble with the poll results. He said, "I hope I'm not called un-American for asking the following: Whose survey was it?" CBS and a Washington polling firm, he was told. Donahue persisted. "And how efficient . . . how productive or useful . . . is a survey taken in the midst of the rubble of people. . . ."

ABC's Brit Hume cut him off. "Don't you think people are going to be more upset in the midst of the rubble than six weeks later?" Hume also noted harsh media criticism of Bush for not intervening during the October coup, and Donahue's complaints about "American might." Hume said, "We in the media are fabulously good about setting up these 'no-win' situations for the President."

January 12, 1990

Earth Day 1990: Truth, Or Media Pollution?

With the media panting with eagerness to play its volunteered role as publicist, professional environmentalists are girding for "Earth Day 1990," a major propaganda event aimed at convincing Americans we live in a messy, dangerous world.

"It will begin at sunrise on April 22, with church bells pealing for the health of the planet," *Time* magazine breathlessly informed readers on December 18. "In tiny chapels and grand cathedrals, Sunday sermons will stress the moral responsibility of environmental awareness." Another article warned that "the planet is in grave trouble. If nations do not take drastic action, it could one day be unfit as a human habitat."

How much credence should we give this dire warning? Should the Earth Day publicists be considered serious scientific prognosticators—or journalistic Chicken Littles?

Perhaps unkindly, we recently ran down some of the predictions made as a scary buildup to the first Earth Day, in 1970. *Life* magazine, a sister publication of *Time*, did a lengthy layout in its Jan. 30, 1970 issue entitled "ECOLOGY: A Cause as Movement." A preface page stated, "Unless something is done to reverse environmental deterioration, say many qualified experts, horrors lie in wait. Others disagree, but scientists have solid experimental and theoretical evidence to support each of the following predictions:

—"In a decade, urban dwellers will have to wear gas masks to survive air pollution."

—"In the early 1980s air pollution combined with a temperature inversion will kill thousands in some U.S. city."

—"By 1985 air pollution will have reduced the amount of sunlight reaching earth by one half."

—"In the 1980s a major ecological system—soil or

water—will break down somewhere in the U.S. New diseases that humans cannot resist will reach plague proportions."

—"Increased carbon dioxide in the atmosphere will affect the earth's temperature, leading to mass flooding or a new ice age."

—"Rising noise levels will cause more heart disease and hearing loss. Sonic booms from SSTs will damage children before birth."

—"Residual DDT collecting in the human liver will make the use of certain common drugs dangerous and increase liver cancer."

We count nine specific predictions in *Life's* list. One has come to pass, partially: AIDS is a disease that humans cannot resist, and in narrow pockets of some communities it has reached "plague proportions." But environmental pollution did not start AIDS, other than in the sense that the first cases seem to have stemmed from unsanitary acts by male homosexuals.

What alarms us about the forthcoming Earth Day is that the media seem on the verge of one of their periodic take-no-prisoners assaults on truth and reason. The pastoral visionaries who dominate the ecological movement are long on condemnation of modern society—and short on suggestions as how man can live in comfort if he is forced to abandon such amenities as electrical power and heat.

Our early warnings are that Earth Day 1990 tends to take dead-aim at the traditional ecological bugaboos of business, nuclear energy and the auto. For instance, Dorian Harewood, who plays an army nurse on the TV series "China Beach," recently told the Associated Press about an in-progress movie called "Solar Crisis," in which she plays an environmental commando. "The story is that the Earth's burning up and we're trying to return the atmosphere to a good condition," Harewood told an interviewer. "One man with a multinational corporation is making money off people's misery and tries to stop us."

Which is not to suggest that the Earth Day planners dislike money. A full-time staff of 20 persons is at work in Palo Alto, California, "plotting strategy as if the event were a political campaign," according to *Time*. To raise the $3 million in estimated costs, planners are licensing the Earth Day logo, which will appear on everything from coffee mugs to windbreakers.

Let's face it: The environmental movement is big business, with some groups putting more emphasis on lawyers, publicity and fund-raising than science. Consider the Natural Resources Defense Council, which in 1989 huckstered the bogus Alar/apple scare.

NRDC's most recent annual report lists as staff members 29 lawyers, four press agents, and nine persons working in "development," a euphemism for fundraising. NRDC's $10 million budget supports lavish offices in Washington and New York—but only nine scientists.

Our advice: when you read the Earth Day 1990 publicity, remember *Life's* 1970 predictions, when the magazine batted an iffy one-for-nine.

January 5, 1990

Liberals Were Wrong About Communism—Can You Believe Them Now?

Even as communism crumbles in Eastern Europe, Americans who incurred the hatred of the liberal establishment because of their determined efforts to resist the spread of that evil system at home and abroad are being denied the honor they are due. In the January 1 issue of *Time* magazine, which honored Mikhail Gorbachev as the "man of the decade," editor-at-large Strobe Talbott declared that "the Soviet threat isn't what it used to be." He added, "The real point, however, is that it never was. The doves in the Great Debate of the past 40 years were right all along." Oh?

Which doves does Strobe Talbott have in mind? These, perhaps?

Jane Fonda, who in 1970 told the students at Michigan State University, "I would think that if you understood what communism was, you would hope, you would pray on your knees, that we would someday become communists."

Walter Cronkite, who was quoted in the *Moscow Literary Gazette* of May 1979, seven months before the invasion of Afghanistan, as saying that "an honest person cannot believe that (the USSR is preparing for war, that it might attack someone)."

Sydney Schanberg, *The New York Times* correspondent in Cambodia in 1975, who four days before the Pol Pot communists captured Phnom Penh and began their bloodbath that resulted in the death of perhaps a quarter of the population of Cambodia wrote: "But these concepts (of freedom) mean nothing to the ordinary people of Indochina, and it is difficult to imagine how their lives could be anything but better with the Americans gone."

John Stewart Service, the American Foreign Service

officer, who in a dispatch from China dated September 28, 1944, informed Washington: "The Communist political program is simple democracy." Service assured his superiors that Mao Tse-tung had no desire to make China socialist, saying, "The next stage in China's advance must be capitalism."

John Kenneth Galbraith, the dovish Harvard economist, who in an article in *The New Yorker* magazine in 1984 toasted the "great material progress" of the Soviet Union. He explained it this way: "Partly, the Russian system succeeds because, in contrast with the Western industrial economies, it makes full use of its manpower."

Bernard Goldberg, CBS correspondent, in a 1986 broadcast from Moscow: "As incredible as it may sound, Soviets not only think they're free, they think they're freer than we are."

These views are typical of the thinking of those who took a benign or even adulatory view of communism and the Soviet Union in the years since the 1917 Bolshevik coup d'etat. As the new candor inside the Soviet Union and the new revolutions in Eastern Europe expose the true inhuman face of communism for all to see, it is galling to see *Time* declare that the holders of these views are now being vindicated. What will we see next? The canonization of Julius and Ethel Rosenberg?

A few days after *Time's* glorification of Gorbachev and the doves appeared on the newsstands, A.M. Rosenthal used his column in *The New York Times* to deliver a strong demurral. Gorbachev, he noted, still insists that he is a "convinced communist" and that communism is his main goal. Rosenthal said that the revolution sweeping Eastern Europe is being fought for the abolition of communism, not for its reform. He argued that *Time's* "man of the decade," Gorbachev, could not have won this honor if the truth about Soviet communism had not been told by the dissidents, year after year. He concluded that the dissidents who fought communism while Gorbachev tried to build it "are the real 'men of the decade.' "

They include not only such renowned giants of the anti-

293

communist cause as Solzhenitsyn and Sakharov, but also the thousands of political prisoners, many of whom are still in prison in the Soviet Union. They should also include the anti-communists in the Free World who successfully fought to keep their own countries free and who tried, not always successfully, to block the communist efforts to enslave Eastern Europe and countries such as China, Korea, South Africa, Vietnam, Afghanistan, Nicaragua and El Salvador. Some of these "dissidents" even dared to dream of liberation of the communist world.

The anti-communists represented the thinking of the vast majority of the American people, but they were an oppressed minority in the media, academia, the entertainment world and important parts of the U.S. government. They were ridiculed as "Neanderthals" and often denounced as "McCarthyites." They did much to keep hope alive in the communist countries when the doves that *Time* says were right all along, were telling us that the victims were content and that it was a mistake to think that they longed for liberation.

December 29, 1989

Time Admits "Tailoring" The News To Push The Causes It Believes In

Time readers blinked at a rare boxed announcement in the magazine's December 18 issue, at the bottom of the letters column. Highlighted by a bright yellow background, it carried the headline, "Editorial Judgments." The first sentence read, "We've received more than 3,400 identically worded postcards referring to this quote in *The Wall Street Journal* from *Time* senior editor Charles Alexander: 'On this issue [the environment] we have crossed the boundary from news reporting to advocacy.' The postcards said, 'Tell your readers about this.'"

Time then admitted, in laughably roundabout fashion, that it tailors "reporting" to fit editors' biases. The box stated, "In all our coverage we try to be balanced and fair in our presentation of the facts and in reporting the range of differing views on the issues posed by the facts. But from the beginning of *Time* over 66 years ago, we have also undertaken—and made no secret of it—to add our own judgments on subjects that truly mattered, from civil rights to arms control." We do not believe this will be news to our regular readers . . . it may be part of the reason they value *Time*. We hope so, because we believe considered journalistic judgments are an important contribution to an informed society. And, yes, our stand on the planet is that we support its survival."

The 3,400 postcards that evoked this extraordinary confession that the largest circulation news magazine in the country tailors the news to serve whatever causes the editors deem important came from members of Accuracy in Media throughout the country. They were addressed to Editor-in-Chief Jason McManus, and they obviously got his attention. Mr. McManus is no doubt right in thinking that many regular readers of his magazine know that it allows the opinions of the editors and reporters to influence the way it reports the news. That is true to some degree in all publications.

At the same time, the editor claims that *Time* in all its coverage tries to be fair and balanced in the presentation of the facts and related opinions. That was not the impression conveyed by senior editor Charles Alexander's statement, which was made at an apocalypse-oriented environmental conference at the Smithsonian Institution in Washington. David Brooks of *The Wall Street Journal*, who first publicized Alexander's confession, along with similar statements by other journalists, wrote, "Throughout the entire conference not a single disagreement deflected the steady breeze of alarmism . . . an acid rain crisis, a toxics crisis, a famine crisis, a population crisis. . . ."

A videotape of the conference confirmed the impression that scare-mongers, not objective scientists, are setting our environmental agenda. *Time's* Alexander, Andrea Mitchell of NBC and other journalists seemed determined to out-do one another in vowing fealty to the "environment." *Washington Post* executive editor Ben Bradlee said he had no problem with what his fellow panelists were saying, but he warned that there was "a minor danger in saying it, because as soon as you say, 'To hell with the news, I'm no longer interested in news, I'm interested in causes,' you've got a whole kooky constituency to respond to, which you can waste a lot of time on."

The claim that *Time* tries to give its readers all the relevant facts and opinions before adding its judgments on matters that are "truly important" doesn't wash. As NBC's Andrea Mitchell suggested at the Smithsonian conference, that kind of coverage may not be effective in getting the results the journalists on the panel desired. Dr. Stephen Schneider, one of the climatologists worried about global warming, shares that concern. He says: "To avert the risk (of global warming) we need to get some broad based support, to capture public imagination. That, of course, means getting loads of media coverage. So we have to offer up some scary scenarios, make some simplified dramatic statements and little mention of any doubts one might have... Each of us has to decide what the right balance is between being effective and being honest."

The *Detroit News* made this editorial comment: "The next time you hear about some scary environmental horror on the nightly news, keep that quote in mind. It goes far to explain the debasement of American environmental science into cheap political theater. Apparently 'being honest' is no longer the test of a good scientist."

And to judge from *Time's* candid advocacy of advocacy journalism, being honest is no longer the test of a good journalist. One might say that this goes far to explain the debasement of much American journalism into cheap political theater. Bear that in mind whenever you read any story in *Time* on something "that truly matters."

December 15, 1989

A Case Of Artful Deception

Anyone who gives a taped interview to a television network becomes a hostage to the professionalism—or honesty—of the reporter or producer who ultimately puts the story together to go on the air. As is true of any newsgathering operation, TV news uses selective quotations. The TV people do their interviews, then pick the snippets of talk they think will best tell the story they are trying to give the public.

So what happens when TV interviewers use quotations out of context? When a person's actual words are used to have him saying something he did not mean? Pat Robertson, the television minister, learned a hard lesson in television practices recently from *ABC News*. As its high-paid executives like to boast, *ABC News* consistently is the top-ranked of the three networks. ABC does not like to admit error. But in this instance Pat Robertson caught ABC in a situation where he could prove it was flat-out wrong.

The incident arose in late October, on the day when another minister, Jim Bakker, was sentenced to forty years in prison for financial corruption. ABC correspondent Rebecca Chase interviewed Robertson from his Virginia Beach headquarters. Chase first asked Robertson for his reaction to what she called "the rather stiff sentence received by Mr. Bakker." Robertson agreed he thought the sentence was stiff, but that he had expected it, or even more, from a judge he noted was known in the Carolinas as "Maximum Bob."

Then ABC's Rebecca Chase asked another question: Did Pat Robertson feel the sentence closed the era of church scandals? Robertson replied, "I am delighted to see it. I think that God really has done a job cleaning his church." Robertson went on to say that "we are starting a new era of religious broadcasting that's going to be very fine in the next decade."

To Pat Robertson's utter astonishment, *ABC News* played games with his quotations. By the time the interview got through the editing process and aired on the *World News*

Tonight program, ABC had him saying he was "delighted" at the Bakker sentence. Of course, Pat Robertson said no such thing. He used the "delighted" quotation in the context of the era of scandals being at an end. By mixing up the answers, ABC got a more dramatic quotation to put on the air. It also made Pat Robertson appear to be gloating over the fact that Jim Bakker might be spending much of the rest of his life in prison. But juggling Pat Robertson's answers was at best sloppy journalism—and at worst a deliberate distortion of what the man said.

Fortunately for Pat Robertson, he had the resources to put the lie to ABC. He had a tape of the full interview. The next morning he played it on his televised *700 Club* and let viewers see the truth for themselves. Exposure of the distortion had immediate impact. *ABC News* realized that Pat Robertson had let hundreds of thousands of Americans in on the misquotation. A night later, anchorman Peter Jennings "clarified" the report, which we applaud. But *ABC News* should not have made such a dumb error, and it should have added several words to its "clarification"—"We did something wrong, and we're sorry."

November 28, 1989

The "Sound Bite" Bites Back

Stephen Hess of the Brookings Institution in Washington, a liberal think tank, knows American politics from the inside. He worked in the Nixon White House, and he has written extensively on the way Americans elect their officials. He is articulate, and readily available, and therefore he is one of the experts regularly asked to provide a 10- or 15-second snippet of an interview that TV people call a "sound bite." Television uses "sound bites" as a means of having someone other than the correspondent or anchorman interpret an event.

Hess is good at sound bites, and he is enormously popular with the networks. He computes that during the 1988 presidential election, television networks or stations asked him for sound bites 301 times. Thus Hess is uniquely qualified to judge how TV networks use these interview fragments.

He gives television news a poor report card in a recent discussion at the Washington Journalism Center which he wryly titled "The 'Sound Bite' Bites Back." Hess raised serious questions about whether what we see on the news each evening is really objective reporting or comments chosen to fit the preconceived notion of the person who produced or reported the segment.

Hess does not accuse TV networks of outright dishonesty. He has never been asked to give a particular opinion. The process is more subtle. He says, "The producer calls to check me out—to see if I am likely to say what they want." If the answer is not satisfactory, the producer says, "I'll get back to you," which Hess recognizes as a code phrase meaning he will not be used.

He says the producer or reporter, when he calls for the sound bite, already has an idea of the shape of the story that will be put on the air. His role, as the sound bite, is to be the "chip in the mosaic" that the network is putting together.

The danger in this process is that television news increasingly is becoming "the gathering of quotes to fit a hypotheses." And more distressing, the shape of a story is often decided by a producer in the studio, rather than by a field reporter who has an intelligent grasp of what is happening.

Hess feels the trend towards prepackaging news has accelerated in recent years as TV networks skimp on their news spending for budgetary reasons. He says he encounters all too many so-called "reporters" who have no journalistic training, and who all too often lack the common sense to realize what they are doing. These persons might give a network a "highly efficient and cost-effective system for producing material," Hess says, but the quality of news reporting suffers enormously. And so, too, he says, does the information recieved by the TV viewer. Hess feels that TV now uses sound bites as a form of news fabrication. Citizens who watch TV, he says, should realize the sound bites are chosen to reinforce a preconceived message and not to give a rounded story.

November 21, 1989

"When The Truth Collides With A Legend, Print The Legend"

Bryant Gumbel, the black co-host of the NBC *Today* show, dropped all pretense of journalistic objectivity when he subjected the Reverend Ralph David Abernathy to an intense grilling over revelations of Dr. Martin's Luther King's extramarital affairs in the fall of 1989. Abernathy, a former confidant of King's, has generated national controversy with his book suggesting that King had sex with two different women and fought with a third on the night before he was assassinated.

Gumbel has not, to our knowledge, ever questioned excessive media coverage of the Reverend Jim Bakker's sexual affair with Jessica Hahn. But he strongly suggested that Abernathy should have kept his mouth shut about this flaw in Reverend King's character. Gumbel, supposedly a newsman dedicated to the public's "right to know," asked Abernathy, "Why do it, when you knew that what you would reveal would give great comfort to those who would like to demean the memory of Doctor King? Why did you give them the weapon?"

Abernathy said he wanted to be honest. He noted none of this was new, and that FBI files as well as a Pulitzer Prize winning book by David Garrow had documented that King had extra-marital affairs. Abernathy said his book would have been rejected as dishonest if he had not dealt with it. But Gumbel noted that black "leaders" such as Atlanta Mayor Andrew Young and the Reverend Jesse Jackson had repudiated the book. Abernathy said this response showed that these leaders "are not concerned about the movement." Gumbel shot back, "Is that fair, Dr. Abernathy?" Abernathy went on to say that Young had not been "fair or honest" to the people of Atlanta and that Jackson "was not honest with Martin Luther King" and that King had wanted to fire him from the Southern Christian Leadership Conference, SCLC. Abernathy said when he took over the SCLC, he suspended Jackson from the organization. Abernathy also said Jackson had been dishonest when he claimed he had cradled King in his arms after the assassination and had gotten King's blood on his shirt.

Gumbel seemed astounded by these remarks. "I'm not sure I'm hearing all this," he said. He would have been even more astounded if Abernathy had referred to published reports that the Reverend Jackson has had his own womanizing problem. A book on Jackson by black journalist Barbara Reynolds notes that Jackson has had relationships with women other than his wife.

When Abernathy proceeded to complain that Young and Jackson had not read his book, Gumbel called for censorship, saying, "I've read the book. Why did you include the pages? It could have just as easily been left out." With his lip quivering, Gumbel made one last plea for censorship. Referring to a line from a movie, Gumbel said that "when the truth collides with a legend, print the legend." He was saying, in effect, that the truth should be suppressed. He was saying that fiction is more important than fact.

But Abernathy quoted from the Bible, saying that the truth will set one free, and that the truth sometimes hurts. The interview concluded with Abernathy telling Gumbel to have a good day. Gumbel said he'd try to.

November 1, 1989

More Phony Numbers
On Housing

At the "Housing Now!" march in Washington in the fall of 1989, a Reverend David Hayden was shown on the *CBS Evening News* saying that there were 3 to 4 million homeless people in this country. *CBS News* correspondent Terence Smith didn't bother to ask where this figure came from. It seems to be the highest figure ever advanced by a spokesman for the homeless.

The Reverend Hayden had also claimed that there were 250,000 at the demonstration itself. Yet the U.S. Park Police put the figure at only 40,000. The evidence suggests that his number of homeless was also greatly exaggerated.

The number of homeless is a matter of dispute. Heritage Foundation policy analyst John Scanlon wrote a report noting that the previous highest figure of the number of homeless had been put at two or three million by activist Mitch Snyder. But Scanlon said that Snyder himself had said the figure is meaningless, and that he supplied it to a Congressional panel because he was trying "to satisfy its gnawing curiosity for a number."

Scanlon's report notes that scientific studies put the number of homeless at somewhere between 250,000 and 600,000. These studies have been conducted by the Housing and Urban Development Department, the National Bureau of Economic Research and the Urban Institute. But Scanlon says the important thing is that most of the homeless are drug or alcohol addicts or released mental patients. He said these people cannot be helped by having the government build more housing.

Scanlon's report was generally ignored by the media. But it was attacked by William Raspberry of *The Washington Post* in an October 6 column, on the eve of the "Housing Now!" march. Raspberry said of Scanlon, "I find it hard to take him seriously." Scanlon said that Raspberry was a victim of media misinformation. He said, "I think Raspberry, like most Americans, has been hearing the other side of the story for so long that when they're confronted with the facts, they're just incredulous."

He added, "Those who call themselves housing advocates and homeless advocates have really been responsible for the problem because they've been painting a picture of the homeless that is inaccurate." Scanlon's report said these advocates have tried to portray the homeless as people middle America can sympathize with.

And their strategy has been successful. He noted that a recent study of media coverage of homelessness was issued by S. Robert Lichter and Linda Lichter. It was titled "The Visible Poor: Media Coverage of the Homeless 1986-1989." It found that only 25 percent of homeless featured in major print or broadcast stories were identified as unemployed, and only 7 percent were identified as drug or alcohol abusers. These are figures significantly at odds with major surveys.

The American people sympathize with the plight of the homeless. But a solution is not possible as long as the media continue to misrepresent the number of those in need, and what their needs actually are.

October 20, 1989

Is San Francisco Still Standing?

For over 22 hours television network news informed viewers throughout the nation about the terrible destruction wrought by the "killer quake" that had hit northern California, registering 6.9 on the Richter scale, just after 5:00 p.m. on October 17, 1989. Four scenes were shown over and over again—the badly damaged buildings in the Marina district, the huge fire that destroyed a city block in the same area when a gas main ruptured, the collapsed mile and a half of two-tier freeway in Oakland, and the collapse of a segment of the upper deck of the Bay Bridge.

A uniformed officer was shown warning the residents that they had only a few hours of daylight and that they had better get busy and make preparations for a prolonged period without water or electricity. There was mention of the smell of leaking gas throughout the downtown area.

Watching the nearly non-stop coverage, millions of viewers were led to believe that the devastation in San Francisco and the Bay area had been widespread and that most of the residents were faced with grim days ahead. AT&T said that it had been unable to handle all the calls from people anxious to know if their family and friends were safe. TV viewers were urged not to call unless it was an emergency.

Those who did succeed in getting through to friends and relatives learned that while people in the Bay Area had been shaken up and many had been terrified, the devastation and hardship in that area that was being described on television was limited to the few sites being shown—the Marina district, the freeway in Oakland and the Bay Bridge. It was obvious that network television could perform a valuable service by telling viewers that the scenes of destruction they had been seeing were not typical of the entire Bay Area and that the overwhelming majority of the residents were safe and suffering only moderate inconvenience. That suggestion was welcomed as a good idea at CBS and NBC, but the news personnel we spoke to at ABC and CNN were seemingly unconvinced that what they had been showing was unrepresentative of conditions throughout the city and the Bay Area.

On October 18, Tom Brokaw began his report on the *NBC Nightly News* saying, "This is the Marina district neighborhood. It was the hardest hit residential area in San Francisco. It was believed that between three and five people died in that apartment house right back there. But I must tell you that most of the damage in San Francisco has been confined to this area, which is about four square miles altogether. I made a helicopter tour of the entire area, and the greatest damage was right here, on the Oakland (sic) Bay Bridge and, of course, on Interstate 880."

Peter Jennings on ABC's *World News Tonight* also decided the time had come to let the public in on what had been a well kept secret. He began his report that night saying, "The good news is this. Despite what you see going on behind me (the demolition of a residence in San Francisco's Marina district) San Francisco is still standing."

The MacNeil/Lehrer News Hour interviewed an engineer who had come to San Francisco to survey the damage, who commented, "We have had had a great deal of trouble finding the earthquake."

Dan Rather of CBS was reluctant to acknowledge that things were not as bad as they had been portrayed. He began his broadcast reciting casualty figures, which later proved to be greatly overstated. He talked of "the killer quake" and said beautiful San Francisco had spent the 20th century "living with fear, living in dread of powerful earthquakes." Late in the broadcast, correspondent Susan Spencer mentioned that some city officials wished that "more was being said about the structures that did not fall."

CNN's *Prime News* was even worse. Anchorman Lou Waters talked about "a surreal day" becoming "an even more eerie night." He said, "There is still no power in the San Francisco area as crews continue to search for escaping gas before any power can be restored." Many in the area had never suffered any power outage, and it had already been restored to most of the residential areas where it had been cut off.

Earthquake experts interviewed on TV pointed out that they try to learn from every quake. The networks ought to do the same. The quake was a big story, but it didn't devastate San Francisco. The networks should have reported that as soon as they knew it, because that was the biggest and best news of all.

October 20, 1989

The Confessions Of A Radical Huckster—Why You Can't Trust TV News

A radical Washington publicist who has represented a medley of far-left causes and communist countries has revealed how he orchestrated The Great Apple Scare of 1989. He is David Fenton, who at only age 37 can claim to be a 20-year veteran of the America-bashing left. Fenton represented the Natural Resources Defense Council (NRDC) which in February 1989 issued a report pushing the false claim that Alar, a chemical growth regulator used on apples, posed a serious cancer risk for American children.

Fenton says the keystone to his scare campaign was the decision to give *60 Minutes* the exclusive right to break the story. *60 Minutes* set off a nationwide panic when it aired a segment on February 26 based on the NRDC report. Mothers dumped apple juice down the drain, and schools pulled the fruit from lunchrooms. Plummeting sales toppled many growers into bankruptcy, and the beleaguered apple industry now puts its losses at more than $200 million.

Now we learn that this was the work of David Fenton, whose PR firm has represented such clients as the communist Sandinista government of Nicaragua, the Marxist regimes of Angola and Grenada, and the ultra-left Christic Institute, a sworn foe of the Nicaraguan freedom fighters. Many of the radicals of Fenton's generation are now embracing environmental extremism as a substitute for communism. They resent the success of our free market economy and delight in any opportunity to throw sand in its machinery.

Fenton's role in depriving apple growers of Alar, a chemical that helped them produce better apples at lower cost, was disclosed in a memo he wrote to his clients, excerpts from which were published in the October 3 issue of *The Wall Street Journal*. He had earlier boasted of his role in an interview in the summer issue of *Propaganda Review*, a leftist magazine.

The NRDC report was based on the false premise that Alar posed a grave cancer risk to children because they eat a lot of apples and drink a lot of apple juice. It employed badly flawed data and sought to exploit the concerns mothers have for the health of their young children. Fenton claimed that most such reports are handed out at a press conference and generate a few print stories. "Television coverage is rarely sought or achieved," he added. But he harked back to Yippie leaders Abbie Hoffman and Jerry Rubin, men he says were "way ahead of their time in understanding how television can be used to effect mass movements." He followed their example.

"An agreement was made with *60 Minutes* to break the story of the report in February," Fenton wrote. Exploiting media contacts, Fenton arranged interviews on morning talk shows and elsewhere to follow *60 Minutes*. Knowing TV's preference for glitz over fact, Fenton worked with actress Meryl Streep to create a front group, "Mothers and Others for Pesticide Limits." She did the talk shows as a talking head who was asked no questions requiring her to go beyond canned answers. Fenton told *Propaganda Review*, "The American public is hungry for celebrities and having one available really helps."

Fenton boasted to *Propaganda Review*, "Over a two-week period, if you turned on the *Today* show or the evening news or *Donahue* you saw it. You heard it on the radio. If you opened your home town newspaper, you read about it four times. It was everywhere."

Three government agencies tried to damp down the hysteria created by Fenton's media campaign. They assured the public that apples were perfectly safe, but it was no use. Fenton's saturation strategy worked. He said, "At that point a phenomenon takes place—the story becomes a myth; it obtains a level of recognition and presence that gives it a life of its own." There were no celebrities on the TV talk shows telling the facts—that the risk of cancer from eating raw apples was zero and that the cancer risk posed by apple juice was far less than that posed by peanut butter.

October 13, 1989

Federal Express's $100 Million Message

An enraged corporate executive has sent ABC the sort of message that cannot be ignored even by the most arrogant network. Frederick Smith, who built the Federal Express Company from an idea into a billion dollar courier empire, has yanked $100 million in advertising to protest a "shallow, scurrilous and deceptive" segment on the *20/20* news show about his company.

In dollar volume, the cancellation might be the largest in TV history. The intent, according to Federal Express vice president Carole Presley, was to send a "message . . . understood by the accountants at ABC."

The segment, aired in July, charged Federal Express with cheating the government on billings. It alleged mass violations of security rules on shipping of classified documents between contractors and the military, and careless handling of explosives. It depicted Federal Express as a place where workers routinely broke open parcels looking for narcotics and used drugs on the job.

The chief ABC witness was a former Federal Express driver in Dover, Delaware. Citing privacy laws, the company refused to say why he no longer is employed. His charges about security violations and drugs were seemingly corroborated by another man who had been fired six years earlier. ABC identified both men as "former employees," but pictured one driving what seemed to be a Federal Express truck. Federal Express calls them malicious and disgruntled.

To underline its statement that Federal Express refused cooperation, *20/20* correspondent Tom Jarriel was shown outside a facility in Dover. "We tried to get Federal Express to tell its side of the story," Jarriel said. He gestured towards the building. "The lights are out, the shades are drawn, but they were here a few minutes ago when a producer was here—but not now. They are locked up tight."

This entire sequence was phony. What *20/20* knew, but did not tell viewers, was that the facility was "closed" because it had never opened. It was still under construction. The persons encountered by producer Chris Harper were actually carpenters finishing work.

Nor did Jarriel mention that Federal Express invited *20/20* to the company's headquarters in Memphis to see how workers are trained to handle hazardous materials, and how it deals with drug problems plaguing many businesses. That invitation wasn't accepted. Evidently the producers of the program thought the false non-cooperation charge would add spice to their story.

The segment ended with correspondent Jarriel smugly claiming credit for Federal Express's discontinuing the classified documents shipment program to take the sting out of his "revelations." Barbara Walters applauded him, saying, "It's satisfying . . . to see that . . . digging into something can have positive results." Federal Express says it stopped the program because of onerous red tape involved.

Federal Express chairman Fred Smith, a tough former Marine pilot who built his company from an idea he conceived while writing a college paper, used Marine-tough language in a letter to John Sias, president of ABC-TV. He said, "ABC's handling of this entire story was . . . an abuse of the public trust and certainly not in keeping with any acceptable standards of professional reporting. . . . If ABC continues to engage in such practices, there is little doubt in my mind that you will lose your viewers in direct proportion to your loss of credibility."

Smith also told Sias, "We have canceled all prime time advertising with you." That included 11 spots on *20/20*, but binding commitments for slots on sports programs will be honored.

Federal Express did not publicize this drastic action. We first contacted the company about the *20/20* segment in August after several employees denounced it as a smear. Public affairs and legal people told us they were too busy finishing a merger with Flying Tigers Airways to comment. So

313

rank-and-file workers and the public didn't hear the strong message Smith had sent ABC.

That led us to call Fred Smith a "wimp" for not defending his company publicly. He quickly proved us wrong. He told us in no uncertain terms that he had taken strong action and enclosed his letter to John Sias to prove it. We compliment him and retract the "wimp" label. We transfer it to Walter Porges, the ABC vice president for news practices, who has referred to himself as "the minister of Truth." When we asked him about Fred Smith's reaction to the program, he said, "We see no reason to go on record telling you business between a customer and us."

October 6, 1989